THE FAITHFUL SAYINGS
IN THE PASTORAL LETTERS

Dr. GEORGE W. KNIGHT, III

BAKER BOOK HOUSE
Grand Rapids, Michigan

Reprinted 1979 by
Baker Book House Company
with permission of Presbyterian and
Reformed Publishing Company
ISBN: 0-8010-5402-8

Printed in the United States of America

TO MY BELOVED WIFE VIRGINIA
AND OUR CHILDREN
GEORGE, VANN, MARGARET, JENNIE, AND HUGH

THE AUTHOR

The author, George W. Knight, III, received his Doctor of Theology degree from The Free University, Amsterdam, the Netherlands. While in Europe he also studied with the New Testament scholars Dr. Herman Ridderbos and Dr. Oscar Cullmann. His B.D. and Th.M. degrees were received from Westminster Theological Seminary, Philadelphia, Pennsylvania. Dr. Knight has taught Bible in colleges and served as pastor of churches in Pennsylvania, New Jersey and Florida. He was a delegate to the 1968 Reformed Ecumenical Synod in Europe, and presently serves on its North American study committee on "Office in the New Testament." The author is Professor of New Testament at Covenant Theological Seminary, St. Louis, Missouri.

TABLE OF CONTENTS

A WORD TO THE READER

The commonly recognized and accepted abbreviations have been utilized throughout the dissertation (*e.g.*, *TWNT* for *Theologisches Wörterbuch zum Neuen Testament* and *TDNT* for the English translation of the same, *Theological Dictionary of the New Testament*). Commentaries on the Pastoral Letters, concordances, grammars and lexicons have often been cited by using merely the author's or editor's last name: full titles are found in the bibliography. The *American Standard Version* (*A.S.V.*) has been used as the basic English translation with modernization of verb forms and pronouns. Other English translations, including at times the author's own, also occur.

INTRODUCTION

The phrase "Faithful is the saying" (πιστὸς ὁ λόγος) elicits one's attention by virtue of its five-fold occurrence in the Pastoral Letters. This repeated phenomenon in the Pastorals is all the more striking because of the absence of this exact phrase, or even anything closely approximating it, anywhere else in Paul or for that matter in the N.T. Equally striking is the addition "and worthy of all acceptation" (καὶ πάσης ἀποδοχῆς ἄξιος) in two of the five occurrences but not at the other three. Coupled with this striking phrase are the sometimes more evident, sometimes less evident, sayings to which it refers. Here indeed is a fascinating situation worthy of serious investigation. And strangely enough here is a situation which has received virtually no intensive and comprehensive study[1]. Thus this dissertation is an attempt to provide at least a beginning in investigating with some measure of care the phenomenon of the faithful sayings in the Pastoral Letters.

The starting point is most naturally the recurring phrase itself, "faithful is the saying". The first part of chapter I seeks to open up the questions attendant upon this phrase and likewise seeks to draw answers from the phrase itself as well as from contextual considerations and usage of the vocabulary elsewhere. The conclusion reached is that the phrase is a citation-emphasis formula which serves to drawn one's attention to the fact that a saying is cited and which serves at the same time to emphasize and commend that saying. Thus even at this stage of the study the conclusion is dawning that that to which the λόγος refers is indeed a "saying", not merely a statement written by the author in the course of his writing of the letter. This preliminary hypothesis will be tested at each saying, and only after all five have been considered may

---

[1] Two examples of the studies devoted thus far to the faithful sayings of the Pastorals are H. B. Swete, "The Faithful Sayings", *Journal of Theological Studies* xviii (1917), pp. 1-7, and J. M. Bover, "Fidelis Sermo", *Biblica* 19 (1938), pp. 74-79. As is evident from the number of pages involved, these are but brief, albeit noteworthy, attempts to explore the question. Also, it must be said, special notes have been devoted to the sayings in various commentaries, but again on a limited scale.

the conclusion finally be drawn that these are truly *sayings* not statements framed in the course of the letter by the author.

The second half of chapter I is devoted to the addition found at two of the five places of the words "and worthy of acceptance". This enlargement is also seen to partake of the nature of a citation-emphasis formula although with more of the quality of emphasis than of citation. The question is raised as to why this phrase is added at only two places and not at the other three. The solution is posed that the addition or omission may well be dependent on the type of the saying or on the content of the saying. The verification of this solution depends upon the ascertainment of the sayings themselves, and thus is postponed until the concluding chapter.

Chapters II through VI take up the sayings themselves, with each chapter devoted to a saying. The sayings are considered in the order adjudged to be the chronological order of the books themselves, namely, 1 Timothy, Titus and then 2 Timothy. For each saying the inevitable questions are raised and the problems common to them all or unique to this or that one are considered. At each location of the phrase "faithful is the saying" one of the first questions raised is that of the "saying" to which this formula refers. Does it precede or follow the formula? And to what extent does it extend? Once the saying is determined, care is taken to determine its meaning and significance, particularly in its setting. Finally an attempt is made to determine the possible origin of the saying. At these as well as at other points of the research one is keenly aware that these questions are inexorably intertwined. The evidence of each saying and of the sayings considered together would seem to be that they were not composed by the author of the Pastorals while drafting the letters but rather were well-known sayings known and used by the Christian church.

The concluding chapter, among other things, seeks to consider the sayings as a whole and in relation to one another. The work of Christ and the place of man in the sayings are especially considered.

This and previous analyses of the sayings have already uncovered certain differences in form and content. Two of the sayings are interestingly marked by the accent of personal involvement and acceptance with the use of verbs and pronouns in the first person plural ("we", etc.). Two of the sayings speak in more general and indirect terms. (The saying on church government, for the reasons noted, stands by itself in reference to the point under consideration). The striking counterpart to this evaluation of the four sayings is that the addition to the formula of the words "and worthy of all acceptance" is found only with the two non-"we"-type sayings and likewise the words are omitted or not added with the "we"-type sayings. This correlation would seem to establish the reason for the addition or omission, *viz.*, the absence or inclusion respectively of the evidence of acceptance in the saying itself.

The faithful sayings are then related to other summaries of the Christian faith within the pages of the Scriptures, *e.g.*, Dodd's evaluation of the *kerygma* as found in Acts and in Paul. Certain perspectives are suggested for a reevaluation of our understanding of the early church.

A concern that has loomed large through this study, as well as any study of the Pastoral Letters, although it has in the main been in the background, is that of authorship. The self-testimony of the letters to the Apostle Paul has been accepted at face value on the background of its canonical standing in the life of the church, and also on the background of one's own and others' painstaking studies into this question. In the concluding chapter this question is related to the occurrence of faithful sayings in the midst of these Pastoral Letters. Although the faithful sayings touch only upon certain aspects of the problems anent the authorship, they do seem to provide some helpful pointers to Luke as an amanuensis for Paul.

Last of all, the sayings show the orientation to Christ of the early church. This orientation is demonstrated by the fact that the sayings either speak in terms of the person and work of Christ, or reflect a teaching or saying of Christ.

With these sayings we have come to the self-conscious creedal/liturgical expressions of the early church of its faith and life.

CHAPTER I

"FAITHFUL IS THE SAYING,
AND WORTHY OF ALL ACCEPTATION"

A. Πιστὸς ὁ λόγος...

The phrase πιστὸς ὁ λόγος occurs five[1] times (1 Tim. 1:15; 3:1[2]; 4:9; Titus 3:8; 2 Tim. 2:11) in the Pastoral[3] Letters of the Apostle Paul[4]. Twice in 1 Timothy only (1 Tim. 1:15; 4:9) the phrase is enlarged by the addition of the words καὶ πάσης ἀποδοχῆς ἄξιος. The phrase in its shorter or longer form is found nowhere else in the New Testament, nor is it found in the Greek Old Testament. Πιστὸς λόγος does occur in Titus 1:9 in the statement ἀντεχόμενον τοῦ κατὰ τὴν διδαχὴν πιστοῦ λόγου.

[1] The indication that the phrase occurs five times is not to prejudge the textual question which arises but rather to indicate the extent of the locations. The textual variant ἀνθρώπινος for πιστός will be considered at the relevant places (1 Tim. 1:15; 3:1).

[2] Whether the phrase really belongs with 2:15 or 3:1 will be considered when that saying and its context are discussed. For convenience, the location of 3:1, selected by Nestle and other editors of the Greek New Testament, is adopted for now.

[3] The commonly accepted term for the designation of 1 and 2 Timothy and Titus is adopted in this study as a matter of convenience and usage without prejudice pro or con as to its accuracy or aptness in designating these letters as a whole.

[4] In the opening section of these canonical letters we find the author's name given as the Apostle Paul. Any scientific investigation must begin with this claim, and hence the burden of proof rests upon those who would deny these letters to the one to whom they are attributed. The denial and the attempt at its proof have been made by a number of men. In some quarters the non-Pauline authorship has become a dogma of New Testament scholarship. However, the tide is turning as it did when others than the so-called Hauptbriefe were regarded as non-Pauline. Most recent works on the Pastoral Letters have affirmed the authorship of Paul, e.g., J. Jeremias, C. Spicq, E. K. Simpson, D. Guthrie, W. Hendriksen, J. N. D. Kelly and H. N. Ridderbos. The author has considered the problem and set forth his reasons for accepting the Pauline authorship in a thesis submitted to the faculty of Westminster Theological Seminary, Phila., Pa., U.S.A., 1957, entitled The Authorship of The Pastoral Epistles. A most devastating refutation of both the Fictional Approach and the Fragment Approach is given by C. F. D. Moule in his recent Manson Memorial Lecture, "The Problem of the Pastoral Epistles: A Reap-

4

In Rev. 21:5 and 22:6 the phrase οἱ λόγοι πιστοί is found in the statement οὗτοι οἱ λόγοι πιστοὶ καὶ ἀληθινοί (εἰσιν)[5]. Dionysius of Halicarnassus (I B.C.) and Dio Chrysostom (I-II A.D.) would appear to be the only other known authors using the phrase πιστὸς ὁ λόγος[6]. The former says γενήσεται δέ μου πιστὸς ὁ λόγος..., which Cary translates "and my claim will seem credible..." (*Dionys. Hal.* 3, 23, 17)[7]. The latter says ἴσως δὲ οὐδὲ φανεῖται πιστὸς ὁ λόγος..., which Crosby translates "and possibly the statement will not even seem credible..." (*Dio Chrys.* 28 [45], 3)[8]. Dionysius also uses πιστὸς εἶναι ὁ λόγος in the statement διὰ μὲν δὴ ταύτας τάς αἰτίας οὐκ ἔδοξε μοι πιστὸς εἶναι ὁ λόγος ("for these reasons, then, this account has not seemed to me to be credible", *Dionys. Hal.* 9, 19, 3[9])[10]. The phrase is known nowhere else in or before N.T. times, although there are certain places where both πιστός and λόγος occur together but not in this construction[11]. W. Nauck strangely, in the face of this evidence, as meager as it may be, says, "Im hellenistischen Schrifttum ist diese Wendung nicht belegt"[12]. If he means by this that the phrase does not occur as

praisal", *Bulletin of the John Rylands Library*, 47 (1965), pp. 430-452. Moule
offers as his solution the postulating of Luke as the amanuensis. *Cf.* also his
earlier proposal along this line in his Excursus II, "Luke and The Pastoral
Epistles", *The Birth of the New Testament* (New York: Harper & Row, 1962),
pp. 220f. Most of those that deny the Pauline authorship admit that they are
Pauline in the sense that they are written by a Paulinist who sought to copy
the so-called genuine letters of Paul. This in itself is ample ground for utilizing
these other letters of Paul to understand the Pastoral Letters.
  5 Rev. 22:6 does not have εἰσιν; Rev. 21:5 does.
  6 W. F. Arndt and F. W. Gingrich, *A Greek-English Lexicon of the New
Testament of Other Early Christian Literature* (a translation and adaptation
of Walter Bauer's *Griechisch-Deutsches Wörterbuch zu den Schriften des
Neuen Testaments...*), (Chicago: The University of Chicago Press, 1957), *s.v.*
πιστός. Hereinafter referred to as Arndt-Gingrich.
  7 *The Roman Antiquities of Dionysius of Halicarnassus* edited by E. Cary
(*The Loeb Classical Library*), II, (Cambridge: Harvard University Press,
1939), pp. 104, 105.
  8 *Dio Chrysostom* edited by H. L. Crosby (*Loeb*), IV, (1946), pp. 208, 209.
  9 Cited by J. J. Wettstein, *Novum Testamentum Graecum*, II (Amsterdam:
Dommerian, 1752), *ad* 1 Tim. 1:15.
  10 *Loeb* (1945), Vol. V, ed. Cary, pp. 356, 357.
  11 In addition to the places already cited, Wetstein (or Wettstein), *loc. cit.*,
gives among others "Xiphilinus' Tiberio. p. 109 – οὐ μέντοι καὶ πιστὸς ὁ λόγος"
which is from the 11th cen. A.D. and therefore obviously too late to be of value
to this study. *Cf.* also M. Dibelius and H. Conzelmann, *Die Pastoralbriefe*
(hereinafter referred to as Dibelius-Conzelmann) *ad* 1 Tim. 1:15. Plato Tim 49b
(πιστῷ καὶ βεβαίῳ χρήσασθαι λόγῳ) and Dio Chrys 25 3 II p. 71 Arnim are the
only references mentioned other than Dionys Hal Ant Rom III 23 17.
  12 W. Nauck, *Die Herkunft des Verfassers der Pastoralbriefe.* Inaugural-
Dissertation zur Erlangung des Doktorgrades (unpublished, Göttingen, 1950),
p. 46.

a "formula" used as it is in the Pastoral Letters before or after a saying, then we can agree with his verdict, but as an absolute negation it runs counter to the evidence.

The lack of an exactly parallel usage in Greek writings has caused Dibelius-Conzelmann and particularly Nauck to turn to Jewish sources. Nauck cites as one possible parallel the Jewish prayer after *Shema'* which is found as an *Anhang* in P. Fiebig's *Berachoth*[13]. This prayer which is given only in German and for which no date is offered except to say that it is "old" hardly offers any instructive parallel or background.

Nauck cites as a definite parallel and as a proof that πιστὸς ὁ λόγος is of Judaistic origin a fragment given by Sukenik in his *Megillot Genuzot*[14] נכון הדבר לבוא לבוא ואמת המשא ומזה יודע לכמה כי לוא ישוב אחור. Part of Nauck's concern to demonstrate that πιστὸς ὁ λόγος is of Judaistic origin stems from the fact that his dissertation seeks to demonstrate that the author of the Pastorals is of Jewish background and rabbinically influenced[15]. This would be one more proof of his argument as a whole. In this particular case he appeals not only to the apparent similarity between the fragment and the phrase but also to his evaluation that in the context of both the Judaistic usage and in that of the πιστὸς ὁ λόγος formula "salvation" is a significant item[16].

---

[13] P. Fiebig, *Berachoth. Der Mischnatractat "Segensprüche" ins Deutsche übersetzt*... Mit einem Anhang, bietend: eine Reihe alter und wichtiger jüdischen Gebete, (*Ausgewählte Mischnatractate in deutscher Uebersetzung*, 3, Tübingen: J. C. B. Mohr, 1906), p. 34: "wahr und fest, gegründet, bestehend, richtig, treu, geliebt, lieb, kostbar, lieflich, furchtbar, gewaltig, ordentlich, angenehm, gut und schön ist dies Wort für uns immer und ewig".

[14] E. L. Sukenik, *Megillot Genuzot*, II, (Jerusalem, 1950), page כג, line ז. Nauck gives as the translation into German: "Fest ist das Wort, dass es eintrifft, und zuverlässig der Spruch und (Gott) weiss genau, dass es (das Wort) nicht hinfallen wird", *op. cit.*, note 32 to page 50. The same text, now designated as 1 Q 27, 1, and commonly known as the "book of mysteries", is also found in D. Barthélemy and J. T. Milik, *Qumran Cave I. Discoveries in the Judaean Desert I* (Oxford, 1955), page 103, plates XXI and XXII, Col. I, line 8, with a French translation, "Assurément la Parole se réalisera et certaine est la Prédiction". I. Rabinowitz in his article "The Authorship, Audience and Date of the de Vaux Fragment of an Unknown Work", *Journal of Biblical Literature* LXXXI (1952), pp. 19-32, dates the work as 166/5 B. C. Of interest to our study is the fact that this statement follows that to which it refers as is occasionally the case with the faithful sayings.

[15] Nauck, *op. cit.*, further notes that the writer makes his point to his Greek readers by the use of Hellenistic words and concepts. The author is then seen to be a Jew who is rabbinically influenced but who uses Hellenistic words and concepts to get his message across to his Greek speaking readers. Although Nauck does not indicate beyond this general description who in particular he thinks the author is, it must be acknowledged that if his case is established no one that is known in N.T. times fits the picture better than the Apostle Paul.

[16] Nauck, *op. cit.*, p. 49. "Ergebnis: Die Bekräftigung der alten Glaubens-

As plausible as Nauck's case may seem, it still lacks the certainty that compels it to be accepted at this point as fact rather than as theory. First of all the similarity may be only that. Not all similarities require relationship or dependence or development from one to the other. Further the examples are few, and in the case of the former much later than the Pastoral Letters. Old Jewish prayers may not be pressed to prove the practice of the N.T. time. It is highly likely that the author of the Pastoral Letters would never have heard or seen these Jewish statements. Even though it may come from the New Testament time, this is likewise true of the statement found in the sectarian fragment. The author of the Pastoral Letters, described and characterized as Nauck has presented him, would hardly have had contact with such a statement, or if he did, would hardly utilize or be influenced by it. And this would be true of the author on almost all the theories of authorship. The statement found in the fragment is also no guarantee for the usage in the main stream of Judaism at that time. Second, the Jewish phrases are used in a different way from the πιστὸς ὁ λόγος phrase in the Pastoral Letters. The πιστὸς ὁ λόγος is a formula of introduction, or citation, or emphasis, or some combination thereof, before or after a particular and varied saying. This is not the case with the Jewish phrases cited by Nauck. Third, one must question whether the πιστὸς ὁ λόγος occurrences are always directly and self-consciously connected with σῴζειν/σωτήρ. It is one thing to note that such concepts and words are in the surroundings of πιστὸς ὁ λόγος and are connected to it by the ongoing characteristic of the continuous account; it is another to ascertain that these sayings and hence πιστὸς ὁ λόγος always and in every case have to do with σῴζειν/σωτήρ. A more definite evalution must await a careful consideration of each λόγος in its context. Admitting, as do Dibelius-Conzelmann, that "noch näher kommt die Stelle aus einem Fragment (bei Sukenik Megilloth Genuzoth)", we must finally enter with them the judgment that an exact parallel is certainly lacking[17].

Since an exact parallel is not to be found in the extra-biblical Greek writings, the LXX or the Jewish writings, the meaning of the phrase must be determined by ascertaining the meaning of its individual words as well as by studying the phrase as a whole in its context.

Πιστός[18] has both a passive and an active meaning in its classical us-

---

sätze des šemaᶜ durch 'Wahr und fest... und zuverlässig ist das Wort' ist in der jüdischen Synagoge ein Bekenntnis der Gemeinde zu ihren גּאַל, zu der unwandelbaren Erlösertreue Gottes". "An allen fünf Stellen, in denen πιστὸς ὁ λόγος vorkommt, steht im unmittelbar voraufgehenden oder nachfolgenden Kontext eine Form von σῴζειν/σωτήρ (hebräisch: גאל) ...", p. 49.

[17] Dibelius-Conzelmann, ad 1 Tim. 1:15, "eine genaue Entsprechung fehlt allerdings".

[18] In addition to the word appearing in classical usage from the time of Homer, it is also found in inscriptions, papyri, LXX, Ep. Arist., Philo, and

age[19]. In a passive sense it means trustworthy, faithful, dependable, inspiring trust or faith. In an active sense it means trusting, cherishing faith or trust, also believing, full of faith, faithful. In the passages previously cited in which the phrase under consideration is found the passive meaning is uniformly found (*Dionys. Hal.* 3, 23, 17, and *Dio Chrys.* 28 [45], 3). The same is true of the other references referred to which had both πιστός and λόγος. In the papyri and other non-literary sources the most frequently observed meaning is the passive one of faithful or trustworthy[20]. Although in the Greek New Testament πιστός has both the passive and active meaning, it is often used, indeed generally so, in the passive sense of faithful[21]. The evidence up to this point makes one conclude that trustworthy or faithful is the meaning for πιστός in the phrase.

What is the ground or basis for the designation πιστός in the phrase? In ascertaining the depth of the meaning of πιστός in its construction with ὁ λόγος one looks first of all for other occurrences with λόγος (*supra*), and for other combinations of πιστός with the definite article and a noun in that same word order. There are three such occurrences of the latter in 1 Cor. 1:9; 10:13; and 2 Cor. 1:18. These three are an exact parallel with the exception of an intervening δέ in the second and third cases, and this addition or difference is immaterial. In all three cases we read πιστὸς ὁ Θεός. Here we have come to the ultimate source of the meaning of πιστός in the New Testament[22]. When once one realizes that the New Testament speaks of πιστὸς ὁ Θεός then other usages of πιστός must be seen in that light. The λόγος is πιστός because it comes from ὁ Θεός who is πιστός. 2 Cor. 1:18 gives this connection when it says πιστὸς δὲ ὁ Θεὸς ὅτι ὁ λόγος ἡμῶν ὁ πρὸς ὑμᾶς οὐκ ἔστιν ναὶ καὶ οὔ ("but as God is faithful, our word toward you is not yes and no"). The demonstration of the faithfulness of God is seen in the consistency, the sincerity of ὁ λόγος[23]. The λόγος which Paul brought

---

Josephus. See Arndt-Gingrich, R. Bultmann, *TWNT*, VI, and Liddell and Scott, *A Greek-English Lexicon*, s.v.

[19] Arndt-Gingrich, R. Bultmann, s.v., *TWNT*, VI, p. 175, cf. the English translation of Bultmann's article in the monograph *Faith*, in the series *Bible Key Words*, p. 34, under Classical usage: "It includes active and passive meanings *trusting* and *trustworthy (reliable)*".

[20] J. H. Moulton and G. Milligan, *The Vocabulary of the Greek New Testament from the Papyri and other Non-Literary*, s.v.

[21] R. Bultmann, *TWNT*, VI, s.v., p. 204, and the note immediately above. Examples are Mt. 24:25; 25:21; Lk. 16:10 f.; 1 Tim. 3 : 11; 2 Tim. 2 : 2.

[22] Πιστός is used as a special attribute of God frequently in the N.T. and LXX (*e.g.*, 2 Tim. 2:13; Heb. 11:11; Dt. 7:9; Is. 49:7).

[23] Cf. A. Plummer, *A Critical and Exegetical Commentary on the Second Epistle of St. Paul to the Corinthians (I.C.C.)*, ad loc., "As in Jn. ii. 18, ix. 17,

was as demonstration of and stemmed forth from πιστὸς ὁ Θεός[24]. There are three other passages which are similar but not exactly parallel (1 Thess. 5:24; 2 Thess. 3:3; and Heb. 10:23). They differ in that two of them have the substantive participle in place of the noun (1 Thess. 5:24; Heb. 10:23). And they differ further in that two of them have something intervening (2 Thess. 3:3 has δέ ἐστιν, and Heb. 10:23 has γάρ). But they are similar to the first three passages in that these three too predicate the πιστός of God.

That there is a correlation between the πιστός in the phrase πιστὸς ὁ λόγος and God as πιστός is further demonstrated by the fact that God as the faithful one is referred to within and as part of one of the sayings (2 Tim. 2:11-13, verse 13). There we read, "he abides faithful; for he cannot deny himself" (ἐκεῖνος πιστὸς μένει, ἀρνήσασθαι γὰρ ἑαυτὸν οὐ δύναται). Here, as elsewhere in the Scriptures, the believer is encouraged to be faithful because God is faithful even if we are faithless. Likewise, the λόγος is πιστός because it is a saying which sets forth the truth of the One who is faithful. Even as God's remaining πιστός means that he cannot deny himself so also the λόγος which is πιστός is a λόγος which cannot be denied.

The similar, although not identical, phrases in Revelation 21:5 and 22:6 (οὗτοι οἱ λόγοι πιστοὶ καὶ ἀληθινοί [εἰσιν]) give further insight into the meaning of πιστός in connection with λόγος and thus also a linguistic insight which is apropos to the Pastorals' phrase. Why are the words faithful and true (genuine)? In the 21:5 passage the ultimate source or origin of the command to write is God[25]. The author is to write ὅτι οὗτοι λόγοι πιστοὶ καὶ ἀληθινοί εἰσιν. The words (λόγοι) that are proclaimed as πιστοὶ καὶ ἀληθινοί are those that precede. These words

---

ὅτι 'in that'; 'God is faithful in that our word toward you is not a wavering between Yes and No.' They have his letters... and there is no inconsistency or insincerity in the Gospel which they possess; it is a reflexion of the faithfulness of God. Chrys. paraphrases, 'Mistrust not what is from God, for what is from God cannot be untrue.' ... God is faithful in the fact that the Gospel which is proclaimed by His messengers is not a Gospel ... of promises which are not fulfilled".

24 F. W. Grosheide, De Tweede Brief aan De Kerk te Korinthe (C.N.T.), ad loc., "Πιστὸς ὁ Θεός... dient ter inleiding van een uitspraak, die uit de trouw Gods voortvloeit. Dat stemt ook overeen met de constructie van de Grieksen zin. Daarom vatten we ook hier op: het feit, dat God getrouw is, maakt, dat (ὅτι leidt een objectszin in), Paulus geeft te kennen, dat zijn apostolisch werk voortdurend in aanraking staat met en de kenmerken draagt van een God, die onveranderlijk is. De trouw Gods is waarborg, dat Paulus' woord met betrekking tot (πρός c. acc.) de Korinthiërs gesproken niet is ja en neen".

25 Although some have held that the angel is particularly the one in view. For this and other questions about the understanding of Rev. 21:5 and 22:6 and contexts see the commentaries, and among others S. Greijdanus, De Openbaring Des Heeren aan Johannes (K.N.T., XIV), ad loc.

9

are "faithful and true" because they are words which God who is faithful has spoken and brought to pass. Not only has he who sits on the throne said, "Behold, I make things new" (21:5a), before this command to write; but also immediately afterwards is added, "and he said unto me, They are come to pass" (γέγοναν, 21:6). Again then we find the significance of πιστός/οι in God who speaks and it is done, who promises and it is fulfilled.

It is likewise in Rev. 22:6. Here even more so than in Rev. 21:5 the designation πιστοί καὶ ἀληθινοί is rooted in the revelation of God. Almost as if to explain the designation under consideration, we have the statement, "and the Lord, the God of the spirits of the prophets, sent his angel to show unto his servants the things which must shortly come to pass. And behold, I come quickly" (22:6,7a). To the words which are faithful and true a response is demanded and a promise given, "Blessed is he that keeps (ὁ τηρῶν) the words of the prophecy of this book" 22:7b). The faithful words are to be kept, that is, to be believed and obeyed[26]. The Lord, the God of the spirits of the prophets (τῶν προφητῶν), has given the words of the prophecy (τοὺς λόγους τῆς προφητείας) of the book by showing unto his servants the things which shall come to pass. Hence, the words are πιστοί in the final analysis as the words that the Lord, who is the God of the spirits of the prophets, has shown unto His servants. The blessedness comes in keeping them because they are the faithful words of the faithful God. This Johannine usage may well imply that when Paul declares that πιστὸς ὁ λόγος he also is declaring that they are words which God, through the Holy Spirit working through Paul, declares to be veritable and true. Certainly the least that can be said is that a λόγος designated as πιστός sets forth the truth of the faithful God.

Within the Pastoral Letters themselves we find two occurrences which are quite important for our study. The first is Titus 1:9. In verses 7 ff. the bishop is described. He is first characterized as God's steward (ὡς Θεοῦ οἰκονόμου) and then various other qualifications are set down. Among these is that of "holding to the faithful word which is according to the teaching (ἀντεχόμενον τοῦ κατὰ τὴν διδαχὴν πιστοῦ λόγου) that he may be able both to exhort in the sound doctrine (ἐν τῇ διδασκαλίᾳ τῇ ὑγιαινούσῃ), and to convict the gainsayers". Ὁ λόγος is considered πιστός just because it is κατὰ τὴν διδαχήν[27]. The very construction of

---

[26] Cf. Arndt-Gingrich, sub τηρέω.

[27] Cf. J. N. D. Kelly, A Commentary on the Pastoral Epistles, ad loc., "That message is trustworthy, i.e. can be relied upon, when it agrees with the teaching, i.e. faithfully reflects 'the pattern of teaching' (Rom. vi. 17) which the Apostle himself had delivered.... It is also noticeable that the primitive kerygma is already beginning to take shape as a fixed body of orthodox doctrine...".

the sentence with τοῦ then κατὰ τὴν διδαχήν and then πιστοῦ λόγου emphasizes this relationship. With διδαχήν Paul has in view not so much the activity of teaching as the material content[28] (*cf.* Rom. 16:17). The faithfulness of the word is related to the fact that it is according to the teaching which has been taught by a faithful servant of God, and hence comes from God who is faithful. Therefore one who is a steward of God[29] must regard this λόγος as πιστός and not only hold to it (ἀντεχόμενον) but also be equipped with it so that he is able to exhort (παρακαλεῖν) and to convict (ἐλέγχειν) objectors. Here then the πιστὸς λόγος is part of the solid core of διδαχή which has been faithfully transmitted and received.

The second occurrence in the Pastoral Letters which demands attention is 1 Tim. 1:12, the immediately preceding context of the first appearance of πιστὸς ὁ λόγος. "I thank him that enabled me", says Paul, "Christ Jesus our Lord, for that he counted me faithful (πιστόν), appointing me to service...". Although it is possible to take πιστός here in the active sense of one who believes, the entire context and the use of the verb (ἡγήσατο) rule this out and point rather in the direction of the passive sense of faithful or trustworthy. Arndt-Gingrich (under πιστός) appeal to Aristophanes, *Plut.* 27 as an example of the use of the verb with the noun in the sense of "consider someone trustworthy" (πιστόν τινα ἡγεῖσθαι). Hebrews 11:11 is a noteworthy parallel in the New Testament because there also πιστός and ἡγέομαι are used together. The passage reads that Sarah "counted him faithful who had promised" (πιστὸν ἡγήσατο τον ἐπαγγειλάμενον).The passive meaning of πιπτός is beyond question. The similarity points to the same sense in the 1 Tim. 1:12 passage. In 1 Cor. 4:1—5 Paul refers to his ministry, as he does in 1 Tim., and also uses the word πιστός in reference to it[30]. There πιστός clearly means faithful.

The context itself is determinative of the meaning of πιστός. Πιστός would seem to hark back to ὃ ἐπιστεύθην ἐγώ (1 Tim. 1:11) and be utilized because of that remark. Paul had said in 1:11 that God had committed the gospel to his trust, had entrusted him with it. He goes on to say in 1:12 that this was done because he was considered trustworthy (πιστός) by the Lord. Why was he so considered? This is what Paul marvels about and explains in this section. He begins by saying (verse 12), "I thank him that enabled (ἐνδυναμώσαντι) me, Christ Jesus our

---

[28] See C. Bouma, *De Brieven van den Apostel Paulus aan Timotheus en Titus* (K.N.T., XI), *ad loc.*
[29] "Let a man so account of us, as of ministers of Christ, and stewards of the mysteries of God. Here, moreover, it is required in stewards (οἰκονόμοις) that a man be found faithful (πιστός). ... he that judges me is the Lord" (1 Cor. 4:1-4).
[30] See the preceding note.

11

Lord, for that he counted me faithful, appointing me to service...". It is God's enabling that has made Paul πιστός. And so before he will thank God for regarding him as πιστός, the Apostle first thanks τῷ ἐνδυναμώσαντί με Χριστῷ 'Ιησοῦ τῷ κυρίῳ ἡμῶν (cf., 2 Tim. 4:17; Philip. 4:13). Paul's faithfulness rests in his being strengthened by him who is faithful, Christ Jesus our Lord[31]. This enabling was the result of the mercy (verse 13) and grace which abounded exceedingly from the Lord and which worked faith and love which is in Christ Jesus (verse 14). Through the superabundant grace of the Lord, Paul was not only given faith (πιστίς) but was also enabled to be faithful (πιστός). This great act of God's salvation leads Paul to the first faithful saying, which has superabundantly been demonstrated in him who regards himself πρῶτος of those sinners who are saved. As one who is considered πιστός by the Christ and who is entrusted with the εὐαγγελίον, he may with this apostolic power from God declare authoritatively πιστὸς ὁ λόγος. Here again we see πιστός intimately related to God and his Son Jesus Christ. Paul is enabled to be faithful and counted faithful by Christ. The whole standard of faithfulness is of God. And thus when Paul declares ὁ λόγος to be πιστός he does so with the keen awareness that it is to declare that the λόγος is so regarded by Him who is faithful. Paul's faithfulness, and that of the λόγος, always is related to God (cf. again 2 Cor. 1:18—22).

Theodore of Mopsuestia saw a relation between the πιστὸς ὁ λόγος and ἀμὴν λέγω in the Gospels[32]. The latter is found in the form ἀμὴν λέγω or in the form ἀμὴν ἀμὴν λέγω on the lips of Jesus[33]. 'Αμήν is used by Jesus with λέγω and with a saying which he wishes to declare. Thus it serves as an introductory formula of asseveration to a λόγος that Jesus says (λέγω). "The point of the Amen before Jesus' own sayings is rather to show that as such they are reliable and true, and that they are so as and because Jesus Himself in His Amen acknowledges them to be His own saying and thus makes them valid"[34]. This usage of Jesus may have provided a background for the origin of the formula πιστὸς ὁ

---

[31] For a rather thorough treatment of this whole passage and the question under consideration see Bouma, op. cit., ad loc.

[32] Theodore of Mopsuestia ad 1 Tim. 1:15, "fidele verbum. simile est dictum quod in euangelio est expressum: amen, amen dico uobis".

[33] For the occurrences and statistics see W. F. Moulton and A. S. Geden, A Concordance to the Greek Testament, s.v. In the Synoptic Gospels with minor variations, e.g. the addition of a γάρ, the rendering is ἀμὴν λέγω..., and in the Gospel of John it is ἀμην ἀμην λέγω... H. Schlier, sub ἀμήν, TDNT, I, p. 337 indicates that Jesus places ἀμήν before His sayings 30 times in Mt., 13 in Mk. and 6 in Lk., and in John's Gospel 25 times in a double form.

[34] H. Schlier, TDNT, I, p. 338.

λόγος[35]. The relationship would then be more of similar concepts than that of direct linguistic relationship.

A final evaluation of πιστός and of πιστὸς ὁ λόγος must await the study of ὁ λόγος and the consideration of the phrase as a whole.

Λόγος is a word found in literary Greek since Homer[36]. It is also a biblical word occurring many times in the Septuagint version, especially for דָּבָר, also for אֹמֶר and מִלָּה[37]. Moulton and Milligan very simply and clearly come to the point in regard to its meaning by speaking of "its ordinary sense of 'word', 'saying'"[38]. The general sense of *word* or *saying*[39] prevails in the New Testament usage, although even within the Pastoral Letters themselves the variegated nuances within this general scope are most evident. Twenty times[40] λόγος occurs in the Pastoral Letters of which five are πιστὸς ὁ λόγος. Within these other fifteen are found the possible meanings of "speech" (1 Tim. 4:12; *cf.* Titus 2:8), "preaching" (1 Tim. 5:17), and "words" (plural) for what a person says, or "message" (2 Tim. 4:15)[41]. Then there is the controverted passage of 1 Tim. 4:5, which among other possibilities some refer to God's creative

---

[35] The evidence is certainly not conclusive. The O.T. אָמֵן is translated usually γένοιτο (see Arndt-Gingrich, *sub* ἀμήν) and not by πιστός. But a change from the personal λέγω to the more indirect and passive λόγος may have influenced the change from the Hebraistic and personal ἀμήν to the more indirect and passive Greek πιστός. Nevertheless, when Paul affirms πιστὸς ὁ λόγος it amounts to the same as ἀμὴν λέγω, except that in Jesus' case the affirmation concerns his own words and is in his own authority. In Paul's case the affirmation is made concerning ὁ λόγος and on the authority of one who found him faithful, even the Lord Jesus Christ.

[36] For a study of the word in the Greek world see A. Debrunner and H. Kleinknecht, *TDNT*, IV, pp. 71-91.

[37] Thayer, *s.v.* For a study of the Hebrew equivalents for λόγος, and of the Word of God in the Old Testament, *cf.* O. Procksch, *TDNT*, IV, pp. 91-100.

[38] Moulton and Milligan, *s.v.*, Liddell and Scott for the Greek language in general, and Arndt-Gingrich for the New Testament in particular agree on dividing the function or meaning of the word into the two large headings of *speaking*, and *computation* or *reckoning* (*cf.* A. Debrunner, *TDNT*, IV, p. 69 f.). To these two divisions Arndt-Gingrich, Cremer and Thayer add the unique usage of ὁ λόγος as referring to Christ.

[39] Liddell and Scott, Vol. II, p. 1058, *sub* VI, similar to Cremer, *s.v.*, speak of λόγος as "*verbal expression* or *utterance* . . . rarely a single *word*, . . . never in Gramm. signif. of vocable (ἔπος, λέξις, ὄνομα, ῥῆμα), usu. of a *phrase*." A Debrunner underscores this evaluation, *TDNT*, IV, p. 74, note 16.

[40] 1 Tim. 1:15; 3:1; 4:5, 6, 9, 12; 5:17; 6:3; Titus 1:3, 9; 2:5, 8; 3:8; 2 Tim. 1:13; 2:9, 11, 15, 17.

[41] For these and other examples *cf.* Arndt-Gingrich, *passim*, *s.v.* Also note the various translations for each of the places where λόγος is found. See note above for the listing.

word, or "the true understanding of God and his relation to creation which is contained in his word (in the Old Testament)"[42]. More often λόγος is used in the Pastorals as the truth or message of God; e.g., 1 Tim. 4:5 (θεοῦ), 4:6 (τῆς πίστεως), 5:17, 6:3 (τοῖς τοῦ κυρίου ἡμῶν Ἰησοῦ Χριστοῦ); Tit. 1:3 (αὐτοῦ), 1:9 (τοῦ κατὰ τὴν διδαχὴν πιστοῦ λόγου), 2:5 (τοῦ θεοῦ); 2 Tim. 1:13 (ὑποτύπωσιν ἔχε ὑγιαινόντων λόγων), 2:9 (τοῦ θεοῦ), 2:15 (τῆς ἀληθείας). Arndt-Gingrich correctly place most of these in the category "of divine revelation through Christ and his messengers" (s.v.). They point out that this Christian message "is called simply ὁ λόγος = The 'Word', since no misunderstanding would be possible among Christians"[43]. When the New Testament writers speak of the word (ὁ λόγος), they have in view that special word, the truth of God, unless the context indicates otherwise[44]. This is so obvious in the one place in the Pastoral Letters, excluding the πιστὸς ὁ λόγος passages, where λόγος appears simply with the definite article (2 Tim. 4:2— κήρυξον τὸν λόγον). Likewise the five-fold reference to ὁ λόγος in πιστὸς ὁ λόγος fits in this same category. The word (ὁ λόγος) is πιστός because it is the word setting forth God's truth. And so ὁ λόγος is used in the phrase πιστὸς ὁ λόγος to indicate that particular saying which crystallizes and enunciates some aspect of the Christian message.

In the phrase πιστὸς ὁ λόγος and in the statements to which it refers is the λόγος in each case oral or written? Some differentiation is made in 2 Thess. 2:15, "So then brethren, stand fast, and hold the traditions which you were taught, whether by word (εἴτε διὰ λόγου), or by epistle (εἴτε δι' ἐπιστολῆς) of ours." Here λόγος in contrast to ἐπιστολῆς

---

[42] C. K. Barrett, *The Pastoral Epistles (The New Claredon Bible*, Oxford: Claredon Press, 1963), *ad loc.*

[43] Page 479. Revising the list given by Arndt-Gingrich, this list of ὁ λόγος with no other qualification, such as adjective or genitive construction, is as follows: Mt. 13:20-23; Mk. 2:2; 4 : 14-20, 33; Lk. 1:2; 8:12 f., 15; Acts 6:6; 8:4; 10:36; 11:19; 14:25; 16:6; 17:11; 18:5; Gal. 6:6; Col. 4:3; 1 Thess. 1:6; 2 Tim. 4:2; 1 Peter 2:8; 3:1; 1 John 2:7. Mark 8:32 is questionable as to meaning. But that the meaning is not always or necessarily intrinsic in λόγος is evident from the variation in 1 Peter 3:1 from τῷ λόγῳ as the truth or message of God to ἄνευ λόγου, without a word, without speaking. See the commentaries. However, even this passage has the definite article ὁ with λόγος when used in reference to God's message and λόγος without the definite article when used for another meaning.

[44] The context, not solely the presence of the definite article, must always be the final determining factor even with this working observation. 2 Cor. 11:6 with its use of τῷ λόγῳ is a good case in point. There is not *the* word of God which is in view but rather Paul's speech or manner of speaking. *Cf.* P. E. Hughes, *Paul's Second Epistle to the Corinthians (The New International Commentary on The New Testament), ad loc.*

(εἴτε ... εἴτε), designates Paul's oral teaching[45]. Compare also 2 Thess. 2:2, "...or by word, or by epistle..." (μήτε διὰ λόγου μήτε δι' ἐπιστολῆς)[46]. The λόγος as Paul's oral teaching is brought out clearly in 2 Thess. 2:5. "Do you not remember, that, when I was yet with you, I told (ἔλεγον) you these things?" In this context the λόγος would seem to indicate not only that which is oral but also that which is preaching or teaching (cf. esp. 1 Thess. 2:13). This is not always strictly involved in the use of λόγος when the oral element is to the fore, nor when λόγος is commended or emphasized. In Acts 15:27, Judas and Silas are sent to confirm that which was written (γράψαντες, verse 23). Along with these things which are written, the apostles and elders sent "Judas and Silas, who themselves also shall tell you the same things by word of mouth" (verse 27, καὶ αὐτοὺς διὰ λόγου ἀπαγγέλλοντας τὰ αὐτά). The emphasis is not first of all on teaching or proclamation (although ἀπαγγέλλω is also used in that sense). It is rather on a reporting or telling orally (διὰ λόγου) of that action which was taken, as a corroboration of it, and also an explanation and even explication of that which was given in writing. A further example of λόγος used as an oral report is that of Acts 11:22, "and the report (ὁ λόγος) concerning them came to the ears of the church which was in Jerusalem" (cf. Lk. 5:15; 7:17).

Since teaching often and preaching especially is oral, and since ὁ λόγος is commonly understood as the Christian message, λόγος itself may designate proclamation or instruction. But it is not this which is most basic to the meaning of the word when contrasted with that which is written but rather simply its oral character. This is made yet clearer by 2 Cor. 10:10, "his letters, they say, are weighty and strong; but his bodily presence is weak, and his speech (ὁ λόγος) of no account". Whether the translation be that of speech, as here (A.S.V. and most English translations) or, as may be conjectured, that of preaching or proclamation, the stress of the contrast of the sentence is upon oral over against written[47]. That λόγος and κήρυγμα may not be simply identified is immediately apparent in 1 Cor. 2:4. "And my speech (ὁ λόγος μου) and

---

[45] Cf. the commentaries of J. Eadie, Wm. Hendriksen (N.T.C.), G. Milligan, L. Morris (N.I.C.N.T.), Van Leeuwen (K.N.T.), and especially J. E. Frame, A Critical and Exegetical Commentary on the Epistles of St. Paul to The Thessalonians (I.C.C.), ad loc.

[46] For the meaning of ὡς δι ἡμῶν and the exact force, therefore, of the terms under consideration see the clear treatment of the various possibilities by Frame, Thess. (I.C.C.), ad loc. The conclusion on these matters does not affect the distinction between λόγος as oral and ἐπιστολῆς as written.

[47] For further consideration of λόγος and of the verse see F. W. Grosheide, De Tweede Brief aan De Kerk te Korinthe (C.N.T.), ad loc. See further 1 Cor. 1:17 and 2:1-5 for Paul's own evaluation of his λόγος.

my preaching (τὸ κήρυγμά μου) were not in persuasive words (λόγοις) of wisdom..."⁴⁸.

Although it is evident that an oral nature may be predicated of λόγος, it may not be done absolutely to the exclusion of the use of λόγος for that which is written⁴⁹. Λόγος is used for that which is written in Luke's description of "the former treatise (λόγον) I made" (Acts 1:1) in referring to his "book", the Gospel of Luke. 2 Thess. 3:14 ("And if any man obeys not our word by this epistle" — τῷ λόγῳ ἡμῶν διὰ τῆς ἐπιστολῆς), and Heb. 13:22 ("But I exhort you, brethren, bear with the word — τοῦ λόγου — of exhortation for I have written — ἐπέστειλα — unto you in few words — διὰ βραχέων") also bear out the use of λόγος in reference to that which is written. Even in the very context where Paul uses λόγος as that which is oral in distinction from that which is written (2 Cor. 10:10), he also goes on in 2 Cor. 10:11 to use λόγος in reference to that which is written, namely his letters (ἐπιστολῶν). "Let such a one reckon this, that, what we are in word by letters (τῷ λόγῳ δι' ἐπιστολῶν) when we are absent, such are, we also in deed when we are present". This close juxtaposition of the usage of λόγος first as oral then as written is clear evidence that the word λόγος itself may not be taken to be exclusively of itself either oral or written. Rather, this proximate alternation demonstrates that it is only the context which determines the particular meaning of λόγος. Apart from such contextual delineation there is no way to ascertain without doubt the specificity of ὁ λόγος.

It is apparent that in those very same books of the N.T. where λόγος is used to refer to that which is oral, it is also used to refer to that which is written (e.g., Acts in which cf. also 2:41; 20:7 to those previously cited; 2 Thess.; 2 Cor. side by side in 10:10 and 11). Thus it must be emphasized that contextual considerations, not etymology or conceptual ideology, are the determining factors in ascertaining the precise shade of meaning of λόγος⁵⁰. Where those factors are absent so is the basis for judgment.

⁴⁸ Cf. Robertson & Plummer, 1 Cor. (I.C.C.), and F. W. Grosheide, 1 Cor. (N.I.C.N.T.), ad loc.
⁴⁹ G. Kittel, TWNT, IV, p. 101, makes this clear when he says: "Paulus unterscheidet einen Brief von dem λόγος als dem gesprochen Wort (2 Th 2,2.15; 2 K 10,10, vgl Ag 15,27), kann aber ebenso – sogar in Selben Satz, 2 K 10,11 – den Brief selbst als Träger und Wiedergabe des λόγος bezeichnen (2 Th 3,14, vgl Hb 5,11; 13,22). Eine Ansprache (Ag 2,41; 20,7), ein Bericht (Ag 11, 22), ein berichtendes Gerücht (Lk 5,15; 7,17) heissen λόγος, ebenso aber auch der zum Buch verfasste Teilbericht (Ag 1,1)".
⁵⁰ A point repeatedly and properly made by James Barr, The Semantics of Biblical Language (London: Oxford, 1961), passim over against an opposite tendency among some writers of Kittel, TWNT as well as some other Biblical scholars. Arndt-Gingrich sub λόγος say, "The expression [λόγος] may take any

We must grant, from the survey before us as well as from the probabilities of the situation, that even though repeated five-fold in the Pastoral Letters and thus in effect a "formula", πιστὸς ὁ λόγος might refer in some cases to that which was oral and in others to that which was written. It would exceed the limits of exegesis to demand *a priori* that the repetition would require the λόγοι to be either all written or all oral because one or more can be demonstrated to be one or the other. Thus, the uniformity of the phrase does not carry with it inherently the uniformity of the form of the λόγος. This is obvious from even a cursory glance at the variety in style and length of those passages to which the formula refers. And this judgment is substantiated by the analogy of Rev. 21:5 and 22:6. There we have two phrases or formulas which, except for the addition of εἰσιν at 21:5, are identical. They occur in the same book and that in fairly close conjunction to one another. They form a most apt parallel for πιστὸς ὁ λόγος because they contain, in a very slightly different form, the words under consideration (οὗτοι οἱ λόγοι πιστοὶ καὶ ἀληθινοί εἰσιν). In Rev. 21:5, most commentators[51] take λόγοι as referring to the oral statement of him "that sits on the throne" in verse 5, *i.e.*, "Behold, I make all things new". Even though the command was to write, the original reference of λόγοι is to that which is oral. And its becoming written does not change the meaning or application of the phrase. That which is written in verse 5b now refers to that which was written in verse 5a which was once spoken of as oral λόγοι. On the other hand, in Rev. 22:6 λόγοι is taken by most commentators[52] as referring to all that which precedes in the book, and hence to that which is written down. It is true that John has been shown these things (verse 6b), and that he has heard and seen them (verse 8), but it is still the emphasis on the words of the book as written which is to the fore[53] (*cf.* verse 7, "Blessed is he that keeps the words of the prophecy of

one of many different forms, so that the exact transl. of λ. depends on the context".

[51] *Cf. e.g.*, Greijdanus (*K.N.T.*), H. B. Swete, Düsterdieck (Meyer), Hendriksen, *More Than Conquerors*, p. 241, E. Lohmeyer (*H.N.T.*), J. Behm (*N.T.D.*), E. Lohse (*N.T.D.*), *ad loc.* I. T. Beckwith, *ad loc.*, thinks it refers to verses 1-5. But even on the view espoused by Beckwith λόγοι refers also to the oral statement of verse 5.

[52] *Cf. e.g.*, Greijdanus, H. B. Swete, Düsterdieck (Meyer), Hendriksen, *op. cit.*, p. 251, J. Behm (*N.T.D.*), E. Lohse (*N.T.D.*), Beckwith, *ad loc.* E. Lohmeyer (*H.N.T.*), *ad loc.*, restricts the phrase to that which immediately precedes. Over against such a view as that of Lohmeyer, Swete (*ad loc.*) argues that "the sayings which he pronounces to be 'faithful and true' ... are, as the sequel shows, the teachings of the entire Book, and not only the noble words with which the last of its visions has just ended (*vv.* 3-5)".

[53] "οὗτοι οἱ λόγοι, *these words:* the λόγοι, *words*, include not only the actual *utterances*, but the whole revelation given in the vision. And while reference is here made directly to what is revealed in the vision immediately preceding

17

this book" — τοὺς λόγους ... τοῦ βιβλίου τούτου, and verse 9, "... that keep the words of this book" — τοὺς λόγους τοῦ βιβλίου τούτου; *cf.* further verses 10, 18 and 19). Here then we have the word λόγοι, in two almost identical phrases in the same book, referring to different kinds of λόγοι; in the one case to that which was oral, in another to that which was written. In the former, λόγοι designates a brief and specific oral statement; in the latter, λόγοι designates the entire book written comprising both what was seen and also what was heard. Thus once more, and this time in the case of a repeated "formula", it is evident that the context determines the meaning. Hence, in the Pastoral Letters, the λόγος itself and the contextual evidence will be determinative of the meaning of λόγος in the "formula" πιστὸς ὁ λόγος in reference to oral or written.

It is evident in the Pastoral Letters that λόγος in πιστὸς ὁ λόγος refers to a statement, to a series of words. In each case there is a particular phrase or group of phrases in view. How shall λόγος be rendered into English to designate in a felicitous way that it refers to such a statement and therefore is used in that way? The best word available is that of *"saying"* (*A.V., R.V., A.S.V., R.S.V.*). It does justice to the fact that λόγος commonly means a word or saying and that it belongs to the family of λέγω (to say). "Saying" does not prejudice the question of oral versus written, but it does recognize, by being a collective noun in the singular, the plurality of words referred to by the singular word λόγος. It further recognizes, by the nuance which the word "saying" contains, the admittedly somewhat aphoristic character of that which is designated by λόγος in these five places. Both the meaning "saying" and the use of λόγος to refer to sayings is found elsewhere in the New Testament (Mt. 19:11; John 4:37; *cf.* also Mt. 19:22; Mk. 7:29; Lk. 1:29; Jn. 2:22, 6:60, 7:36, 15:20, 18:9, 19:8)[54], as well as in Paul (*cf.* Rom. 13:9 and 1 Cor. 15:54)[55]. Λόγος in reference

(219-225), it is clear that all is included which is presupposed and culminates in that vision of the coming of the new Jerusalem, that is, the revelations of the whole book; this is shown by the general scope of the following clauses, and especially by the express designation, 'the words of the prophecy of this book'" (Beckwith, *ad loc.*).

54 See Thayer, *s.v.*, where this list is further expanded. Thayer definitely groups πιστὸς ὁ λόγος in the Pastorals in this category as do Cremer, *s.v.*, and Liddell-Scott.

55 Lock, *ad* Titus 3:8, takes the position that Paul is "quoting some well-known saying" and gives this as a more probable solution "as all the sayings have a gnomic and rhythmical character and bear on salvation". He then adds, "*cf.* Ro 13⁹ ἐν τούτῳ τῷ λόγῳ ἀνακεφαλαιοῦται, 1 Co 15⁵⁴ τότε γενήσεται ὁ λόγος ὁ γεγραμμένος".

E. Walder, "The Logos of the Pastoral Epistles", *The Journal of Theological*

to a proverb, maxim or saying is a not unusual phenomenon in classical Greek[56].

The question is often asked whether πιστὸς ὁ λόγος as used in the Pastoral Letters is a citation[57] formula or a formula of emphasis[58]. And the matter is usually tendered as an either/or proposition. On the contrary, the proper solution to this natural inquiry is the answer that it is both. It is this answer alone that does justice to both elements of πιστὸς ὁ λόγος.

Studies, xxiv (1923), pp. 310-315, repudiates the rendering of ὁ λόγος ·in the impersonal sense of "the saying" and of ὁ λόγος as referring to a saying in the five-fold formula. He attempts to prove that ὁ λόγος in πιστὸς ὁ λόγος and elsewhere in the Pastorals is used in the Johannine sense of the personal Word of God, on the analogy of πιστὸς ὁ θέος, πιστὸς ὁ κύριος. Lock's critique, *ad* Titus 3:8, is a most adequate reply: "but in 1³ it does not suit the following words, ἐν κηρύγματι: in 1⁹ the personal Logos could scarcely be described as 'faithful *according to the teaching*'; in the phrase πιστὸς ὁ λόγος the personal use would be appropriate in 2 Ti 2¹¹, but it is not needed there; it seems tautologous in 1 Ti 1¹⁵, and very inappropriate in 1 Ti 3¹ and here; whereas the explanation of it as a quotation is appropriate in each passage".

[56] For the references see Thayer, p. 380, 2c, and Liddell-Scott, II, p. 1059, VII, 2. As examples note the following: Aeschylus, *The Seven Against Thebes*, *Loeb*. ed., ἀλλ' οὖν θεοὺς τοὺς τῆς ἁλούσης πόλεος ἐκλείπειν λόγος (but then, 'tis said, a captured city is forsaken by its gods); Plato, *Phaedrus*, 240 C, ἥλικα γὰρ καὶ ὁ παλαιὸς λόγος τέρπειν τὸν ἥλικα (*Loeb* ed., translates, or rather paraphrases, The old proverb says, 'birds of a feather flock together').

[57] *E.g.*, *Dibelius*, 2nd ed., Jeremias. The question as to the origin of these λόγοι must be postponed until after they have been considered individually. Of course the question of whether πιστὸς ὁ λόγος is a citation formula is intimately related to whether these λόγοι are cited by Paul or are his own creation. It must be acknowledged that Paul could refer to his own saying which he had coined as a λόγος and with a citation formula, although this is less likely than if the λόγοι were the creations of others. The discussion above only deals with what may be gathered from πιστὸς ὁ λόγος itself. The confirmation or repudiation of this will have to await the evaluation of the λόγοι themselves.

[58] Bernard, Bouma, Bover (see below in this note), Calvin, Dibelius 3rd ed. by Conzelmann, Fairbairn, Nauck, *op. cit.*, Ridderbos, Schlatter, Simpson, G. Kittel, *TDNT*, IV, p. 118, Note 199. Kelly takes a somewhat middle position when he says that it "is used to introduce, or follow, a citation . . . to which he wishes to draw attention". The difficulty of the false distinction is pointed up in the fact that the 3rd ed. by Conzelmann prefers "Beteuerung", but indicates that the 2nd ed. by Dibelius alone took the position of "Zitationsformel". J. G. Duncan, "Πιστὸς ὁ λόγος," *The Expository Times*, XXXV (1923), p. 141, holds that the expression "is simply a method of calling attention to and specially emphasizing . . . a truth . . .", and that the sayings are probably coined by the writer. J. M. Bover, "Fidelis Sermo", *Biblica*, 19 (1958), uses the language of "que tan encarecidamente recomienda el Apóstol con esta llamada de attencion".

19

In favor of the phrase as a citation formula, stress has been placed on the word λόγος as meaning a saying and the obvious "saying" which is cited. Mostly before, but sometimes also after a saying is cited, the formula πιστὸς ὁ λόγος is used to draw attention to the fact that here is something, *i.e.*, a saying, which has been cited or quoted. And indeed all that has been said is true and does do justice to both the λόγος in the formula and the λόγος which is indeed cited. The author could have used πιστός without λόγος, or in some other combination, if he merely wanted to emphasize that what he had written or was going to write was faithful. Therefore proper regard must be given to λόγος as indicative of a saying which is being seth forth.

On the other hand, the author did not have to use the word πιστός, but could have utilized λόγος in some other combination, if he simply wanted to indicate that here was a λόγος (a saying). But he does use πιστός. And thus this makes the formula more than a mere indication of citation. In the nature of the case, it makes it a formula which speaks with an emphasis, *i.e.*, that the λόγος is πιστός. Πιστὸς ὁ λόγος does not merely call attention to the fact that here we have a λόγος; but it says with emphasis that here we have a saying which is regarded as πιστός. This is further borne out by the fact that πιστός is a predicate rather than an attributive adjective and that as a predicate adjective it is placed before the articular noun for emphasis (for a fuller treatment, see *infra*).

The formula does not only contain λόγος and refer to a λόγος, nor does it only contain πιστός and call something πιστός, but rather the formula points to a λόγος cited and says with emphasis that this λόγος is πιστός. The formula is therefore of itself not just a citation formula and not just an emphasis formula, but a combined citation-emphasis formula. Its five-fold repeated usage in these letters demonstrates beyond reasonable doubt not only that πιστὸς ὁ λόγος is a formula, rather than just another phrase, but also that it is a citation-emphasis formula.

It is natural to ask the question as to the origin of the repeated formula πιστὸς ὁ λόγος. Is the formula formed by Paul himself or does he use a formula created by others? On the one hand it may be conjectured that πιστὸς ὁ λόγος was not Pauline but was as much taken over from others as the sayings themselves may have been. The single instance in Titus 1:9 is just the exception that indicates how foreign πιστὸς ὁ λόγος is to Paul. The usage in Titus 1:9 merely reflects then a borrowing of the usage in the five-fold formula which was itself borrowed. Likewise, the absence of such a formula or anything very close to it in any other of Paul's letters may be pleaded as an indication that it is not original with Paul. The very similar formula in Rev. 21:5; 22:6 may point to a general usage in the New Testament age. However, the absence of such formulas elsewhere also speaks against such a theory. The evidence is very thin and the conjectures are just that.

On the other hand the formula certainly can not be absolutely denied to the author, the Apostle Paul. Paul has used both ὁ λόγος and πιστός elsewhere in his writings, as the study has shown. One who has used ὁ λόγος and who has used πιστὸς ὁ θεός, πιστὸς ὁ καλῶν, πιστὸς ... ὁ κύριος can certainly not be denied the possibility of saying πιστὸς ὁ λόγος. Further, the use of πιστοῦ λόγου in Titus 1:9 points to the author's known combination of these words. But even this affirmation of the possibility and probability concerning the formula is not absolutely without doubt, although it seems to be the case. The use of πιστός in 1 Tim. 1:15 fits in the context where Paul uses ἐπιστεύθην (verse 11) and πιστόν (verse 12; cf. also ἀπιστία — verse 13, and πίστεως — verse 14). The formula would seem to flow forth from and fit within that passage, the first occurrence, as the self-conscious creation of Paul. No matter what the origin of the phrase, as it is used and found in the Pastorals it is thereby Pauline. It is used with the authority of an apostle who can authoritatively cite the λόγος and not only indicate that it is πιστός but also pronounce it such.

Πιστὸς ὁ λόγος is often translated, following the Greek word order, with the words, "Faithful is the saying". Translators and commentators uniformly and universally recognize that the copulative verb ἐστίν, although omitted, is understood and properly supplied in translation[59]. Being in the predicate rather than the attributive position, πιστός may be thereby stressed and emphasized[60]. And further, πιστός has the predicate position of being before the articular noun rather than after it. N. Turner observes that "when the predicate occurs before the articular noun it tends to be emphatic"[61]. This is certainly true in 1 Cor. 1:9, 10:13; 2 Cor. 1:18; 2 Thess. 3:3, cf., 1 Thess. 5:24, in all of which πιστός is a

---

[59] See R. W. Funk, *A Greek Grammar of the New Testament and Other Early Christian Literature* (A Translation and Revision of the ninth-tenth German edition of F. Blass and A. Debrunner, Chicago: The University of Chicago Press, 1961), p. 70 f. *Cf.* for similar examples 1 Cor. 1:9, 10:13; 2 Cor. 1:18.
[60] A. T. Robertson, *A Grammar of the Greek New Testament in the Light of Historical Research* (London: Hodder & Stoughton, 3rd ed., 1919), p. 656, makes just such a point with some emphasis. "The distinction between the attributive adjective and the predicate adjective lies in just this, that the predicate presents an additional statement, is indeed the main point, while the attributive is an incidental description of the substantive about which the statement is made". H. W. Smyth, revised by G. M. Messing, *Greek Grammar* (Cambridge: Harvard University Press, 1959), p. 295, says essentially the same thing with however a note of qualification: "This is called the predicate position, which often lends emphasis".
[61] N. Turner, *A Grammar of New Testament Greek by J. H. Moulton*, Vol. III, Syntax, (Edinburgh: T. & T. Clark, 1963), p. 225.

predicate adjective before the articular noun. In all these passages Paul is emphasizing that God, the Lord, is faithful (πιστός). So in the formula πιστὸς ὁ λόγος, Paul is saying with emphasis that ὁ λόγος is faithful or trustworthy (πιστός). This grammatical insight lends further weight to the evaluation of the formula as one of emphasis (see *supra*) as well as one of citation.

B. ... καὶ πάσης ἀποδοχῆς ἄξιος

Twice (1 Tim. 1:15; 4:9) πιστὸς ὁ λόγος had added to it by the conjunction καὶ the identical phrase πάσης ἀποδοχῆς ἄξιος, ("worthy of all acceptation"). 'Αποδοχή occurs nowhere else in the New Testament. Not only is ἀποδοχή confined to the Pastoral Letters but also the adjective, ἀποδεκτός (1 Tim. 2:3; 5:4). The verbal form, ἀποδέχομαι, is not found in the Pastorals or in Paul generally but only in Luke (Lk. 8:40; 9:11; Acts 2:41; 18:27; 21:17; 24:3; 28:30). 'Αποδέχομαι is a compound of δέχομαι which is found in most of Paul's letters[62] as well as in other parts of the N.T.[63]

'Αποδοχή is found from Thucydides (V B.C.) on, although only once is it found in his works. It is not found in the LXX or other Greek versions of the O.T. and Apocrypha[64]. Thus, "apart from a single refer. in Thuc., it is only Hellenistic, and therefore comparatively late"[65]. One reference often cited as illustrative of the meaning of ἀποδοχή is 1, 5, 5, in Polybius (II B.C.) where it is found often. The citation is τοτ' ἤδη καὶ πᾶς ὁ συνεχὴς λόγος ἀποδοχῆς τυγχάνει παρὰ τοῖς ἀκούουσιν ("they will give ear to all the subsequent narrative")[66]. The evidence for the occurrence, usage and meaning of the term, as well as the phrase (which shall be discussed *infra*), is plentiful[67].

The consensus of lexicons[68] as well as of the commentators[69] agrees on

---

62 1 Cor. 2:14; 2 Cor. 6:1; 7:15; 8:17; 11:4,16; Gal. 4:14; Eph. 6:17; Philip. 4:18; Col. 4:10; 1 Thess. 1:6; 2:13; 2 Thess. 2:10.

63 Mt., Mk., Lk., Jn., Acts, Heb., and James.

64 G. Abbott-Smith, *A Manual Greek Lexicon of the New Testament* (Edinburgh: T. & T. Clark, 3rd ed., 1937), *s.v.*, and especially note its absence from Hatch and Redpath, *Concordance to the Septuagint*.

65 W. Grundmann, *TDNT*, II, p. 55.

66 Polybius, *The Histories*, 1, 5, 5 (*The Loeb Classical Library*, I, ed. by E. Capps, T. E. Page, W. H. D. Rouse, Eng. trans. by W. R. Paton, London: Heinemann, MCMXXII, p. 14).

67 See Arndt-Gingrich, Cremer, Liddell & Scott, Moulton & Milligan, and Thayer, *s.v. Cf.* F. Field, *Notes on the Translation of the New Testament* (Cambridge: The University Press, 1899), p. 203, who shows by numerous examples how the word is a favorite with later Greek authors, especially with Diodorus Siculus, generally in the phrases ἀποδοχῆς ἄξιος, ἀξιοῦσθαι, τυγχάνειν.

68 Arndt-Gingrich, "*acceptance, approval*", Cremer, p. 686, "*recognition, acknowledgment, approval*, and, indeed, *willing, ready acknowledgment*", Lid-

22

the essential meaning of the word. W. Grundmann gives as the meaning of this word that of "acceptance". He affirms that it is a substantive of ἀποδέχομαι, and then goes on to say, "Like the verb, however, it usually denotes friendly reception and therefore approval or appreciation"[70]. He paraphrases πάσης ἀποδοχῆς ἄξιος with the words "worthy of approval and high estimation".

The meaning of ἀποδοχή is borne out by the meaning of the verb ἀποδέχομαι itself. "In the N.T. it occurs only in the Lucan writings and in the general sense of 'friendly reception' "[71]. The most significant passage is that in which the verb is used with λόγος, i.e., Acts 2:41, οἱ μὲν οὖν ἀποδεξάμενοι τὸν λόγον αὐτοῦ ἐβαπτίσθησαν, καὶ προσετέθησαν ἐν τῇ ἡμέρᾳ ἐκείνῃ ψυχαὶ ὡσεὶ τρισχίλιαι ("they then that received his word were baptized: and there were added in that day about three thousand souls"). Here the meaning is that of accepting what is offered, of receiving it into the mind, in short, of believing the word (Codex D even has the textual variant πιστεύσαντες at this point). Since ἀποδέχομαι means much the same as the simple form δέχομαι, it is relevant to note that δέχεσθαι τὸν λόγον τοῦ Θεοῦ is a recurrent phrase in Acts (8:14; 11:1; 17:11; cf. Jn. 1:21; 1 Th. 1:6; 2:13)[72]. Here also δέχομαι is the equivalent of faith, receiving that which is given. So ἀποδοχή in the phrase under consideration is a believing receiving of the λόγος which is πιστός.

Ἄξιος properly means "bringing up the other beam of the scales", "bringing into equilibrium", and therefore "equivalent". The use of ἄξιος shows that two distinct magnitudes are equal or equivalent; an act "deserves" praise or punishment. So in the N.T.: μισθοῦ, τιμῆς, τροφῆς, πληγῶν, δεσμῶν, θανάτου ἄξιος, Mt. 10:10; Lk. 10:7; 12:48; 23:15, 41; Acts 23:29; 25:11, 25; 26:31; Rom. 1:32; 1 Tim. 5:18; 6:1; Rev. 16:6. Hence the meaning of "worthy". As Inschr. Priene, 59,3: ἐπιστοφῆς ἄξιος, "worthy of consideration", so I Tim. 1:15; 4:9: πάσης ἀποδοχῆς ἄξιος, "worthy in any wise to be received"[73]. Ἄξιος when used in the sense of worthy is usually found with the genitive of the things to which it refers. In 1 Tim. 1:15 and 4:9 this is also the case; there ἄξιος is found

---

dell & Scott, "acceptance, approbation, favour", and Thayer, "reception, admission, acceptance, approbation", all s.v.
[69] Cf., Bengel, Bernard, Bouma, Dibelius-Conzelmann, Fausset, Hendriksen, Lock, Spicq, ad 1 Tim. 1:15.
[70] W. Grundmann, TDNT, II, p. 55.
[71] Ibid.
[72] Ibid., p. 54.
[73] For this portion of the discussion of ἄξιος the author has utilized the work of W. Foerster, TDNT, I, s.v., p. 379.

23

in relation to πάσης ἀποδοχῆς in the genitive. The λόγος is worthy *of* πάσης ἀποδοχῆς.

The phrase ἀποδοχῆς ἄξιος is represented in extra-biblical Greek writings and it may be spoken of as one generally used. Field shows how it is a favorite one with later Greek authors[74]. In fact, Moulton and Milligan say that "Fields's examples (*Notes*, p. 203) show how much of a formula this ἀποδοχῆς ἄξιος (as 1 Tim. 1[15]) had become"[75]. Perhaps one of the most interesting occurrences for our study is the inscription from Ephesus, which Moulton and Milligan date *circa* A.D. 148, in which "an ἀγωνοθέτης named Priscus is styled δοκιμωτάτου καὶ πάσης τειμῆς καὶ ἀποδοχῆς ἀξίου"[76]. This inscription may reflect an older and established usage at Ephesus and may therefore give some indication why Paul uses the phrase now under consideration. It is noteworthy that the phrase πάσης ἀποδοχῆς ἄξιος is only used in 1 Timothy (1:15; 4:9) which is sent to Timothy and the church at Ephesus (1 Tim. 1:3). The inscription itself uses the phrase in relation to the games. Paul's reference to athletics and the games to illustrate the Christian life is well known. And of the two occurrences of πάσης ἀποδοχῆς ἄξιος, one is used in connection with bodily exercise (1 Tim. 4:8 & 9). However, these considerations may not be unduly pressed as conclusive both because of the late date of the inscription (*circa* A.D. 148), and also because the phrase is so widely known in other Greek writings outside of Ephesus. Paul could well have known and used the phrase apart from any known usage in Ephesus. But then again he may have used it because he knew it would be particularly fitting and would make the impact he desired in Ephesus. It is difficult to give a decisive answer to this question.

---

[74] Field, *op. cit.*, p. 203. See also Arndt-Gingrich, and Moulton & Milligan, *sub* ἀποδοχή. B. Hicks, in his article "On Some Political Terms Employed in the New Testament", *The Classical Review* I (1887), p. 4, adds to the evidence when he writes: "Thus in addition to the instances of the phrase ἀποδοχῆς ἄξιος cited by Field on 1 Tim. i.15, we may quote the following from an Ephesian inscription now at Oxford: Τίτου Αἰλίου | Πρίσκου, ἀνδρὸς δοκμωτάτου, καὶ | πάσης τιμῆς καὶ ἀποδοχῆς ἀξίου (Baille, *Facs. Inscr. Gr.* No. 2; see Waddinton, *Fastes*, p. 225). Other examples of the same phrase may be found in the *Corpus Inscriptionum Atticarum*, ii. 628 *fin.* (1st century B.C.); Keil, *Sylloge Inscriptionum Boeot.* xxxi. 14; *Corpus Inscr. Gr.* 2349 *b*, compare 3524, line 29; also in the well-known decree in honour of Menas at Sestos, about B. C. 120 (Dittenberger, *Sylloge*, No. 246, lines 13-14): τῆς καλλίστης ἀποδοχῆς ἀξιούμενος παρ' αὐτῷ". W. A. Oldfather and L. W. Daly, "A Quotation from Menander in the Pastoral Epistles?", *Classical Philology* 38 (1943), pp. 202-204, raise the question, but their answer is not conclusive.

[75] Moulton and Milligan, *The Vocabulary of the Greek Testament*, *sub* ἀποδοχή.

[76] *Ibid.* For a fuller text see note 74; also W. Dittenberger, *Sylloge Inscriptionum Graecarum*, 2nd ed., p. 656, 20 f., and in the 3rd ed., p. 867, 21.

Again the question may be raised, as it was for πιστὸς ὁ λόγος, whether this phrase πάσης ἀποδοχῆς ἄξιος was merely utilized by Paul or taken over as an existing formula used and recognized in the Christian community. It is recognized that (πάσης) ἀποδοχῆς ἄξιος is known and used in extra-biblical writings, and also as a sort of "formula". Now the question is more specific: Had it become a "Christian formula", or was it simply used by Paul on his own volition? There certainly is no evidence for its being a generally utilized formula in the Christian community. In the N.T. it is found in 1 Tim. 1:15 and 4:9. The evidence would seem to point to Paul's simply using a well-known Greek phrase as part of his own vocabulary rather than his taking over a "Christianized formula". The presence of the related adjective ἀποδεκτός (only in 1 Tim. 2:3; 5:4 in the N.T.) indicates that the writer of these letters is conversant with and employs the ἀποδεχ(κ)-forms. The use of the simple form δέχομαι in most of Paul's letters makes Paul's utilization of the root δεχ(κ) — with the prefix ἀπο — a rather natural expansion of his vocabulary. Certainly ἀποδοχῆς can not be ruled out as a normal expression for the writer of the Pastoral Letters.

In regard to ἄξιος, there are several examples of its use in Paul[77]. For Paul to use ἄξιος is quite in accord with his previous practice. Again it is striking that in the Pastoral Letters ἄξιος, as in the case of the phrase πάσης ἀποδοχῆς ἄξιος, occurs only in 1 Timothy. In addition to this phrase, it is found only in 5:18 and 6:1, and the former is set forth as a quotation. Thus 5:18 does not represent the writer's own style or vocabulary. In 6:1 we read, πάσης τιμῆς ἀξίους. This formulation, like that of the phrases in 1:15 and 4:9, is also like the Ephesian inscription (. . . πάσης τειμῆς καὶ ἀποδοχῆς ἀξίου). Thus, aside from the quotation in 5:18, the only instances of ἄξιος in 1 Timothy are in phrases which are quite similar to parts of the Ephesian inscription. Hence, the influence of that phrase, which had also left its mark in the Ephesian inscription, may possibly be seen not only in 1:15 and 4:9 but also in 6:1. This combined incidence gives further credence, although it is still short of conclusive, to the possibility that Paul used, or at least was influenced by, a well-known and recognized Ephesian formula when he said πάσης ἀποδοχῆς ἄξιος.

In what sense does πάσης qualify ἀποδοχῆς? The two alternatives which are proposed are those of *extensive* or *intensive*. The *extensive* or *universal* sense would translate the phrase *"worthy of all* (universal)

---

[77] Ἄξιος in Paul is found at Rom. 1:32; 8:18; 1 Cor. 16:4; 2 Thess. 1:3; 1 Tim. 1:15; 4:9; 5:18; 6:1.

acceptation"[78], or "worthy to be accepted by all"[79]. The *intensive* sense would translate the phrase "worthy of full acceptance"[80] or "deserving whole-hearted acceptance"[81]. The commentators are quite divided as to their understanding[82]. Many commentators merely offer the alternatives, or favor one but leave the other possibility open[83]. The grammars, such as those of Robertson, Moulton-Turner, and Blass-Debrunner-Funk, offer little help on this particular question.

The older English commentators such as Bernard and Ellicott seem to be most certain and emphatic on the extensive sense to the exclusion of the intensive. Bernard (*ad* 1 Tim. 1:15) states: "We thus translate: *worthy of all* (universal) *acceptation*. As always in such constructions in St Paul, πᾶς is used *extensively*, not *intensively*, and the phrase is equivalent to 'acceptation by everyone' ". One wonders whether the matter is one of semantics, because Ellicott, who is just as definite, comes closer to an intensive meaning while at the same time repudiating it. Ellicott says, " *'all* (i.e. *every kind of*) *acceptation*' . . . an excellent translation . . . πᾶς with abstract nouns, commonly denoting *extension* . . . , rather than *intension*"[84]. And Alford states briefly, "*all* (all possible, i.e., universal)".

So among those who would plead for an extensive or universal meaning there seem to be two groups. One group refers the all to everyone, all men universally and extensively and the other group thinks that the all means every kind of or all possible acceptation. This latter group consistently repudiates the intensive sense of the highest or fullest acceptation, but at the same time comes quite close to that meaning.

---

[78] J. H. Bernard, *The Pastoral Epistles (Cambridge Greek Testament)*, *ad* 1 Tim. 1:15.

[79] Alternative presented by Barrett, *ad* 1 Tim. 1:15.

[80] Hendriksen, *ad* 1 Tim. 1:15.

[81] Kelly, *ad* 1 Tim. 1:15.

[82] Those favoring the extensive or universal view are Bernard, C. J. Ellicott, *The Pastoral Epistles of St Paul* and perhaps Alford. Spicq, "Il est possible que dans cette construction πᾶς ait un sens extensif plus qu'intensif...", *ad* 1 Tim. 1:15. Those favoring the intensive view are Bengel, Bouma, Fausset (in Jamieson, Fausset & Brown), Huther, Kelly, Scott and White.

[83] Barrett, "*words that merit full acceptance* (or perhaps, '... are worthy to be accepted by all'); Gealy (*Interpreter's Bible*), "*worthy of full* [i.e., wholehearted or universal] *acceptance*"; Lock, "πάσης, 'entire', perhaps combining the thought of 'wholehearted', cf. [16], and 'universal', cf. [24]". Hendriksen favors the intensive but at the same time brings in the extensive.

[84] Ellicott, *ad* 1 Tim. 1:15. Bracketed as an example of extension is "'omnium totius animae facultatum' Beng." which is rendered in the English translation of Bengel as "by all the faculties of the whole soul". This seems closer to the intensive than Bernard's meaning of extensively. Ellicott refers to his notes on Eph. 1:8 in his commentary on Ephesians. Therein he objects to "'summa sapienta' (Rosenm. Eadie)" and declares "πᾶς, as Harless correctly observes, always denoting *extension* rather than *intension*".

It must be said over against those who hold that Paul in particular or Greek in general does not use πᾶς with an abstract noun without an article in the intensive sense that this is an unproven absolute negation which is contradicted by the facts. Both Thayer[85] and Bauer-Arndt-Gingrich[86] recognize the intensive usage, and the latter in particular give extra-biblical examples as well as examples in the N.T. in general, in Paul and in the Pastorals. J. M. Bover in his full article on "Uso del adjetivo singular πᾶς in San Pablo"[87] as well as B. Beicke in *TWNT* (V, *sub* πᾶς)[88] also recognize this intensive usage. Acts 24:3 would seem to present a clear case of the intensive meaning ("we accept it in all ways and in all places, most excellent Felix, with all thankfulness" — πάντῃ τε καὶ πανταχοῦ ... μετὰ πάσης εὐχαριστίας). Obviously πάντῃ and πανταχοῦ, especially the latter, set forth the extensive idea, i.e., by everyone, everywhere in every way, especially when it is introduced by a verb in the first person plural, "we". To take then the πάσης in this sentence in any sense of the extensive would make the addition of the prepositional phrase of which it is a part almost redundant and a tautology, at least so far as the πάσης is concerned. But if πάσης is taken in the intensive sense, it completely fits the context and rounds out the thought[89]. This one example may suffice to show that the intensive use of πᾶς is utilized in the N.T. White says clearly: "Other

[85] Thayer, *ad* πᾶς, "or it signifies *the highest degree, the maximum*, of the thing which the noun denotes". Thayer refers to Ellicott on Eph. 1:8, but there Ellicott repudiates this very sense.

[86] Arndt-Gingrich, *ad* πᾶς, "to denote the highest degree *full, greatest, all*". Cf. J. Eadie, *A Commentary on the Greek Text of The Epistle of Paul to The Ephesians* (Edinburgh: T. & T. Clark, 3rd ed., 1883), *ad* Eph. 1:8, who cites other examples from the classics as well as from the Scriptures, among which is 1 Tim. 1:15. The editors and translators of *The Loeb Classical Library Series* at the classical passages in question in most cases agree by means of their translation with Eadie's appeal to these passages as examples of the idea of intension with the word πᾶς. The fact that one may disagree with one or two of the scriptural or classical examples does not negate the proof that the others offer of the idea of intension in the use of πᾶς.

[87] *Biblica*, 19 (1938), pp. 411-434. On page 423 he speaks of such a category in the following words: "*Sentido de plenitud*. Hay gran multitud de textos, en que el adjetivo *todo* expressa plentitud o integridad y puede sustituírse por *pleno* o *entero*. A este género pertenecen los siguientes: Rom. 15,13 ... 2 Cor. 9,8 ... Eph. 4,2 ... Eph. 6,18 ... Col. 1,11 ... 1 Tim. 1,15 = 4,9: Fidelis sermo et omni acceptione dignus. Tit. 2,15 ... En estos y otros ejemplos parecidos algunos dan a *todo* el sentido de *sumo* o *maximo*".

[88] Page 886, Reicke speaks of the "Adjektivishes πᾶς " "ohne Artikel" and then further says: "E l a t i v e B e d e u t u n g : *völlig, hochst, all, lauter*. Im NT nur bei Abstrakten..." And after citing examples, including several from Paul, he concludes by adding: "In der Prof. Gräz kommt dieses πᾶς auch bei sachlichen Gegenständen vor...".

[89] This is uniformly recognized by the modern English translations.

examples in the Pastorals of the use of πᾶς (= *summus*) with abstract nouns (besides ch. iv. 9) are 1 Tim. ii.2,11, iii.4, v.2, vi.1, 2 Tim. iv.2, Tit. ii.10,15, iii.2)"[90].

The fact that πᾶς in the type of construction under consideration may be used intensively does not of itself prove that it is used intensively in 1 Tim. 1:15 and 4:9. Further light may be gained from 1 Tim. 6:1. There we read: "Let as many as are servants under the yoke count their masters worthy of all honor (... τοὺς ἰδίους δεσπότας πάσης τιμῆς ἀξίους ἡγείσθωσαν). This passage is helpful because of its similarity in vocabulary and form. The extensive meaning, worthy of honor by everyone, would seem to be ruled out by the direct restriction which Paul makes that servants are to make this evaluation of their masters over against themselves. The servants are not admonished to regard their masters worthy of receiving honor from someone else or from everyone but from themselves as their servants. ("Οσοι . . . δοῦλοι . . . τοὺς ἰδίους δεσπότας . . . ἡγείσθωσαν). Nor is the extensive sense of worthy of every kind of honor satisfactory even though it is possible and plausible. What Paul has in mind is not the variety of the honor, but the fullness or depth and sincerity of the honor that the masters should be counted worthy of receiving. That the intensive idea is in view is borne out by Paul's parallel treatments of the same relationship in Eph. 6:5—8 and Col. 3:22—24. There the depths of the intensiveness which is in view in πάσης τιμῆς ἀξίους is underscored and expressed in other ways by the phrases "with fear and trembling, in singleness of your heart, as unto Christ . . . doing the will of God from the heart" (ἐκ ψυχῆς, Eph. 6:5-6), and "work heartily (ἐκ ψυχῆς), as unto the Lord" (Col. 3:23). The attitude of honor which is in view is that which springs from the inner heart or soul of a man and is that which is likened to his attitude to Christ.

Not only does this similar statement in 1 Tim. 6:1 point in the direction of the intensive sense by its close similarity to 1 Tim. 1:15 and 4:9 but so also does the Ephesian inscription (ἀνδρὸς δοκιμωτάτου, καὶ πάσης τειμῆς καὶ ἀποδοχῆς ἀξίου) to which they both have similarities. In this inscription, in which πάσης modifies not only τειμῆς but also ἀποδοχῆς, the force of the πάσης would seem rather obviously to refer to the fullness of the honor and acceptance of which the man was worthy rather than to the various kinds of the same. And so both the passage in 1 Tim. 6:1 and the Ephesian inscription point to the presumption, at least, of an intensive meaning in 1 Tim. 1:15 and 4:9 for the πάσης.

Paul's intent in adding the πάσης is not primarily that all the Ephesian Christians or all men everywhere might recognize that this saying was

[90] N. J. D. White, *The Expositor's Greek Testament, ad* 1 Tim. 1:15. Arndt-Gingrich, *sub* πᾶς, give essentially the same list with one or two omissions.

worthy of every kind of acceptance, but rather that he might indicate that it is worthy of the fullest, most whole-hearted acceptance[91]. This is substantiated by the fact that Paul is concerned about personal appropriation by the very nature of the saying to which this phrase refers. This emphasis on the intensive does not rule out the extensive in any way at all. Probably the antithesis is a false one, or at least overstated. That one should respond with all acceptation, *i.e.*, fully, carries with it that one should respond extensively with all one's faculties, heart and mind alike.

Further, the continual thrust of the Gospel message and of the particular sayings to which this phrase refers is always universalistic in its offer and demand. Indeed all men are called upon to render full and unqualified acceptance. The saying of 1 Tim. 1:15 speaks of Christ as come into the world to save sinners. Sinners, not just Jews or Ephesians, but sinners everywhere, sinners extensively are called upon fully to accept this saying as faithful. Therefore both it and the Christ of which it speaks are worthy of not all kinds of acceptance or faith, but unreserved and complete acceptance and faith. Moreover, the very context of the second instance of the phrase, which is joined to the phrase and the saying of which it speaks by "for" (γάρ), speaks of "the living God, who is the Savior of all men, specially of them that believe". Here the universalistic appeal is stated clearly and that in terms of the necessary response of belief and acceptance. The acceptance (ἀποδοχῆς) of which the saying is worthy (ἄξιος) is that of "wholehearted and universal *personal appropriation* with no reservation of any kind"[92].

Πάσης ἀποδοχῆς ἄξιος is joined to πιστὸς ὁ λόγος in both places (1 Tim. 1:15; 4:9) by the conjunction καί. Hence, this addition strengthens the initial formula at these two places by making the formula a fuller and more emphatic one. The addition πάσης ἀποδοχῆς ἄξιος makes explicit that which is implicit in πιστὸς ὁ λόγος, *i.e.*, that the λόγος is a saying which one must fully accept for oneself. Πιστὸς ὁ λόγος has this note within it, but its thrust is more on the intrinsic nature and value of the saying and its truth (πιστός). Certainly a saying of such a nature and value demand the response of faith, but it is just this response

---

91 "Πάση zonder lidwoord: alle mogelijke, de grootste en hoogste; dat gezegde verdient algeheele en volkomen aanvaarding zonder eenige restrictie", Bouma, *ad* 1 Tim. 1:15. "*All* – all possible: to be received by all, with all the faculties of the soul, mind, and heart", A. R. Fausset, *ad* 1 Tim. in *A Commentary Critical, Experimental and Practical on the Old and New Testaments* by R. Jamieson, A. R. Fausset, and D. Brown, Vol. VI (reprinted by Eerdmans, Grand Rapids, 1948).
92 Hendriksen, *ad* 1 Tim. 1:15.

(ἀποδοχῆς) which "and worthy of all acceptation" delineates and specifies.

One is immediately led to ask why the addition "and worthy of all acceptation" is attached to the other formula in two of the five times that "faithful is the saying" occurs, but not in the other times. In the case of Titus 3:8 a partial answer may be that the words, "and concerning these things I desire that you affirm confidently, to the end that they who have believed God may be careful to maintain good works", take the place of "and worthy of all acceptation", at least formally and perhaps also materially. This then leaves only two instances out of the five in which "faithful is the saying" is not supplemented (1 Tim. 3:1; 2 Tim. 2:11). There are several answers that can be conjectured. It may be proffered that the addition is restricted to 1 Timothy and thus the answer lies within the nature and vocabulary of that letter over against the other two. This suggestion is unlikely and is made less so by the fact of the addition already mentioned at Titus 3:8. And then the question remains why 1 Tim. 3:1 is not enlarged by the addition. The addition or omission of πάσης ἀποδοχῆς ἄξιος may possibly be only a stylistic variation, addition or omission with no other explanation needed. With more plausibility it may be assumed that there is something inherent in the form or content of the saying itself that explains the addition in certain cases. Again, there may be something inherent in the form or content of the saying to which the addition is not added that makes the addition inappropriate or at least less apropos. Either the positive or the negative factors just mentioned might provide the key to Paul's thought and usage pattern, or even possibly a combination thereof. But no conclusive answer can be given until the sayings themselves are ascertained and their meanings carefully understood. Only then can similarities between those sayings which have πάσης ἀποδοχῆς ἄξιος and those sayings which do not have it be used to detect a possible solution to the rationale of the addition or omission[93].

To the study of the λόγοι themselves our study must now turn.

---

[93] See the concluding chapter.

CHAPTER II

1 TIMOTHY 1:15 AND ITS SAYING

The first[1] instance of both the formula πιστὸς ὁ λόγος and of the saying to which it refers is 1 Timothy 1:15. At this location there exists the textual variant of *humanus* (ἀνθρώπινος) for πιστός. This variant is found only in Latin in the Old Latin Mss. *mon* and *r*[1], and then in Ambrosiaster mss. (according to Jerome), Julian-Eclanum, Vigilus, and sometimes Augustine[2]. This evidence is exceedingly weak and late, and not one biblical manuscript in Greek testifies to this reading, and only two in Latin. Lock is the only scholar who seems seriously to advance the idea that ἀνθρώπινος (*humanus*) is "possibly right"[3]. The paucity and lateness of the evidence over against the strength and earliness of the evidence for πιστός points with certainty to πιστός as the authentic reading. Westcott and Hort say in their "Notes on Select Readings"[4] in

---

[1] The author considers the order of the Pastoral Letters to be 1 Timothy, Titus and 2 Timothy. The λόγοι will therefore be considered in that order. This is not the place to discuss at length the reasons which may be adduced for such an order. Suffice it to say that this order seems to do the most justice to the interrelationships of the letters on the basis of both their Pauline authorship and also of the positioning of the letters in a period after the close of Acts. 2 Timothy would therefore refer to another or second imprisonment, Paul having been released from the first imprisonment recorded at the end of Acts. *Cf.* further the introductory sections of the commentaries by Guthrie and Hendriksen, and also Guthrie's *New Testament Introduction, The Pauline Epistles*, the section on the Pastorals, and Zahn's *Introduction to the New Testament*, Vol. II, the Pastoral section. Almost all scholars who affirm the Pauline authorship and who place the Pastorals beyond the time of Acts advocate the order of 1 Timothy-Titus-2 Timothy.

[2] See especially the critical Greek New Testaments edited by Aland-Black-Metzger-Wikgren, and by Souter.

[3] Lock's only argument, which is quite weak and which is readily answered by Nestle-Aland, Souter and Westcott and Hort as mentioned above in the course of the discussion, is as follows: "The MSS authority is not strong, but the correction from πιστός is unlikely (but *vid.* W.-H., *Notes on Select Readings* on 3[1]), whereas the assimilation to πιστός in 4[9], II 2[11], Tit 3[8], where there is no variant, is very probable. It is therefore possibly right, and the meaning will be 'true to human needs'..." (p. xxxvi).

[4] B. F. Westcott and F. J. A. Hort, *The New Testament in the Original*

31

commenting on 3:1 that "the same reading, probably transferred from this place, occurs at i 15 ...". This solution does rather adequately explain the derivation of the variant.

The λόγος itself is recognized by all to be that which follows the formula. The form and character of this saying make it stand out immediately as that to which Paul has reference. And there is also general consensus that the λόγος ends with the words σῶσαι, so that ὅτι Χριστὸς ᾿Ιησοῦς ἦλθεν εἰς τὸν κόσμον ἁμαρτωλοὺς σῶσαι ("that Christ Jesus came into the world to save sinners") comprises the saying. Thus, ὧν πρῶτός εἰμι ἐγώ is regarded as a personal application by Paul but not part of the saying as such[5]. The ὅτι ("that") attaches the saying to the formula and thus it is a recitative ὅτι introducing a quotation[6]. The ὅτι then is not part of the quotation but serves as the connecting link.

The saying begins with the names Χριστὸς ᾿Ιησοῦς in that particular order. It may well be asked why the saying has the order "Christ Jesus" instead of "Jesus Christ". In the Pastorals "Christ Jesus" is found 25 times and "Jesus Christ" 6 times (in the Nestle text; at 7 places "Jesus Christ" occurs as a variant). Hendriksen points out that this is in accord with the ever increasing tendency in Paul for "Christ Jesus" to become the most used order[7]. Although this indicates that the Pastoral usage is

---

Greek, Introduction, Appendix (Cambridge & London: Macmillan & Co., 1881), p. 132. The "Notes on Select Readings" appears as the major portion of the Appendix.

    [5] *Cf., e.g.,* Bouma, Huther and Kelly *ad loc.*

    [6] H. B. Swete, "The Faithful Sayings", *Journal of Theological Studies,* xviii (1917), p. 1. For the use and significance of ὅτι *recitativum* see Arndt-Gingrich, Moulton & Milligan and Thayer *sub* ὅτι, and Blass-Debrunner-Funk, section 397 and especially section 470, and A. T. Robertson, p. 1027 f.

    [7] *Cf.* note 19 page 51 in Hendriksen's commentary. There Hendriksen gives the overall statistics of the N.T. and the particular situation for Paul. "In Paul's epistles the order 'Christ Jesus', though not so prominent at first, gradually takes over, so that in the end the order 'Jesus Christ' becomes the exception and 'Christ Jesus' the rule. ... To account for this phenomenon it has been suggested that at first the Aramaic 'Jesus, the Christ' was rendered into the Greek rather literally, supplying the order in which the proper name Jesus is followed by the appellative Christ, indicating his office. After a while the term Christ began to be felt increasingly as a second proper name next to Jesus. Being now on a par with the name Jesus, the flexible character of the Greek language made it possible to reverse the order; hence, 'Christ Jesus' or 'Jesus Christ, with no difference in meaning". See further, S.V. McCasland, "Christ Jesus", *Journal of Biblical Literature* 65 (1946), pp. 377-383. McCasland points out that Χριστὸς ᾿Ιησοῦς occurs in the N.T. only in

accord with the other letters of Paul, the question first asked still remains.

Before one can answer the question concerning the word order of Χριστὸς Ἰησοῦς a beginning, at least, must be made on ascertaining the meaning of Χριστός. As is often the case, these two questions are interrelated. Χριστός in the New Testament generally is the Greek equivalent of the Hebrew "Messiah", the anointed one. Thus Jesus is referred to as "the Christ", *i.e.*, the promised and expected one of the Old Testament (*cf., e.g.*, Mt. 16:16; Acts 2:36; 3:18,20; etc.). It is he who is anointed with the fullness of God's Spirit and declared to be the one God has sent to accomplish his work[8].

the letters of Paul and in Acts. He further lists as the only three occurrences in Acts, Acts 3:20, 5:42, 24:24 (*cf.* 18:5, 28). An examination of these Acts' passages shows them to be themselves unusual in Acts. Acts 3:20 is in Peter's discourse and has the reverse order as a textual variant. Acts 5:42 as well as 18:5, 28 have τὸν Χριστὸν Ἰησοῦν. Acts 18:5 occurs in a speech of Paul and 18:28 may represent the influence of Paul through Priscilla and Aquila on Apollos. Acts 24:24 is a description by Luke of the essence of Paul's message. Thus the order Χριστὸς Ἰησοῦς, with Χριστός without the article, is virtually limited to Paul in the N.T. *Cf.* Paul Feine, *Jesus Christus und Paulus* (Leipzig: Hinrichs, 1902), p. 35. McCasland says that Χριστὸς Ἰησοῦς is an inversion, but contrary to Hendriksen (*supra* this note) goes on to say "that the inversion could not have been made at all unless 'Christ' had originally been an appellative..." and "that 'Christ' must still be an appellative in order to permit the inversion" (*op. cit.*, p. 382). "It was not customary for Greek writers to invert double names..." but "the flexibility of Greek idiom permits adjectival and appellative forms to precede or follow the proper names they modify at will" (*idem*). "'Christ' was at first an appellative, a verbal adjective, meaning 'the anointed one', modifying the proper name 'Jesus'" (p. 383). McCasland's case can be strengthened by observing that when Paul uses the expression "the Lord Jesus Christ" or "our Lord Jesus Christ" with κύριος in the first position that then Ἰησοῦς is always next and Χριστός last. This is probably to be explained by a desire to have the "titles" on either side of the name Jesus rather than one title after the other. McCasland goes on to admit (p. 383) that the name "Jesus Christ", in this order, had possibly become a double proper name in certain N.T. writings. The final solution of the matter is probably "that both [Christ Jesus and Jesus Christ] are practically proper names: and neither has lost the whole implication of office", B. B. Warfield, *The Lord of Glory*, (New York: American Tract Society, 1907), p. 243 note 27.

8 For a rather comprehensive treatment of the meaning of Χριστός both from its O.T. origins and from its application to Jesus see G. Vos, *The Self-Disclosure of Jesus* (Grand Rapids: Eerdmans, 1954), "The Christ", pp. 105-117. See also C. C. Torrey, "Χριστός", *Quantulacumque* edited by Casey, Lake & Lake (London: Christophers, 1937), pp. 317-324, and O. Cullmann, *The Christology of the New Testament* (Philadelphia: Westminster, 1959), pp. 111-136. For one of the most recent treatments of the title in Paul see W. Kramer, *Christ, Lord, Son of God* (Studies in Biblical Theology, 50, Naperville, Ill.: Allenson, 1966). Kramer excludes from Paul's writings 2 Thess., Col., Eph., and the Pastorals. F. Hahn, *Christologische Hoheitstitel. Ihre Geschichte im frühen*

In the usage of Paul Χριστός begins to become a personal name which Paul uses for Jesus[9]. However, this process of Χριστός beginning to become a personal or proper name with Paul need not entirely obliterate the fact that the name was first applied to Jesus and is still applied to Jesus as a title because he is the Messiah. Warfield puts it aptly when he says: "But this obvious use of 'Christ' as a name of dignity by no means implies that it is not employed practically as a proper name. Its implications of Messiahship remain present and suggestive, but it has become the peculiar property of Jesus who is thought of as so indisputably the Messiah that the title 'Messiah' has become His proper name"[10].

McCasland contends that the form "Christ Jesus" rather than "Jesus Christ" is only explicable if Χριστός is an appellative[11]. Paul Feine suggests that the inversion is made to emphasize Χριστός[12]. Others, such as Warfield, have taken the position that the two forms are

Christentum (Forschungen zur Religion und Literatur des Alten und Neuen Testaments 83, 1963) is a very recent treatment of the title from the viewpoint of the synoptic Gospels.

[9] For the two divisions of title or personal name and the passages designated for each see Arndt-Gingrich, sub Χριστός. The presence or absence of the definite article is not significant as a guide for title or personal name respectively, as Χριστός is obviously used anarthrously for a title. Warfield, The Lord of Glory, p. 240 note 23, sets forth some of the literature and the opposing viewpoints on title versus personal name. Cf. further Cullmann, Christology, who recognizes Χριστός as still a title at places in Paul contra V. Taylor, The Names of Jesus (London: Macmillan & Co., 1954), pp. 21 & 22, who holds that in Paul and the Pastorals Χριστός is almost always a personal name. For the ongoing discussion and recent bibliographical material see W. Kramer, op. cit., and F. Hahn, op. cit.

[10] Warfield, Lord of Glory, p. 239 f. Prof. Dr. John Skilton has pointed out in a private conversation that the people of Jesus' day expected not many Messiahs but one personal Messiah and that this expectation of one personal Messiah would provide the occasion for the application of the title to the person as his unique proper name. The observation is borne out by the anarthrous usage of Μεσσίας explained by an anarthrous Χριστός in John 4:25. This observation would strengthen Warfield's judgment. Cf. also Cullmann, Christology: "Already the letters of Paul, the oldest Christian writings we possess, have a tendency to fix the word Christ as a proper name, although the passages in which Paul writes 'Christ' before Jesus (i.e., 'Christ Jesus') serve as a reminder that he is still aware of its real meaning. Christians of the New Testament period did not completely forget the meaning of the title Messiah ..." (p. 112). This view is faulted by Kramer, op. cit., Par. 61, pp. 203 ff.

[11] See note 7. Cullmann, Christology, p. 134, essentially agrees with the evaluation of Χριστός as an appellative. In commenting on Χριστός becoming a proper name with Paul, he says: "We can see at least the beginnings of this development in Paul's writings, although his occasional practice of putting 'Christ' before 'Jesus' shows that he was still clearly aware that the title is not a proper name". See also note 10.

[12] Paul Feine, Jesus Christus und Paulus, p. 36. The German text could be rendered in English as follows: "The ground of this combination is a feeling

34

practically the same[13]. It must be recognized, however, that placing Χριστός first in Greek style would perhaps tend to give it some slight emphasis. Even if the order be discounted as insignificant, the saying nevertheless speaks of the anointed one, the Christ, the Messiah. Ἰησοῦς is the proper name for the incarnate Son of God. It speaks of Him in his particularity as a human being, a Palestinian Jew, as Jesus of Nazareth[14]. But this name also is not without its significance. This name is given by God as the name which his Son should bear not only in the flesh but from henceforth. "And she shall bring forth a son; and you shall call his name Jesus; for it is he that shall save his people from their sins" (Mt. 1:21, cf. 1:25; Lk. 1:31; 2:21). Jesus is to be the great Joshua to whom Moses and all the prophets have pointed. In Jesus God has come to help and to save. All that the name Jesus signifies in Matthew 1:21 the saying in 1 Tim. 1:15 explicitly says again, not only by using the name Jesus but also by saying that he "came into the world to save sinners"[15]. This becomes evident when one realizes that the saying is rooted in sayings of Jesus made concerning himself during his earthly ministry which we find and know in the context of the Gospels. He speaks of his consciousness of having come into the world to save. To designate specifically who it is that has come to save the saying in 1 Tim. 1:15 uses the name Ἰησοῦς.

Bengel has come quite close to the meaning of Χριστὸς Ἰησοῦς when he said: "Christ Jesus -Christ, as promised: Jesus, as manifested"[16]. The saying speaks of the Anointed One who is the incarnate Son of God and the Savior of sinners, Jesus[17].

---

of need on Paul's part to throw the Messianic aspect of Jesus into the foreground". Cf. Greijdanus, Romeinen (K.N.T.), ad 1:1.

[13] The Lord of Glory, p. 243, "it is difficult to trace any difference in the implications of their use".

[14] See W. Foerster, Ἰησοῦς, TDNT, III, pp. 284-293, especially p. 287.

[15] For a consideration of how much Paul knew about the "earthly" Jesus and how concerned he was about him as such see the able doctoral dissertation of B. C. Lategan, Die Aardse Jesus In Die Prediking van Paulus volgens sy briewe (Rotterdam, 1967). This dissertation which is written in Afrikaans has a summary in English, pp. 267-273. Lategan's thesis is that Paul knew about and was concerned about the "earthly" Jesus. Of course, this question does not loom so large when one considers that this is a saying that Paul cites.

[16] Ad 1 Tim. 1:15: "Christus, promissus: Jesus, exhibitus".

[17] For the Christology of the Pastoral Letters see G. Sevenster, De Christologie van het Nieuwe Testament (Amsterdam, 2nd ed., 1948), pp. 282-287. Sevenster's treatment is much more balanced than that of H. Windisch, "Zur Christologie der Pastoralbriefe", Z.N.W. 34 (1935), pp. 213-238, which Sevenster correctly criticizes. Sevenster treats the Pastorals separately from the Pauline letters because he regards them in the present form as not from Paul (p. 142, note 2). However, he says several times that the Christology of the Pastorals is similar to Paul's letters (pp. 282 twice, 283, 284). The differences he regards as minimal (p. 284).

No evaluation of Christ Jesus in this saying and in the Pastorals would be quite adequate without a consideration of 1 Tim. 2:5[18]. In this passage Χριστός Ἰησοῦς as to his person is particularly designated as a man (ἄνθρωπος) and as the one mediator between God and men (εἷς καὶ μεσίτης θεοῦ καὶ ἀνθρώπων). Because the author so specifically designates Χριστός Ἰησοῦς as ἄνθρωπος and μεσίτης, one may assume that these characteristics are also in view when the author thinks of Χριστός Ἰησοῦς in the saying in 1 Tim. 1:15[19]. This is borne out further by the fact that the work of Χριστός Ἰησοῦς in both passages is almost identical, although the words used to describe that work are different[20].

The saying describes that which Χριστός Ἰησοῦς has done as ἦλθεν εἰς τὸν κόσμον. Bouma notes that the aorist tense indicates a particular past time and fact. The aorist tense signifies that which Christ Jesus has done. He has come, and the place where he has come is into the world. Dibelius and others are correct and have performed a good service when they point out that ἦλθεν εἰς τὸν κόσμον as a phrase does not automatically contain within itself the notion of preexistence per se[21]. It is one thing to point that the phrase ἦλθεν (ἔρχεσθαι) εἰς τὸν κόσμον itself does not imply preexistence and it is another to make this evaluation of the phrase when it is used by Christians with Christ Jesus as the subject.

[18] The objection might be raised that it is inappropriate to refer to other portions of the Pastorals to explain a saying which was probably not composed by the author of the Pastorals. But such an objection fails to realize that the saying is not a foreign body in the thought and theology of the letters. It is cited just because it says what the author wants to say then and there in a way in which he wants to say it. It is quoted just because it aptly expresses his theological or christological idea and because he quite agrees with both the form and content. Thus it is not only legitimate but necessary and wise to understand a saying in the context of one who has used it. Further, in the particular case of Χριστός Ἰησοῦς, one must remember that the words in that order are practically restricted to Paul (including the Pastorals). Therefore one must go to Paul and these Pastorals if one would understand the use of the form in the N.T. usage.

[19] Even though this is the only passage in which he speaks of Christ as "Mediator".

[20] Cf. "to save sinners" and "who gave himself a ransom for all" (1 Tim. 2:6), especially as they are preceded by the words of verse 4 that "God our Savior" "would have all men to be saved". For the meaning of the words τὸ μαρτύριον καιροῖς ἰδίοις ("the testimony [to be borne] in its own times") see R. Schippers, Getuigen van Jezus Christus in het Nieuwe Testament (Franeker: Wever, 1938), pp. 148 ff.

[21] Cf. also Weiss (Meyer series) who points to Rom. 5:12 and 1 Tim. 6:7 as places where coming into the world (εἰς τὸν κόσμον) obviously does not have preexistence in view, nor is it inherent in the phrase. Similarly done by Wohlenberg, and Lock who adds John 6:14. Windisch, op. cit., p. 222, negates the idea that the preexistence of Christ Jesus is in view here in the Pastorals.

Is it not, as a matter of fact, evident that the uniform usage of that phrase *with* reference to Christ Jesus is to both his preexistence and also his incarnation and earthly work?[22] Six times in the Gospel of John (1:9; 3:19; 11:27; 12:46; 16:28; 18:37) it is said that Jesus comes into the world[23]. When John 1:9[24] speaks of the true light, even Jesus Christ, "coming into the world" in the context of John 1:1, the thought of his preexistence (1:1) and his incarnation (1:14) is evidently present and intended by the phrase[25]. In John 3:19 Jesus is again referred to as the light, and as the light which "is come into the world" (τὸ φῶς ἐλήλυθεν εἰς τὸν κόσμον). This light is God's only begotten Son (verses 16,17 and 18). This is the Son who has been with God and is sent into the world (ἀπέστειλεν ὁ Θεὸς τὸν υἱὸν εἰς τὸν κόσμον, verse 17). He is previously identified as "he that descended out of heaven, the Son of man" (ὁ ἐκ τοῦ οὐρανοῦ, ὁ υἱὸς τοῦ ἀνθρώπου, verse 13). Jesus says of himself in John 12:46, "I am come a light into the world" (ἐγὼ φῶς εἰς τὸν κόσμον ἐλήλυθα). His coming is in correlation to God's sending (verses 44,45 and 49). And the result of Jesus' coming and his being sent by the Father is that the one that beholds Jesus beholds God (verse 45; *cf.* 1:14, 18). This is true because as John 1:14 and 18 indicate the Word (or the Son) has become flesh with the glory of the only begotten Son of the Father, declaring the Father with whom he has eternally dwelt. "I came out from the Father, and am come into the world: again, I leave the world, and go unto the Father" (ἐξῆλθον παρὰ τοῦ πατρὸς καὶ ἐλήλυθα εἰς τὸν κόσμον πάλιν ἀφίημι τὸν κόσμον καὶ πορφεύομαι πρὸς τόν πατέρα), Jesus says explicitly in John 16:28. Here his coming into the world is clearly seen to be the converse of his coming from the Father. And coming from the Father bespeaks his preexistence. Again the meaning of coming into the world in reference to Jesus is seen by his

---

22 *Cf.* Wohlenberg who makes this wise distinction.
23 John 6:14 is not included because it speaks in terms of "the prophet" (ὁ προφήτης) rather than of the Messiah, and especially because it is the evaluation of the people in general rather than that of Jesus or his disciples. It is the latter evaluation which above all is germane to the evaluation of the faithful saying of the Christian community found in 1 Tim. 1:15. The evaluation of the people in general may not have been the same as that of Jesus and his disciples.
24 H. Sasse, *TDNT*, III, p. 889 f. in his list of the subjects of (εἰσ)ἔρχεσθαι εἰς τὸν κόσμον gives "'every man,' Jn. 1:9 . . . , unless ἐρχόμενον is here to be linked with τὸ φῶς". See however, Hendriksen, *Gospel of John (N.T.C.)*, and Grosheide, *Johannes*, I, (*K.N.T.*), *ad loc.*, who take this phrase as referring to Jesus and give convincing reasons for doing so. One point that especially needs to be noted is that the whole first chapter speaks of the coming of the Logos and the Light. See especially Grosheide for the discussion and literature. *Cf.* further J. Sickenberger, "Das in die Welt Kommende Licht", *Theologie und Glaube* 33 (1941), pp. 129-134.
25 Also noted by A. Oepke, *TDNT*, II, *sub* εἰς, p. 423.

37

use of the reverse expression "leaving the world". For Him both coming into the world and leaving the world are but opposite sides of coming out from or going unto the Father. It is this particular aspect which makes coming into the world mean much more when applied to Jesus than it can when applied to anything or anyone else. It is indeed this aspect which demands the understanding of preexistence as well as incarnation when this phrase is applied to Jesus[26]. This uniform usage in John's Gospel, which is the only other place in the N.T. where the expression is found, demonstrates that the concepts of preexistence and incarnation are in view. One cannot affirm the incarnation and deny the preexistence because they are correlative. There is no good reason to deny that these concepts are in view in the usage in 1 Tim. 1:15 also (cf. 3:16).

A further correlation between the concept of coming into the world in 1 Tim. 1:15 and in John's Gospel in reference to Jesus is the reason given for his coming. In 1 Tim. 1:15 this is specifically stated, i.e., "to save sinners". In those passages in John's Gospel which we have just surveyed in which the aspect of being sent by God the Father is mentioned there too the soteriological is stated as the reason for Jesus' coming. In 3:17 we read: "For God sent not the Son into the world to judge the world; but that the world should be saved through him" (οὐ γὰρ ἀπέστειλεν ὁ Θεὸς τὸν υἱὸν εἰς τὸν κόσμον... ἀλλ' ἵνα σωθῇ ὁ κόσμος δι' αὐτοῦ). Likewise in John 12:46 and 47: "I am come a light into the world, that whosoever believes on me may not abide in the darkness ... for I came not to judge the world, but to save the world" (ἐγὼ φῶς εἰς τὸν κόσμον ἐλήλυθα... οὐ γὰρ ἦλθον ἵνα κρίνω τὸν κόσμον ἀλλ' ἵνα σώσω τὸν κόσμον). And the soteriological is implicit in the context of several of the other occurrences (1:9, cf. 1:12f.; 11:27, cf. 11:25f.; 16:28, cf. 16:27,30).

In what sense or with what meaning does κόσμος occur in 1 Tim. 1:15? Commentators are rather divided as to the meaning. Some state that "κόσμος is here to be understood not in a moral, but in a physical sense"[27]. Others say that it "indicates not merely a change of location,

---

[26] See also John 18:37 and 11:27. For a fine discussion of the meaning of the coming of Jesus in John's Gospel see J. Schneider, *TDNT*, II, p. 671 f. Schneider says: "the Johannine Christ maintains: ἀπ' ἐμαυτοῦ οὐκ ἐλήλυθα (7:28; 8:42). The basis of His Messianic claim is the certainty: οἶδα πόθεν ἦλθον καὶ ποῦ ὑπάγω (8:14). His coming rests on His divine mission (8:42). Here is the foundation of His claim.... The point at issue ... is simply whether Jesus is the Messiah. John's Gospel is designed to demonstrate the contention of Jesus that the Messiah of God has come in Him".
[27] J. J. van Oosterzee, in *Lange*; also Huther.

a 'descent' from one place to another (from heaven to earth), but a *change of state and of moral and spiritual environment"*[28]. The lexicons[29] relate a wide variety of meanings for κόσμος including the two suggested. Our attention is naturally drawn to the Johannine usage in view of the fact that only in John does the phrase under consideration occur outside of 1 Tim. 1:15. Here we are on fertile ground indeed as κόσμος is a word frequently used by John. But here too we are met by the overwhelming richness of variety in meanings[30]. Therefore the outcome can not be determined by the various meanings of κόσμος in John but by the particular meaning or meanings associated with the instances where John speaks of Jesus as coming into the world.

Six times in the Gospel of John (1:9; 3:19; 11:27; 12:46; 16:28; 18:37), the author, Jesus, or his disciples[31] speak of His coming into the world. John 1:10 is especially helpful in determining the meaning of κόσμος in verse 9 because it uses that very term three times ("He was in the world, and the world was made through him, and the world knew him not"). The first two instances make it clear that the κόσμος is this earth and its mankind which God has created. The third instance makes it clear that it is the realm of mankind which, though created by the Word, became alienated from the life of God. It is the human race as sinful, blind, hostile to God and His Word, the realm of evil: "and the world (κόσμος) knew him not". This is the world into which the true light, the Word came. In John 3:19 we read: "And this is the judgment, that the light is come into the world, and men loved the darkness rather than the light; for their works were evil". The world is characterized as that of men who do evil works and who love darkness and who therefore hate the light which enters into their midst. Similarly verse 17 speaks of God not judging the world, although it is sinful and could be judged, but sending His Son "that the world should be saved through him". Here obviously the world designates sinful men. Martha's statement in John 11:27 seems to indicate the realm of human history. At John 12:46 Jesus says: "I am come a light into the world, that whosoever believes on me may not abide in the darkness". The whole concept of Jesus as the light here as also in 1:9 and 3:19 is indicative of the moral contrast between the world in the darkness of the realm of evil and Jesus as the one who brings light to and for sinful men. Again verse 47 speaks of his not judging the world but coming "to save the world". This is explanatory of the way in which he

[28] Hendriksen; *cf.* also Bengel's description of the κόσμος as "full of sin".
[29] See Arndt-Gingrich, who give eight primary meanings plus several subordinate ones.
[30] See first of all the fine additional note of Westcott on John 1:10 who notes in order the different meanings and the progression from one to another. See also the clear delineation of Hendriksen in a note on John 1:10.
[31] See note 23.

brings light to the world. He enlightens men by saving them. Thus the world into which he enters and which he comes not to judge but to save is both the earthly sphere and the race of sinful men. The saying in 16:28 would certainly seem to have the place or locale in view. But verse 33 makes clear that it is not only the place as such but the place as one of tribulation and one which Jesus has overcome. The world, the realm of evil men, shall harass them, but Christ has conquered this world of evil. "To this end have I been born", says Jesus, "and to this end am I come into the world, that I should bear witness unto the truth" (18:37). The world here, as in verse 36, is certainly this earth. But it is not simply that, it is the world which is contrasted with the kingdom and which is in need of the truth to which Jesus bears witness. Jesus describes his coming into the world in term of his bearing witness unto the truth. The world of which he speaks is then a world which needs the truth because "the whole world lies in the evil one" (1 John 5:19).

The usage even in these passages is not completely uniform, but the general emphasis is certainly upon the world as the sinful human race and the place of its abode[32]. "The fact that this divinely anointed Savior 'came into the world' indicates *not merely a change of location,* a 'descent' from one place to another (from heaven to earth), but *a change of state and of moral and spiritual environment*" (Hendriksen, *ad* 1 Tim. 1:15). Such is the conclusion to which the evidence of the usage of the phrase in John's Gospel leads. Such an understanding of κόσμος in John is essentially that of Paul[33].

---

[32] Cremer, *sub* κόσμος, p. 368 f., gives a compact yet full survey of the use of κόσμος in John in the following words: "As employed by *John,* κόσμος may be deemed one of those words in which (particularly in its use in the connection of the exposition) the chief features of a writer's circle of thought are concentrated. It denotes *the ordered entirety of God's creation... humanity itself, as it presents itself within this order* ... But the world is an order of things characterized by the ungodly conduct of mankind, by sin and by estrangement from God. ... Into such an order of things the Saviour entered, John i.9,10, iii.19, viii.12, ix.5, xii.46, ix.39, xvi.28, xviii.37, iii.17, x.36, xvii.18, 1 John iv.9,14, but not as one who originated within, and took His rise from, this order, and had a corresponding character... therefore He also quitted it again ... not, however, without having broken its power, xvi.33, ἐγὼ νενίκηκα τὸν κόσμον, cf. 1 John iv.4,5, having become the propitiatory sacrifice for the sins of the whole world ... in order to save it..." *Cf.* also H. Sasse, *TDNT,* III, pp. 868-895 for an extensive treatment of κόσμος, and in relation to John and the phrase coming into the world see especially pp. 894 and 889. See also R. Bultmann, *Theology of the New Testament* (New York: Scribners, 1955), Vol. II, pp. 15 ff.

[33] For the substantiation of this evaluation see R. Bultmann, *op. cit.,* p. 15 and other sections therein indicated, who says, "As for Paul, so for John the *kosmos* means primarily the world of men; on it the judgment falls that it is evil and would be lost were it not for the coming of the 'Son' "; and

There is one aspect of the use of κόσμος in the Johannine writings and in 1 Tim. 1:15 which must yet be highlighted and has heretofore in this survey not received adequate emphasis. And that is that the κόσμος is the realm or theater of God's redemptive action in Christ. It is the place where redemption is accomplished[34]. This is evident in 1 Tim. 1:15. Christ Jesus came into the world to save sinners. He came into the world to accomplish redemption here. He came to save sinners who have sinned in this world and must be reached in this world. This concept is also present in John's usage, especially when there is reference to Christ coming into the world.

In John 1:9 and context, Jesus is the true light that comes into the world.[35] He comes as a light shining in the world of darkness, *i.e.*, under the bondage of sin and the prince of darkness. Even as darkness is symbolic of bondage and death, so Jesus as the light is the one who brings life (verse 4). He comes to men, and thus into the world, that they might receive him, and in doing so they might become the children of God by being born of God. Again in John 3:19 and context Jesus is come into the world to save the world. It is only by being in the world that he is lifted up on the cross (verse 14). The presence of Christ in the world thereby places men before the decision to choose for him the light or to remain in the darkness of their sin (verses 18 ff.). Christ's descent from heaven and presence in the world brings him to the arena where he is lifted up (verses 13, 14) and it also brings men thereby to the arena of decision. Thus the world becomes the place where redemption is accomplished, and also where it is either received or rejected. Martha's confession of faith in Jesus, "Yes, Lord: I have believed that you are the Christ, the Son of God" is elaborated on by saying that she believes this about him as "he that comes into the world" (John 11:27). For her the Christ, the Son of God, the Lord Jesus whom she now acknowledges is the one who enters this κόσμος to accomplish his Messianic work. Her confession, and particularly her "yes, Lord", are an answer of affirmation to Jesus' proclamation that he is the resurrection and the life and that he that believes in him shall live.

"I am come a light into the world, that whosoever believes on me may not abide in darkness", says Jesus pointedly in John 12:46. Here again Jesus comes as a light into this world of darkness to provide deliverance through the response of faith. He says expressly that he has come (ἦλθον) to save the world. That is the reason for his presence in the

see also H. Sasse, *TDNT*, III, p. 894, who says, "...the Johannine writings... hardly contain a thought on κόσμος which is not at least implicit in Paul's doctrine of the world..."

34 *Cf.* H. Sasse, *TDNT*, III, p. 894.

35 See H. Ridderbos, "The Structure and Scope of the Prologue to the Gospel of John", *Novum Testamentum*, VIII (1966), pp. 180-201. See also note 24.

world. But man's response to Jesus' life and words in this world will determine whether he is saved or judged (verses 46-50). His disciples experience and know the redeeming love of the Father because of their love for Jesus and their belief that he has come forth from the Father and into the world (John 16:26-30). The disciples may have good cheer, comfort, peace and strength, because Christ "has overcome the world" (ἐγὼ νενίκηκα τὸν κόσμον). Christ has been victorious over the great opponent, here personified as the κόσμος[36].

Finally, John 18:37 depicts the world as the place to which Christ has come so that there he may bear witness to the truth ("to this end have I been born, and to this end am I come into the world, that I should bear witness unto the truth"). Into this world he was born, and in this world he lives and dies under Pontius Pilate to bear witness to God's truth. And that action in this world calls those in this world to hear and respond to Christ's voice (verse 38b). Christ comes into this world that here he may bear witness and that here men may respond to his voice.

1 Tim. 1:15 tersely ties these ideas together. It says in effect that the world in which men have sinned and are in the bondage of darkness and death is the place where Christ came to save. The world is the place where Christ Jesus accomplishes his salvation; the world is the place where sinners are saved by what Christ Jesus has already done.

Ἁμαρτωλούς (sinners) is used here as a substantive. The word is extremely rare in Greek literature[37]. In the LXX it is common both as an adjective and as a substantive, occurring 94 times out of which 68 are in the Psalms. It is predominantly used for the Hebrew רָשָׁע (72 out of the 94 times)[38]. "The statistics show us that the רְשָׁעִים of the Psalms for the most part underlies the ἁμαρτωλός of the LXX"[39]. In the Psalms they are the opposite of the pious, righteous and godly (cf. Psalm 1). In short, "he does not regard or follow the Law as an absolutely binding expression of the will of God (Ps. 50:16 f.)"[40].

In the N.T. the word is found 47 times, with most of the occurrences being in the form of the substantive. The Gospels utilize the word, in the main, in the Pharisaic sense, which is a hardening and absolutizing of the LXX usage just noted[41]. Sinners then are the irreligious, unobser-

---

[36] H. Sasse, *TDNT*, III, p. 894 f.
[37] For the references see the helpful article of K. H. Rengstorf, *TDNT*, I, p. 317 f.
[38] See Hatch-Redpath, *s.v.*, and Rengstorf, *TDNT*, I, p. 320.
[39] Rengstorf, *TDNT*, I, p. 321.
[40] *Ibid.*
[41] *Cf., e.g.,* Mk. 2:15,16(*bis*); Mt. 9:10,11; Lk. 5:30; Mt. 11:19; Lk. 7:34; Lk. 15:12.

vant people who did not observe the Law in detail[42]. Paul also knows this in its particular form as a distinction between Jew and Gentile. He says in Gal. 2:15, "We being Jews by nature, and not sinners of the Gentiles". But Paul, although he knows and can use ἁμαρτωλός in this sense and with this distinction, knows and uses the word generally in another sense, i.e., that all men are sinners before God[43]. Although John's Gospel is virtually restricted to the Pharisaic usage[44], the synoptic Gospels show an understanding of other senses of the term[45]. For example, Luke knows the word for those who are especially wicked. The woman of the streets in Lk. 7:36 ff. is designated in particular as a ἁμαρτωλός (verses 37, 39). And it is said that her sins are many (verse 47). Jesus, although using the term at times in the Pharisaic sense perhaps because he recognized its relative value as rooted in the O.T., seeks to bring home in his ministry the truth that being a sinner is the condition that all stand in before God and not merely that which distinguishes one group of men from another. This truth he brings home with forcefulness in Lk 13:2,3; "Do you think that these Galilaeans were sinners above all the Galilaeans, because they have suffered these things? I tell you, No; but, except you repent, you shall all in like manner perish". This statement says in effect that all are ἁμαρτωλοί and all will perish except they repent. This is the basic presumption of his preaching of repentance. Jesus says that the righteousness of those who esteem themselves righteous is inadequate for entrance into the kingdom. Entrance into that kingdom demands righteousness that far exceeds that righteousness (Mt. 5:20). By means of the parable of the Publican and the Pharisee (Lk. 18:9 ff.) Jesus drives this lesson home. Jesus relates that the Publican "smote his breast, saying, God, be merciful to me a sinner"[46]. He does not have the Publican designate himself as a sinner in relation to others and their judgments, e.g., the Pharisee, but in relation to God. The Publican realizes that he is guilty before God and that only God can forgive him. At the same

---

[42] Arndt-Gingrich, s.v. See also the literature cited there.
[43] "through the one man's disobedience the many were made sinners" (Rom. 5:19).
[44] In John's Gospel the word is found only in the 9th chapter in connection with Jesus' healing of the blind man. Some of the Pharisees raise the question: "How can a man that is a sinner do such signs?" (verse 16). This is on the background of the assertion that Jesus is not from God because He did not keep the Sabbath according to their "commandments". Thus they say: "we know that this man is a sinner" (verse 24). The healed man answers them twice using the word sinner in response to their use of it (verses 25 & 31). His response in verse 31 seems more in line with the usage of the LXX O.T. than the more hardened Pharisaic usage.
[45] Cf. K. H. Rengstorf, TDNT, I, pp. 317-33, for his treatment of the various views, and also Thayer, sub ἁμαρτωλός.
[46] "The sinner" (τῷ ἁμαρτωλῷ, Lk. 18:13).

time, of course, the contrast with the Pharisee in the parable brings the judgment that the Pharisee is also a sinner. It says that the Pharisee needs to acknowledge that he is a sinner and that only then will he find acceptance with God (verses 9 & 14). Jesus says that the thought that they were righteous is not acknowledged by God. The Pharisee is not adjudged righteous by God (verse 14).

On this background we come to understand this part of the saying found in all the synoptic Gospels (Mk. 2:17; Mt. 9:13; Lk. 5:32), which may well be reflected in 1 Tim. 1:15. Here Jesus speaks of the great purpose of his coming as that of calling sinners. Because of the controversy with the Pharisees in the background, he uses the language that he has not come to call the righteous but sinners. This must not be construed as a judgment on Jesus' part that the Pharisees are truly righteous[47]. No, rather it is used as a foil over against them. That the religious leaders are sinners who need to repent and that Jesus regards them as such is seen from Jesus' direct address to them in Mt. 21:32. Jesus has come to save those who are sinners, who are lost[48], who know it, and who repent of their sinfulness[49]. "Thus we can see already how Jesus transcended the view that only certain individuals or groups are sinners, replacing it by the conception which regards the emphasising of human autonomy, even under the guise of service of God and devotion to Him, as that which makes man a sinner who needs divine forgiveness and grace"[50].

It is the meaning of sinners in the universal sense of the term that is found in 1 Tim. 1:15. And thus we also see that the early church has understood Jesus' saying in the sense indicated above. Paul indicates this understanding when he adds the words "of whom I am chief" to the saying. The "of whom" (ὧν) has ἁμαρτωλούς as its antecedent. Paul regards himself as one of those sinners whom Jesus came to save. And it is Paul the Jew and the once righteous Pharisee that so regards himself. This is the Paul who could say of himself: "as touching the law, a Pharisee; as touching zeal, persecuting the church; as touching the righteousness which is in the law, found blameless" (Philip. 3:5,6). Therefore we see that the sinners in view in the saying are not the Gentiles in contrast to the Jews, not the lawless in contrast to the law-abiding and the Pharisees, for then would Paul be excluded, but that it is those who are guilty before God — men as such without exception.

---

[47] For the question of "righteous" and "sinners" see H. N. Ridderbos, *The Coming of the Kingdom* (Philadelphia:Presbyterian & Reformed, 1962), p. 220.

[48] "For the Son of man came to seek and to save that which was lost (τὸ ἀπολωλός) (Lk. 19:10).

[49] Luke adds to the statement of Jesus "I am not come to call the righteous but sinners" the words "to repentance" (5:32). For the note of repentance see also Mt. 21:32.

[50] K. H. Rengstorf, *TDNT*, I, p. 332.

44

The New Testament view of the universality of sin, and thus of the fact that all men are sinners, is most clearly spelled out by Paul. It is delineated in Romans 3 (verse 9, ". . . Jews and Greeks, that they are all under sin . . .", and verse 23, "for all have sinned . . ."). All men, and thus all sinners, are characterized as not being righteous (verse 10), as not seeking after God (verse 11), as not being good (verse 12), as falling "short of the glory of God" (verse 23). The words and phrases synonymous to ἁμαρτωλός in the development of Paul's argument in Romans 5 deepen the conception. In verse 8 Paul says, "But God commends his own love toward us, in that, while we were yet sinners, Christ died for us". Those who are called sinners are further designated as ungodly (ἀσεβῶν, verse 6), enemies (ἐχθροί, verse 10) of God, those who need to be declared righteous (δικαιωθέντες, verses 1 & 9) because they are now guilty, and those who need to be reconciled to God (κατηλλάγημεν, verse 10) because they are alienated from God. The sinner is not only such because he is made a sinner through Adam's disobedience (Rom. 5:9) in which he sinned (Rom. 5:12), but also through his own bent of heart, attitude and actions (Rom. 3:10 ff.). Rengstorf (*TDNT*, I, p. 328) summarizes the meaning in these words: "The term is used to describe men from the standpoint that, apart from action on God's part, all without exception are separated from Him by sin, so that the reference is to guilty humanity which is without Christ and therefore unreconciled". Being without Christ they are without hope because as sinners they have no other prospect than the reception of the wages of sin which is eternal death (Rom. 6:23).

The word ἁμαρτωλούς (sinners) is probably placed before the verb in the saying for emphasis[51]. The saying seeks to throw into relief and into the foreground who it is that Christ has come save and what their condition is.

The infinitive (σῶσαι) is an aorist rather than a present, most probably to express the purpose of Christ's coming as a once for all act[52]. Christ Jesus came to accomplish salvation, and he has done that[53]. The concept "to save" is rich with meaning in both its negative and positive aspects[54]. The negative aspect is evident in this passage in ἁμαρτωλούς.

[51] So Bouma. Also Lenski, who says "verb and object are transposed so as to emphasize both"; *cf.* Calvin.
[52] Blass-Debrunner-Funk, sections 338 & 335; see also Robertson, pp. 856 ff.
[53] Lenski speaks of "to save" as an "effective aorist" and then also as a "constative aorist".
[54] For very helpful treatments of this subject see Thayer, Cremer, *sub voca* and Hendriksen, *ad loc.* G. Vos has a rather full and clear description in his *The Self-Disclosure of Jesus* (Grand Rapids: Eerdmans, 1954), pp.

It is sinners that Christ came to save. It is that which constitutes them sinners from which Christ saves them. Mt. 1:21 speaks of Jesus as coming to save his people "from their sins" (ἀπὸ τῶν ἁμαρτιῶν αὐτῶν). This includes deliverance from the ultimate outcome and wages of sin, *i.e.*, eternal death (Rom. 6:23; James 5:20) and destruction (*cf.* the contrasts of 1 Cor. 1:18; 2 Cor. 2:15; 2 Thess. 2:10). And this salvation is that of deliverance from the alienation and wrath of God (Rom. 5:9). But σῴζειν does not only have a future or eschatological aspect. The deliverance is also here and now[55]. It is deliverance from the present death of sin (Eph. 2:5,6). And to be saved means to be delivered from the present slavery of sin (Rom. 7:24,25; Gal. 5:1) and to be forgiven of the present guilt of sin (Eph. 1:7; Col. 1:14). But to accentuate the negative without the positive element would be to miss the real heart of the meaning of spiritual salvation in the New Testament. The sinner is not merely removed from a bad situation to a neutral ground but to a positive sphere of goodness and blessing. The state of salvation is the opposite of the state of perishing or being lost (*cf.* Lk. 19:10; Jn. 3:16,17), but just because of that it is the opposite in a positive direction.

To save means to remove the sinner from the realm of sin and death to the realm of life and holiness. In 2 Tim. 2:18, Paul speaks of the Lord delivering him "from every evil work" and therefore that he "will save [him] unto his heavenly kingdom". Salvation is thus the reality of the possession of eternal life (1 Tim. 1:16; Rom. 6:23; John 3:16,17). The life which is entered into through salvation is not only future but also present (Eph. 2:5; Gal. 2:20; 2 Cor. 5:17). And this life is characterized by righteousness (Rom. 5:9—11; 2 Cor. 5:21) and freedom (Gal. 5:1). Christ Jesus came sinners to save. He came to deliver from sin and to give righteousness and life, now and forever.

The saying has been crystallized and it is repeated because the knowledge of this truth is necessary for belief unto salvation (2:4; 2 Tim. 3:15). But salvation is not just knowledge. It is Christ Jesus that

---

255-268. See also the full article by W. Wagner, "Über ΣΩZEIN und seine Derivata im Neuen Testament", *Z.N.W.*, VI, (1905), pp. 205-235, especially for 1 Tim. 1:15 see p. 218. Some of the most recent articles are those of W. C. van Unnik, "L'usage de σῴζειν 'sauver' et de ses dérivés dans les Évangiles synoptiques" in *La Formation des Évangiles* (1957), pp. 178-194, and W. Foerster and G. Fohrer, *TWNT*, VII, pp. 956-1024 with a literature list. For σῴζω in the Pastoral Letters in the latter see p. 995 f.

[55] Thayer, *s.v.*, expresses the thought quite well when he says: "Since salvation begins in this life (in deliverance from error and corrupt notions, in moral purity, in pardon of sin, and in the blessed peace of a soul reconciled to God), but on the visible return of Christ from heaven will be perfected in the consummate blessings of ὁ αἰὼν ὁ μέλλων, we can understand why τὸ σῴζεσθαι is spoken of in some passages as a present possession, in others as a good yet future".

saves sinners. He does so, in short, by becoming the mediator between God and man (2:5) and accomplishing the salvation by providing Himself as the ransom (ἀντίλυτρον, 2:6; *cf.* 1 John 3:5). The translation from death to life and immortality is wrought in Christ Jesus as Savior abolishing death and bringing life and immortality (2 Tim. 1:10). Salvation is always in and through Christ Jesus (2 Tim. 2:10).

This saying as a whole summarizes and epitomizes the Gospel[56]. It focuses on the work of Christ and gives as the reason for the incarnation of Christ the salvation of sinners. The focal point of interest is not that Christ Jesus came into the world, as amazing as that is, but rather that He came into the world "sinners to save". This gospel in a sentence is but slightly different from the announcement made concerning Jesus in Mt. 1:21 ("You shall call his name Jesus, for it is he that shall save his people from their sins") and from Jesus' own indication of His life's mission in Luke 19:10 ("For the Son of man came to seek and to save that which was lost").

Paul cites this saying at this point to emphasize what he has just written and what he writes afterwards[57]. As Kelly says, "The quotation... seems to Paul aptly to epitomize what he had been saying". He is keenly aware that he has been a great and terrible sinner (verse 13) and yet now he has not only received mercy (verse 16), but also has been counted faithful (verse 12), entrusted with the Gospel (verse 11) and appointed to Christ's service (verse 12) as an apostle (verse 1). How can this be? It can happen because Christ Jesus came into the world to save sinners, all kinds, the worst kind not excepted. And so Paul also has been saved. In fact Paul can cite his own case as an example and proof of the truth of this saying ("Christ Jesus came into the world to save sinners, of whom I am chief"[58]). Because Paul regards himself as chief (πρῶτος) of sinners who are saved, he can appeal to this as irrefutable evidence that Christ does and will save sinners as such, if they only believe. He explicates this thought in verse 16, "howbeit for this cause I obtained mercy, that in me as chief might Jesus Christ show forth all his longsuffering, for an example of them that should thereafter believe on him unto eternal life".

---

[56] One of the best expositions of this passage is to be found in the sermon of B. B. Warfield, "The Saving Christ", *The Person and Work of Christ* (Philadelphia: Presbyterian and Reformed Publishing Co., 1950), pp. 549-560.

[57] For an able discussion of the progress of thought in 1 Timothy 1:3-20 see B. B. Warfield, "Some Exegetical Notes on 1 Timothy", *The Presbyterian Review*, VIII, (1887), pp. 500 ff.

[58] For a list and evaluation of almost all the interpretations of the phrase "of whom I am chief" see Hendriksen, *ad loc.* See for an evaluation on Paul's part of himself 1 Cor. 15:9; Gal. 1:13; Eph. 3:8.

Paul responds to the saying personally in its reference to saving sinners by immediately applying its significance to himself, "of whom I am chief". He responds personally as he would have others respond ("worthy of all acceptation"). Paul says in effect that since Christ has saved the chief of sinners it is obvious that he can save all others who "thereafter believe on him" (verse 16). And he ends this paragraph which is centered in the saving work of Christ for sinners with the response of praise in the form of a doxology (verse 17).

The question of the origin of this saying remains. The similarity to Luke 19:10, "the Son of man came to seek and to save that which was lost" (ἦλθεν ... σῶσαι τὸ ἀπολωλός), has already been noticed. Further similarities may be noted elsewhere in the Synoptics (e.g., Mk. 2:17, note ἦλθον ... ἁμαρτωλούς, also Mt. 9:13; likewise Lk. 5:32, ἐλήλυθα ... ἁμαρτωλούς). The differences with 1 Tim. 1:15 are also evident, the most striking being that the phrase "came into the world" is not used in reference to Jesus. Hence there is no exact parallel in the Synoptics. The phrase "came into the world" draws one to the Gospel of John for only there is the phrase used with reference to Christ Jesus apart from 1 Tim. 1:15[59]. Other parallels are seen in John, e.g., 3:17 (... ἀπέστειλεν ὁ Θεὸς τὸν υἱὸν εἰς τὸν κόσμον ... ἵνα σωθῇ ὁ κόσμος δι' αὐτοῦ) and 12:47 (... ἦλθον ... ἵνα σώσω τὸν κόσμον). But then in John's usage Χριστὸς Ἰησοῦς in this order never occurs as it does often in Paul. And the word ἁμαρτωλός is virtually unknown in John's Gospel and particularly in the sense used in 1 Tim. 1:15. Thus no exact parallel is found in John's Gospel.

We are then brought to the recognition that some words or concepts, as well as the main thrust of the saying as a whole, are found in both the Synoptic Gospels and John's Gospel. In the Synoptic Gospels the similar sayings are those in which Jesus speaks of his own person and work (e.g., Mt. 9:13; Mk. 2:17; Lk. 5:32; 19:10). The Johannine parallels too are generally statements made by Jesus about himself (cf. 12:46; 16:28; 18:37). The ultimate source would therefore seem to be found in Christ Jesus himself. Kent (ad loc.) states the solution tersely: "Here the reference almost certainly is to the statement of Jesus, uttered on several occasions (Matt. 9:13; Luke 19:10). Such truths as these probably were often repeated in the Christian assemblies, and were thus well known"[60].

[59] Swete, "The Faithful Sayings", J.Th.S. xviii (1917), p. 2: "The phrase ἦλθεν (ἔρχεται) εἰς τὸν κόσμον used with reference to the Advent is peculiarly Johannine (or, shall we say? Ephesian)".
[60] Likewise Parry (ad loc.) and Easton (ad loc.), "The 'faithful saying', a Christian watch-word from the very beginning, goes back to Jesus himself (Mk. 2,17, etc.)". Kelly (ad loc.) also, "The words, however, echo Christ's own statement to Zacchaeus (Lk. xix.10) ...".

The saying finding its ultimate source in Christ utilizes a combination of Synoptic and Johannine language. Lock (*ad loc.*) preserves the necessary and essential balance with his observation that "the whole phrase implies a knowledge of Synoptic and Johannine language (cf. Lk. 5^{32}, Jn. 12^{47}), and is a witness to their essential unity, but does not imply direct quotation from either".

The last question which this and the other sayings raise is that of the form of the saying. Some commentators conjecture part of a hymn or some liturgy, others conjecture some primitive creed or a part thereof; many commentators offer either as a possibility. Eight words provide too small an amount of evidence upon which to decide the issue with any degree of certainty.

CHAPTER III

1 TIMOTHY 3:1 AND ITS SAYING

Two problems present themselves at this passage. One is whether πιστός or ἀνθρώπινος is the original reading. The other is whether the formula πιστός (or ἀνθρώπινος) ὁ λόγος refers to what precedes or what follows. These two problems are not necessarily related, but in all probability, as will be seen, the two interact and this interaction may help point the way to the solution of both questions.

Ἀνθρώπινος in Greek is found only in one Greek MSS., Codex D* (VI cen.), and in the Latin form humanus in the Old Latin version, manuscripts d(V/VI cen.), m(IV-IX cen.) mon(X cen.), g(IX cen.), and in Ambrosiaster mss. according to Jerome, Augustine, and Sedulius-Scotus[1].

The external evidence is thus exceedingly weak and in the Greek is almost non-existent. The major recent modern English translations (R.V., A.S.V., R.S.V., new A.S.V.), and most commentators[2], and especially editors of critical Greek New Testaments (Nestle-Aland, Kilpatrick, Tischendorf, von Soden, Westcott-Hort, Aland-Black-Metzger-Wikgren) have chosen πιστός as the original reading and placed ἀνθρώπινος as a textual variant. There are however notable exceptions, such as Moffatt's translation, and especially the New English Bible New Testament (and therefore the Greek New Testament text which underlies it edited by Tasker)[3]. To this list may be added Wohlenberg (ad loc.), Easton

---

[1] According to the textual apparatus of the Greek New Testament edited by Aland-Black-Metzger-Wikgren, also in part according to Tischendorf, Alford, and Westcott and Hort. Manuscript g of the Old Latin version has both humanus and fidelis (humanus vel fidelis). The dates for the manuscripts and for the writers who are cited as textual evidence here and later in the discussion are by and large the dates given in the first named critical Greek New Testament in its Introduction.

[2] Alford, Barrett, Bengel, Bernard, Bouma, Chrysostom, Dibelius-Conzelmann, Ellicott, Falconer, Gealy, Guthrie, Hendriksen, Huther, Jeremias, Kelly, Lenski, Scott, Spicq.

[3] In the appendix to The Greek New Testament being the text translated in The New English Bible, 1961, edited by R. V. G. Tasker, which appendix is entitled "Notes on Variant Readings", p. 440 re 3:1, the following note is

(ad loc.), Zahn[4], Lock[5] with hesitation and Westcott and Hort as a "noteworthy rejected reading". The argument for ἀνθρώπινος is offered that it can explain the substitution of πιστός but not vice versa[6]. The occurrence of πιστός elsewhere in there formulas would readily explain why a scribe could change ἀνθρώπινος into πιστός. But it is affirmed that no scribe would substitute ἀνθρώπινος for πιστός. Those who take the reading ἀνθρώπινος associate the formula with what follows (3:1b)[7]. They declare that πιστός is not apt to refer to what follows in that 3:1b does not deal with salvation or the heart of the Christian faith. Some argue that the quotation itself (3:1b) is a common saying of the Greek world and not specifically Christian or religious at all. Thus they affirm that this also makes πιστός inappropriate and ἀνθρώπινος fitting[8]. The meaning of ἀνθρώπινος is taken to be that of "human", "common", or "popular"[9].

The external evidence is, however, overwhelmingly in favor of the reading πιστός, i.e., all Greek MSS. except D*. And further, the origin of ἀνθρώπινος can be explained with πιστός as the original reading. Westcott and Hort have already suggested in their "Notes on Select Readings" that ἀνθρώπινος has entered the text as a substitute for πιστός

given: "Although less widely attested than πιστός, the variant ἀνθρώπινος, found in D* g m, and Ambrosiaster, was regarded as original. The change to πιστός would have been easy in view of the frequent occurrence of the expression πιστὸς ὁ λόγος in the Pastoral Epistles, but the change of πιστός to ἀνθρώπινος seemed unlikely. Paul was understood by the translators to be quoting a proverbial saying and showing its relevance to the Christian ministry". The footnote or marginal reading in the Greek text itself ad loc. reads: "πιστὸς ὁ λόγος, construed either in this position or as the conclusion of the preceding paragraph". The note ad loc. to the English text of the *New English Bible* itself reads slightly differently: "*Some witnesses read. Here are words you may trust, which some interpreters attach to the end of the preceding paragraph*".

4 Theodor Zahn, *Introduction to the New Testament, Vol.* II, (Edinburgh: T. & T. Clark, 1909), p. 124, note 6 to page 92.

5 *Commentary on the Pastoral Epistles*, page xxxvi.

6 Moffatt has a note to his translation: "It is much more easy to understand how it was altered to πιστός for the sake of uniformity with i.15, etc., than vice versa". Lock says (p. xxxvi), "The MSS authority is not strong, but the correction from πιστός is unlikely ... whereas the assimulation to πιστός ... is very probable".

7 *Moffatt Translation, N.E.B.*, Easton, Lock, Wohlenberg and Zahn.

8 *E.g.*, Lock ad loc., "If these words apply to the following paragraph, the variant ἀνθρώπινος would seem more appropriate, the writer quoting a saying applicable to all overseership in human life ('allgemeinmenschlich,' Wohlenberg) and applying it to the Christian Church". Similarly Zahn, *ibid.*, and Scott, ad loc.

9 *E.g., N.E.B., Moffatt.*

"perhaps due to an assumption that the clause belongs to what follows"[10]. Scott *(ad loc.)* in the *Moffatt N.T. Commentary* series over against Moffatt states that case similarly but more fully: "But the mass of textual evidence is against it, and it has all the appearance of being substituted by some early editor who assumed, from the other instances in the Epistles, that the formula, 'It is a faithful saying', must have a direct religious reference. In itself, however, the formula means nothing more than that the saying in question may be relied on, whatever may be its nature". This argument in one form or another has satisfied the vast majority of exegetes[11] and is indeed a reasonable solution. That the substitution of ἀνθρώπινος is a plausible reaction is verified by the reactions of certain commentators. They say, in effect, that the formula is πιστὸς ὁ λόγος if it goes with what precedes, but that it must be ἀνθρώπινος if it goes with what follows, or at least that πιστός is unsuitable to refer to what follows[12]. Lenski *(ad loc.)* rebutts the contention of Zahn and others that ἀνθρώπινος is the correct reading because the saying is a *locus communis*, a current secular expression of the day, that whoever aspires to an ἐπισκοπή desires an excellent task, by pointing out that there is no such or similar saying to be found and that ἐπισκοπή itself is found only rarely in secular sources, and then, we may add, in a different sense (also Wohlenberg in the Zahn series). Likewise Bouma *(ad loc.)*, who says, "Niet afkomstig uit heidensche kringen, want in het profane Grieks is het woord ἐπισκοπή zoo goed als niet gevonden. ... Ook daarom kan de lezing ἀνθρώπινος niet de oorspronkelijke zijn, want dat woord veronderstelt bekendheid in veel ruimer kring". Both external textual evidence and internal considerations show πιστός to be the correct reading.

The question of relationship still remains. Does πιστὸς ὁ λόγος refer to what precedes or to what follows? Here again the commentators and others who have dealt with this question are divided[13]. Schlatter *(ad loc.)*

---

[10] Alford, Bernard, Ellicott and Lenski suggest that the Old Latin has influenced D* and caused the ἀνθρώπινος. The reason suggested by W.-H. and Scott would still be the ultimate cause but the process then would be through the Old Latin.

[11] So e.g., Bouma, Dibelius-Conzelmann, Falconer, Gealy, Guthrie, Hendriksen, & Kelly.

[12] E.g., Lock (note 8) and Falconer *(ad loc.)*.

[13] Those that refer the formula to what *precedes* are: among the editions of the Greek New Testaments only Westcott and Hort; marginal references of the *R.V.*, *A.S.V.*, and *N.E.B.* (if πιστός); of the commentators, Chrysostom, Barrett, Dibelius-Conzelmann (?), Falconer, Lock, Parry, Robertson, Schlatter von Soden, White; Spicq also lists "saint Jean Damascene, Theophylacte, ... Hillard, ... Brown"; Bover, "Fidelis Sermo", *Biblica* 19 (1938), pp. 74-79, esp. pp. 76 ff., J. G. Duncan, "Πιστὸς ὁ λόγος", *The Expository Times*, xxxv (1923),

52

maintains that ὁ λόγος always refers to the word of proclamation and that what follows cannot therefore be referred to but rather what precedes. Bover (*op. cit.*) argues that πιστὸς ὁ λόγος refers to what precedes because the other "faithful sayings" have reference to salvation. Therefore all these sayings must refer to that which is soteriological and hence this saying too. Parry takes a similar position: "to be taken with the preceding words, and occasioned by σωθήσεται". Von Soden argues similarly but also adds his view that all other occurrences of πιστὸς ὁ λόγος except 1 Tim. 1:15 occur after the saying[14]. Westcott and Hort, in their "Notes on Select Readings", come close to expressing the view that the formula goes with what precedes because it cannot refer to 3:1b; ". . . an assumption that the clause belongs to what follows [was] rightly condemned by Chrys.". Schlatter's argument is not valid, as chapter one on πιστὸς ὁ λόγος makes evident. Λόγος is not always used in the sense he requires nor is this the case in the formula. The argument of Bover and von Soden, also Parry, is one of an *a priori*. It assumes that because some of the sayings have a soteriological reference that all of them must have it and thus this one too. Even though this may prove to be the case with others of the sayings, it must not be imposed as a norm without exception. The givens in the immediate context of this formula must be given primary attention before an outside norm is applied. No prejudice or presupposition must disallow a saying about the ἐπισκοπή.

The note of bias is not on one side only. Scott (*ad loc.*) examples this in his comment: "Many expositors, both ancient and modern, would place the formula, 'It is a sure word,' at the end of the previous chapter; but there is nothing in the pedantic allegory of the trespass of Eve which can ever have passed from mouth to mouth as a watchword of Christian wisdom". The question is not which reference fits in one's scheme for the "faithful sayings" or which reference one regards as the better statement. The question is simply which one is in fact the λόγος.

The association of πιστὸς ὁ λόγος with 3:1b rests first upon the

p. 141. Those that refer the formula to what *follows* (3:1b) are: all recent editions of critical Greek New Testaments, and all well-known modern English translations, *cf.* also the Dutch *Nieuwe Vertaling*; of the commentators, Ambrosiaster (*humanus*), Theodore of Mopsuestia, Alford, Bengel, Bernard, Bouma, Calvin, Dibelius, Easton (ἀνθρώπινος), Ellicott, Fairbairn, Fausset, Guthrie, Hendriksen, Holtzmann, Huther, Jeremias, Kelly, Kent, Lenski, Liddon, van Oosterzee, Ridderbos, Scott, Simpson, Spicq, Weiss, Wohlenberg (ἀνθρώπινος); also Swete, "The Faithful Sayings", *Journal of Theological Studies*, xviii (1917), pp. 1-7.

14 *Ad loc.*, "kann nicht zum Folgenden gehören, da es nach II 2.11 T 3.8 I 4.9 1.15 stets zur Bekräftigung eschatologischer Hoffnungen gebraucht; überdies ausser 1.15 stets dem zu bekräftigden nachfolgt wie ein ἀμήν, dort aber mit einem ὅτι der Gegenstand angeschlossen wird . . .".

judgment that 3:1b, "If any man seeks the office of a bishop, he desires a good work" (εἴ τις ἐπισκοπῆς ὀρέγεται, καλοῦ ἔργου ἐπιθυμεῖ), is indeed a saying. Even Lock (*ad loc.*) and Barrett (*ad loc.*), who regard the end af chapter two as that which is referred to by πιστὸς ὁ λόγος, recognize this fact, as well as Gealy (*ad loc.*) who seems to be unsure as to which the formula refers. Most others who take the view that the formula refers to that which precedes are silent on this point. Spicq (*ad loc.*) further argues that without πιστὸς ὁ λόγος beginning this section, it appears to begin too abruptly. That 3:1b is a statement of importance in this section and one upon which Paul places great emphasis is seen not only by the whole development of verses 2 ff. but also by the reference to verse 1 in the οὖν (therefore) of verse 2.

It has been insisted that the statement of 3:1b about a man desiring the office of a bishop is inappropriate for a λόγος which is regarded as πιστός. It is this attitude coupled with the recognition that 3:1b is however a saying which has caused some to opt for ἀνθρώπινος (*e.g.*, Wohlenberg, Lock possibly, *ad loc.*). A similar attitude explains the textual variant (ἀνθρώπινος, *humanus*) itself, but at the same time shows that those same copyists recognized that the formula referred to 3:1b. Thus Ambrosiaster (IV cen.) with his *humanus* and Theodore of Mopsuestia (IV-V cen.) with his *fidele* both referring to 3:1b lived at about the same time as Chrysostom (died 407) with his πιστός referring to the end of chapter 2. To say that πιστὸς ὁ λόγος could not have arisen in the early church or would not be used by the Apostle Paul to refer to 3:1b is to misunderstand both. That there was a lively and deep interest in church order is evidenced not only by the third chapter of 1 Tim. itself, as well as 1 Tim. 5:17 ff. and Titus 1:5 ff., but also by many passages throughout Acts, Paul's letters and other N.T. letters (*cf.* Acts 6:1 ff., 14:21 ff., 15:2 ff., 20:17 ff.; Rom. 12:6 ff.; 1 Cor. 12:28; Philip. 1:1; 1 Thess. 5:12 ff.; Heb. 12:7 & 17; 1 Peter 5:1 ff., etc.).

The verdict must be entered with most of the Greek New Testament editors, commentators and modern English translations that πιστὸς ὁ λόγος refers to 3:1 as the saying. In the words of Kelly, "neither ii.15 nor any of the verses immediately preceding strikes one as a maxim which might have been current in the apostolic Church, whereas iii.1b has all the style and ring of a proverbial saying . . .".

Paul introduces the new subject matter (3:1 ff.) with the solemn citation-emphasis formula and the saying to which it refers (3:1b). The saying is to underscore the value of the work of the office of the bishop[15].

---

[15] Bengel (*ad loc.*) puts it this way: "*This is a true saying* – This preface is used, because it does not seem so to the world". Perhaps there were some, as has heen mentioned *supra*, who did not regard the whole matter properly.

The saying itself is a condition of first class, assumed to be true[16]. The protasis is stated in εἴ τις ἐπισκοπῆς ὀρέγεται, and the apodosis in καλοῦ ἔργου ἐπιθυμεῖ ("If a man seeks the office of a bishop, he desires a good work").

The form of the saying is interesting. It begins with the words "if a man" (εἴ τις). However, as further research indicates, the form does not of itself give any definite help in understanding the saying[17].

[16] Robertson, *Word Pictures*, IV, p. 572; *cf.* also E. DeWitt Burton, *Syntax of the Moods and Tenses in New Testament Greek* (Edinburgh: T. & T. Clark, 3rd ed., reprinted 1955), pp. 100 ff.

[17] Εἴ τις does occur in the LXX in comparative, historical and other formulations but not in so-called casuistic laws. In what may be called casuistic laws because they specify in concrete cases whether a man is guilty or not, or what sort of fine he must pay in a given case, or what he may do in a given case, or whether he is clean in a given case, etc., the formula "if anyone..." often occurs (it is not, however, the only form used for such casuistic rules). In the LXX the formula is never εἴ τις, but ἐάν τις occurs about 22 times and various other formulations of the same idea are found such as ἐάν ἄνθρωπος, ἐάν ψυχή, etc. Nowhere among the O.T. examples is there a close parallel to 1 Tim. 3:1.

In the N.T. the formula ἐάν τις also occurs in rules which could be called casuistic. Especially in Paul's writings εἴ τις occurs in sentences which may be called casuistic in the sense that Paul is stating a general rule about a specific situation. The fact that εἴ τις is used here whereas only ἐάν τις is found in the O.T. for such rules is probably connected with the fact that εἴ takes over some of the uses of ἐάν sometimes in the N.T. (*cf.* Blass-Debrunner-Funk, section 372,3). For a study of some of these casuistic sentences see E. Käsemann, "Sätze heiligen Rechts im Neuen Testament", *Exegetische Versuche und Besinnungen*, II (Tübingen: J. C. B. Mohr, 1960), pp. 70 ff. Examples of specific passages where εἴ τις is used are 1 Cor. 3:17,18; 14:37,38; 16:22; Gal. 1:9; 2 Thess. 3:10,14; and also 1 Cor. 7:12,13 and 1 Tim. 5:4,16 (with a further specification of "brother", "woman", or some other word). There is a noteworthy difference between these examples and 1 Tim. 3:1. In most of these examples the second part of the statement is in the form of an imperative − "If any (εἴ τις) ... *let* (imperative) ..." This aspect is missing from 1 Tim. 3:1. It does *not* say: "If a man seeks the office of a hishop, *let him* ..." Rather, it affirms that "he desires a good work". One may virtually say that these other uses of the εἴ τις formula have a reaction or counter action in the second part of the statement. This again is not true of 1 Tim. 3:1. One is brought to the conclusion that 1 Tim. 3:1 is not some sort of casuistic rule or law.

Εἴ τις states the truth of the saying in a most general way ("if any man"). This use of εἴ τις in this saying is in this respect in accordance with the usage throughout the N.T. (see the complete listing in Moulton & Geden's *Concordance*, p. 262 f. under εἴ τις).

The evidence is lacking to say whether or not this saying originated in response or reaction to some problem about the office or about those seeking it. Probably it arose as a positive encouragement to any man (εἴ τις) to consider this good work (καλοῦ ἔργου).

55

Εἴ τις is apparently used to make the saying general or indefinite ("if *any* man").

Ἐπισκοπῆς is the key word in the saying. Ἐπισκοπή occurs only rarely in secular Greek. In none of these occurrences does it mean a position or office as an overseer. All of these occurrences postdate the saying[18]. The sense of office is in view in two passages in the O.T. (Num. 4:16 and Psalm 108[9]:8)[19]. It is this latter passage which is utilized in the only other N.T. occurrence of the term with the general sense of office, *i.e.*, Acts 1:20. Beyer (*TDNT*, II, p. 608) is right when he says: "The term ἐπισκοπή in 1 Tim. 3:1 does not derive from Ac. 1:20 or its OT orginial. It is newly coined on the basis of the title ἐπίσκοπος which had meantime established itself in the early Church. This is the more easily possible, of course, because ἐπισκοπή is clearly used for 'office' in the language of the LXX". The relationship between ἐπισκοπή and ἐπίσκοπος is most evident in 1 Tim. 3:1 and 2. And this relationship bears out the contention of Beyer stated above. There have been those who have insisted that ἐπισκοπῆς in 3:1 refers in general to the office of one who is an overseer (such as Wohlenberg, and Zahn, *Introduction*, section 37, note 6). They would not restrict the saying to a church office at all. For them, the saying praises the office of any overseer, civil, political, etc. But then, as Weiss points out so well, it would be necessary for 3:2 to read τὸν ἐπίσκοπον τῆς ἐκκλησίας. Rather than doing this the text proceeds from the saying of 1b with its word ἐπισκοπῆς, by means of the use of οὖν in verse 2, and begins to speaks of τὸν ἐπίσκοπον without qualification. It is evident from this connection that ἐπισκοπή is speaking of the office of the ἐπίσκοπος in the life of the Church. Ἐπισκοπή is used in 1 Tim. 3:1 with the meaning, position or office of an ἐπίσκοπος, an overseer or bishop in the life of the Church[20].

Ὀρέγεται, which occurs in the N.T. only in the middle form, means literally to stretch oneself, reach out one's hand, and then figuratively to aspire to, strive for, to desire[21]. The thing which is in view is, as here, in the genitive case[22]. The word occurs only three times in the N.T. (here,

---

[18]   Arndt-Gingrich, *s.v.*, give as the first item of information about ἐπισκοπή the following: "Lucian, Dial. Deor. 20,6 = 'visit'; Dit., Or. 614,6 [III A.D.] = 'care, charge'; Etym. Gud. 508,27 = πρόνοια; LXX". Other than these secular occurrences, ἐπισκοπή is found in a Christian inscription of Lycaonia (IV A.D.) describing a bishop. See Moulton and Milligan, *ad* ἐπισκοπή.

[19]   H. W. Beyer, *TDNT*, II, p. 607.

[20]   Beyer, *TDNT*, II, p. 608; Arndt-Gingrich, *s.v.*

[21]   Arndt-Gingrich, also Thayer, *s.v.*

[22]   Thayer, Arndt-Gingrich, *s.v.* Also Robertson, *Grammar*, p. 508, and Blass-Debrunner-Funk, section 171,1, which point out that verbs of emotion (Robertson), verbs meaning "to strive after, desire" and "to reach, obtain" (Funk) take the genitive. This is true not only for ὀρέγεται in this verse (ἐπισκοπῆς) but also for ἐπιθυμεῖ (καλοῦ ἔργου).

1 Tim. 6:10 and Heb. 11:16). In 1 Tim. 6:10, the context demands a bad sense for the entire thought, but this does not demand that this is inherently the case for the verb itself. In Heb. 11:16 the word is obviously used in a good sense. Field elicits several examples from Greek writers to show that the word "has a special application to such objects as a man is commonly said to *aspire to*"[23]. The whole context of the saying is one in which the verb ὀρέγομαι in connection with ἐπισκοπή is commended in the terms καλοῦ ἔργου ἐπιθυμεῖ. Thus the commendation sets aside at once any thought that this is an ambitious seeking or striving which is self-centered, or which seeks honor or position for oneself. Paul would not have used or commended even facetiously a saying which had in view sinful grasp for power. If he had used it at all in this sense, it would have been to rebuke such an attitude. The nature of the aspiring is determined by the characterization that it is the desiring of a work (ἔργου) and particularly of a work that may be described as "good" (καλοῦ ἔργου)[24].

The saying thus commends the aspiring to the office of a bishop as the desiring of a good work. Ἐπιθυμεῖ, which is similar in meaning to ὀρέγεται, is also used in both a good (*e.g.*, Hebr. 6:11) and a bad sense. It means to desire or to long for with the genitive of the thing desired[25]. It is comparable to the English expression, to set one's heart upon (Thayer). Here the thing desired or longed for is a καλοῦ ἔργου. The commendation of the saying and the good thing desired both point to ἐπιθυμέω here as used in a good sense. Ἐπιθυμέω may be used to provide a slight change from the nearly synonymous previous verb (ὀρέγομαι) for stylistic reason, or to emphasize the inner desire for the good work as such. The latter is more likely the case.

The saying describes that which is desired and hence the ἐπισκοπή as a ἔργον, indeed, as a καλὸν ἔργον. This is the reason that the saying commends and praises anyone aspiring to the office of the bishop, because that person desires a good work, not just an honor or position[26].

---

23 Field, *Notes*, p. 204. Therefore, he repudiates "The idea of an *ambitious seeking*, which does not belong either to the word itself or to its connexion".

24 This sets aside the ingenious and esoteric theory of Swete, *op. cit.*, p. 3, which suggests that the saying is "the *apologia pro vita sua* of some φιλοπρωτεύων at Ephesus, who excused his eagerness for office by pleading, καλοῦ ἔργου ἐπιθυμῶ". Swete assumes that "the writer of the Epistle endorses the saying, not without subconscious irony". Not only does the inherent meaning of the saying itself refute this theory, but also the formula by which it is cited and emphasized. Both these considerations make Swete's proposal entirely incongruous.

25 See note 22.

26 The fathers of the Church agree on stressing this aspect. Theodore of Mopsuestia *ad loc.* says: "bene opus dixit et non 'dignitatem,' nec enim dignitates sunt ecclesiasticae functiones, sed opus". The editor, H. B. Swete, adds in note 16 to this comment the following: "Thdt.: διδάσκει μὴ τιμῆς ἀλλ'

The desire for this good work springs forth from the redeeming activity of the Savior Jesus Christ "who gave himself for us, that he might redeem us from all iniquity, and purify unto himself a people for his own possession, zealous of good works" (ζηλωτὴν καλῶν ἔργων; Titus 3:14). But the καλοῦ ἔργου spoken of in 1 Tim. 3:1 is not just another good work or deed to which all may aspire or which all may do. The qualifications which follow in verses 2 and following make that abundantly evident. In fact the saying is not speaking of some deed, or action, or merely some particular ethical matter, but rather of work in the sense of a task. The saying has in mind the office of a bishop or overseer as an occupation or task (Moffatt translates "an excellent occupation"; the R.S.V., "a noble task"). In aspiring to the office of the bishop, one desires the good task or occupation of the bishop or overseer. Ἔργον is used similarly in 2 Tim. 4:5, "do the work of an evangelist (ἔργον ποίησον εὐαγγελιστοῦ), fulfil your ministry"; cf. also 1 Thess. 5:12, 13, "But we beseech you, brethren, to know them that labor among you, and are over you in the Lord, and admonish you; and to esteem them exceeding highly in love for their work's sake" (διὰ τὸ ἔργον αὐτῶν), and Eph. 4:12, "unto the work of ministering" (εἰς ἔργον διακονίας).

The stress of the second half of 1 Tim. 3:1 does not fall on ἔργου alone but on the καλοῦ, or rather on καλοῦ ἔργου together as one concept. Καλός means good, noble, praiseworthy or excellent. The office or task of the bishop is spoken of as qualitatively good in accord with its purpose[27].

The origin of the saying is hardly to be found in a general saying of the day. The fact that ἐπισκοπή is found only rarely in profane Greek, postdating the saying, and in other senses than its use here tells against such a general origin. The connection between ἐπισκοπή in the saying and

---

ἀρετῆς ὀρέγεσθαι · μὴ τὴν ἀξίαν ποθεῖν, ἀλλὰ τῆς ἀξίας τὸ ἔργον ἐπιζητεῖν. Chrys. had already suggested this weighty remark. It occurs also word for word in S. Jerome (ep. 69), and is repeated in slightly varying forms by Pelagius..., Primasius and Sedulius". Chrysostóm had said in his Homily X on 1 Tim. 3:1 ff.: Εἴ τις ἐπισκοπῆς ὀρέγεται, οὐκ ἐγκαλῶ, φησί · προστασίας γὰρ ἔργον ἐστίν. Εἴ τις ταύτην ἔχει τὴν ἐπιθυσίαν, ὥστε μὴ τῆς ἀρχῆς καὶ τῆς αὐθεντίας ἐφίεσθαι μόνον, ἀλλὰ τῆς προστασίας, οὐκ ἐγκαλῶ · Καλοῦ γὰρ ἔργου ἐπιθυμεῖ, φησίν ("If a man desire the office of a Bishop,' I do not blame him, for it is a work of probation. If any one has this desire, so that he does not covet the dominion and authority, but wishes to protect the Church, I blame him not. 'for he desires a good work'.").

27 Arndt-Gingrich, s.v. In the Pauline usage, and in the Pastoral Letters where both καλός and ἀγαθός are used in reference to ἔργον, one may question whether there is, at this place at least, a distinction between the two. W. Grundmann, TDNT, III, p. 549, says that "In Paul the first use is absolute and the term is synonymous with τὸ ἀγαθόν" and cites as an example Romans 7:18 and 21.

ἐπίσκοπος in verse 2 also negates the thought of some common popular saying of the day. The ἐπισκοπή in view in the saying is the office of the ἐπίσκοπος of the church which is spoken of in verses 2 and following.. The citation-emphasis formula of 3:1a seems to be used generally in the Pastorals for a special Christian saying and would be very unlikely in application to a saying of the day. These considerations point away from a popular non-religious saying as the basis for this statement. The saying would also not seem to be the creation of the author of the Pastoral Letters, the Apostle Paul. Ὀρέγομαι is found three times in the N.T. (1 Tim. 3:1; 6:10; Heb. 11:16). In 6:10, the context demands a bad sense. Thus only in Heb. 11:6 and 1 Tim. 3:1 does the word occur in a context which makes clear that the word has the good rather than the bad sense. 1 Tim. 3:1 is the only place in Paul's writings where the verb ἐπιθυμέω is used in a good sense, although there are the two examples of Philippians 1:23, "having the desire (τὴν ἐπιθυμίαν ἔχων) to depart and be with Christ; for it is very far better " and 1 Thessalonians 2:17 (ἐν πολλῇ ἐπιθυμίᾳ) where the noun is used in a good sense in Paul's writings. This solitary occurrence (1 Tim. 3:1) is more significant because ἐπιθυμέω is used in a good sense elsewhere in the N.T. outside of Paul's writings[28]. Ἔργον is found widely in Paul in general and in the Pastorals in particular, as is καλός. In a very real sense the Pastorals are noted for their usage of καλὰ ἔργα[29]. But even in the midst of this trend the singular καλοῦ ἔργου is significant. Although the Pastorals use the combination καλὰ ἔργα in the plural and the combination ἔργον ἀγαθόν in the singular, nowhere else in the Pastorals is the combination καλοῦ ἔργου in the singular to be found. The same is true for the entire Pauline corpus. In the entire N.T., the form exists in only three other places (the parallel passages Mt. 26:30 and Mk. 14:6, and John 10:33).

Ἐπισκοπή occurs only four times in the N.T. (Lk. 19:44; Acts 1:20; 1 Tim. 3:1; 1 Peter 2:12). The first and last occurrences have the meaning of visitation. The Acts 1:20 passage is governed by the LXX of Psalm 108(9):8. However, the word ἐπίσκοπος is found in the N.T., with the exception of 1 Peter 2:25, in Paul's letters (Philip. 1:1; 1 Tim. 3:2; Tit. 1:7), or in a Pauline situation in Acts 20:28. Thus ἐπισκοπή, because it is not found in Paul, would point away from Paul, but the fact that the related word ἐπίσκοπος is used most widely in the N.T. by Paul would point towards Paul as the most likely candidate of the N.T. writers to use it, particularly in writing the Pastorals. A similar evaluation could be given for καλοῦ ἔργου on the basis of its uniqueness as a combination

---

[28] See F. Büchsel, *TDNT*, III, p. 170.
[29] See W. Grundmann, Καλός, *TDNT*, III, p. 549, in his special section on the Pastorals citing the statistics given by Jülicher in his *Einleitung in das NT*[7] (1931), p. 169.

in the singular and also because of the frequency of καλὰ ἔργα in the Pastorals. The verbal forms tend to point away from Paul. This tendency is enhanced by the obvious factor that 3:1a gives every impression of being a saying rather than a statement of the author. Further, it is introduced by the citation-emphasis formula which is most apt in reference to some saying cited with emphasis by the author rather than in reference to a statement of his own. The vocabulary of the saying does not tie in with any other particular author of the N.T. in any significant way. The use of the ἐπισκοπή-ἐπίσκοπος concept and the combination of καλοῦ ἔργου point in the direction of Christians who have been influenced by the Apostle Paul himself in view of the fact that of all the N.T. authors his vocabulary, although different in other respects, most closely approaches these two concepts. A Judaistic origin for the saying is virtually ruled out by the use of ἐπισκοπή. This is so since the word ἐπισκοπή reflects the use of ἐπίσκοπος for the church overseer. And ἐπίσκοπος[30], at least as a word, reflects a more Grecian background and usage, even though in the Pastorals and in the N.T. in general it is equivalent to the πρεσβύτερος[31].

[30] It is one thing to acknowledge that ἐπίσκοπος is a commonly known Greek word used for those who supervise and it is another to say that the office here designated by this Greek word finds its origin in those Greek examples. The former is indisputable; the latter is highly doubtful. There are those who see a similarity, and some even a dependence, to the *mebaqqer* in the Qumran Scrolls and the Damascus Document. Certainly there is a similarity, although also significant differences. Such differences make dependence highly questionable. This dubiousness extends also to the linguistic relationship (so Schweizer). And then there is the large question of dependence or transference from Qumran (Damascus) to the N.T. community. See, among others, H. W. Beyer, *TDNT*, II, pp. 599-622 (ἐπίσκοπος), especially his discussion of the origin of the episcopate on p. 618 and his evaluation of Jeremias' view of the Damascus *mebaqqer* as the model for Christian bishops; B. Reicke, "The Constitution of the Church in the Light of Jewish Documents" in *The Scrolls and the New Testament* edited by K. Stendahl (London: SCM Press, 1958), pp. 143-156; finally, E. Schweizer, *Church Order in the New Testament* (*Studies in Biblical Theology*, No. 32, London: SCM Press, 1961), pp. 200-202 (section 24i). Schweizer's critique is sober and at the same time brings in other views and literature in a very compressed statement. Ridderbos (*ad* 1 Tim. 3:1) summarizes the question when he says "Het is echter de vraag, of wij, ongeacht nog de taalkundige gelijkstelling van מבקר en ἐπίσκοπος, hier van een zodanige overeenkomst in de zaak kunnen spreken, dat het in de Qumran-litteratuur bedoelde ambt in ruimer ('Farizees'?) verband als voorbeeld van de nieuwtestamentische kan dienen". And he gives point to the summary when he asks, "Is hier meer dan een algemene analogie van het leiderschap in een religieuze gemeenschap?"

Further, and more pointedly, the particular word in the saying, ἐπισκοπή (not ἐπίσκοπος) apparently has no parallel in the Qumran literature.

[31] See the lexicons. *Cf.,e.g.,* H. W. Beyer, *TDNT*, II, p. 619: "... Greek Christianity introduced ἐπίσκοποι ..., as at Ephesus and Philippi. These were

The saying thus speaks not just of the office of a civil overseer or even of a religious overseer (Jewish or otherwise) but of the ἐπισκοπή, the office of the ἐπίσκοπος, the overseer in the Christian church who can be spoken of as an ἐπίσκοπος, or his office as ἐπισκοπή without further qualification. The saying would seem to originate from a Christian community, and probably one influenced by Paul.

One can only conjecture or theorize as to the rationale which prompted such a saying. Therefore, suffice it to say that the saying exalts the office of ruler and emphasizes its value. The office of ἐπίσκοπος is one that is commended as something to be aspired to, for those who possess the qualifications and characteristics outlined in the verses that follow the saying. The fact that in the early church there has developed a saying about the ἐπισκοπή indicates how very basic and important this office was considered to be for the life and well-being of the church. That such is the case is not at all strange when one considers that on his very first missionary journey Paul returns to cities that had mistreated him badly to appoint elders in every church (Acts 14:23). And this high view of those who rule over the church is seen throughout the N.T. (Acts 15; Acts 20:17ff., esp. 28; Philip. 1:1; 1 Thess. 5:12,13; Heb. 13:7,17)[32]. This evaluation is enhanced even more by Paul's citing this saying with the strong citation-emphasis formula, faithful is the saying. This places the saying in the category of those statements that the Apostle Paul would particularly single out and emphasize. And no doubt he cites the saying at the beginning of the third chapter because it is an excellent summary and introductory statement to the qualifications for the ἐπίσκοπος. If indeed the ἐπισκοπή is such a καλοῦ ἔργου then it follows (οὖν) that the ἐπίσκοπος must be all that the verses 2 and following require him to be. Paul takes the agreed upon evaluation of the Church as the foundation or ground for specifying the requisite qualifications. Such an office, such a work, demands such qualifications.

simple, widely known titles, yet not precisely defined and therefore in their very breadth of meaning capable of a new and specific use".

[32] Contra, among others, R. Sohn, A. Harnack, and E. Hatch who pitted the charismatic against the concept of officers and viewed the latter as a later development of the church. For a discussion of this question with a thorough Biblical answer to the concept mentioned above see H. N. Ridderbos, *Paulus* (Kampen: Kok, 1966), pp. 489 ff., pp. 522 ff., and in regard to presbyters and bishops, pp. 510 ff. This discussion and emphasis is important because the influence of the position first mentioned is still felt in New Testament studies. *Cf.* also the article by H. N. Ridderbos, "Kerkelijke orde en kerkelijk recht in de brieven van Paulus" in *Ex auditu verbi* (feestbundel G. C. Berkouwer), (Kampen: Kok, 1965), pp. 194-215.

CHAPTER IV

1 TIMOTHY 4:9 AND ITS SAYING

The first question that arises here is whether the saying precedes[1] verse 9 or follows[2] it. Alford argues that unless verse 10 is the saying it "comes in disjointedly and unaccountably". Guthrie prefers verse 10 on the basis that it "is more theologically weighty than verse 8 and would therefore be admirably adapted for current catechetical purposes". We must agree with him, against Ellicott and Huther, that the use of the conjunction γάρ itself, apart from other considerations, is "by no means conclusive" against verse 10 "since a parallel occurs in 2 Tim. ii.11", unless one at the same time rules out that verse as a saying on the same basis.

What then are the arguments in favor of verse 8 as the saying? It is recognized by almost all that the verse sounds and looks more like a proverbial saying than verse 10. Guthrie even seems to admit this. The unique character of verse 8, at least as contrasted and compared with verse 10, is strengthened by a consideration of its vocabulary. Verse 10 contains no unique words, whereas verse 8 contains one *hapax legomenon* (γυμνασία) and one word (σωματική) not found elsewhere in these letters or elsewhere in the Apostle Paul. This evidence is not overwhelming but it does point to verse 8 rather than verse 10 as the saying. Further, verse 8 is more stereotyped in form and would be wider in application than the experience of verse 10[3]. It seems rather doubtful that the

---

[1] The following find the saying in some portion of that which precedes verse 9, *i.e.*, all or some part of verse 8: Barrett, Bernard, Bouma, Chrysostum, Dibelius[2], Ellicott, Fairbairn, Falconer, Fausset, Gealy, Hendriksen, Holtzmann, Huther, Jeremias, Kelly, Kent, Lenski, Liddon, Lock, van Oosterzee, Parry, Ridderbos, Robertson, Scott, von Soden, Spicq, Weiss, White, Wohlenberg; *N.E.B.* margin, and Swete, *op. cit.*, p. 3 f., Bover, *op. cit.*, p. 77. 1 Tim. 3:16 has been chosen as the saying by some, but the distance and intervening statements make this virtually improbable.

[2] The following find the saying in some portion of that which follows verse 9, *i.e.*, all or some part of verse 10: Alford, Easton (who regards "especially of believers" an addition to the citation – "and by no means a graceful addition"), Guthrie, Simpson; *N.E.B.* text, *Moffatt's Translation*.

[3] Lock, *ad loc.*

subjective experience which begins verse 10 would be a saying. Some have found the saying in verse 10 beginning with ὅτι, but the jump necessary is against such a view[4]. The total sense of verse 10 and especially the connection afforded by the introductory word εἰς τοῦτο γάρ are best explained as a taking up of the thought of verse 8. Verse 10 then offers a confirmation of the saying of verse 8. The conjunction "for" (γάρ) joins verse 10 to verse 8[5]; not to verse 9, because such a connection has little relevance[6]. Thus the εἰς τοῦτο γάρ with its reference back to verse 8 expresses that unto which and for which it is said in verse 10 "we labor", etc.[7]. The verbs thus have a double reference in verse 10. We labor because (ὅτι) we have hoped in God, that is, because our hope is grounded upon God. But at the same time, we labor εἰς τοῦτο. The εἰς τοῦτο refers back to the thought expressed in verse 8[8]. To labor picks up the thought of exercise. Thus the τοῦτο would seem to have particular references to εὐσέβεια[9]. The neuter form of τοῦτο which does not agree in gender with the feminine εὐσέβεια or any other word in verse 8 (or verse 9) makes it clear, however, that τοῦτο has reference to the whole complex in view. These considerations taken together indicate that the verses are best understood in their context when verse 8 is seen to be the saying and verse 10 as taking up the thought of the saying and building upon it.

The next question is the extent of the saying in verse 8. Some take all of verse 8 to be the saying[10], some 8b and following (from ἡ δὲ εὐσέβεια...)[11]. The entirety of verse 8 is to be adjudged the saying

---

4 Holtzmann: "darum aber gehen sie, noch daher sammt den Zwischensatz εἰς τοῦτο γάρ κ.τ.λ., noch lange nicht auf das folgende ὅτι (Hofmann)".

5 Among others Holtzmann: "γάρ: Begründung des Vorigen, d.h. des grossen Werthes (Vs. 9) der in Vs. 8 ausgesprochenen Wahrheit"; Huther: "The particle γάρ shows that this verse is to serve as a reason or confirmation of the preceding thought that godliness is profitable for all things, having a promise of this and the future life"; and Kelly.

6 Even Bouma, who relates verse 10 in a formal way to verse 9, says "maar zakelijk óver vs 9 heen voor den inhoud van vs 8".

7 Bouma (also Thayer and Arndt-Gingrich) cites Mark 1:38 as an example of this usage. This is a good example in that εἰς τοῦτο not only occurs and exemplifies the usage here, but also γάρ. "And he says unto them, Let us go elsewhere into the next towns, that I may preach there also; for to this end came I forth" (εἰς τοῦτο γάρ ἐξῆλθον).

8 Dibelius-Conzelmann: "εἰς τοῦτο ist wohl am besten auf den Inhalt von 8, auf das τέλος der christlichen γυμνασία zu beziehen, denn mit κοπιῶμεν wird doch γυμνάζειν aus 7 aufgenommen".

9 Lenski: "'This thing' = what Paul is speaking about, This thing of true godliness. Also Robertson: "To this end (eis touto). The godliness (eusebeia) of verse 8..."; cf. also Bernard, and Barrett.

10 E.g., Bouma, Jeremias, Lock, White.

11 E.g., Ellicott, Liddon.

rather than just 8b. There are several considerations which favor the inclusion of 8a as part of the saying and which are against its exclusion. The case is not a hard and fast one, and the considerations are not absolutely conclusive (this explains why there is a division of opinion), but they do lend some more weight to taking verse 8 as a whole rather than just verse 8b.

Having admonished Timothy to exercise (γύμναζε) himself unto godliness, Paul proceeds to give the reason for this imperative. Immediately thereafter we find in 8a the statement that "bodily exercise (ἡ σωματικὴ γυμνασία) is profitable for a little". The argument is taken up by the "for" (γάρ) at the beginning of verse 8. Then to this is contrasted the thought of verse 8b, that "godliness is profitable for all things" with the use of δέ. The value and importance of exercise (γύμναζε) unto godliness (εὐσέβεια), verse 7b, is thus proven by showing that godliness (εὐσέβεια) is profitable for all things (verse 8b) in contrast to bodily exercise (γυμνασία) which is but profitable for a little. Now it is possible that Paul merely interjected the thought of verse 8a about bodily exercise because of his reference to exercise in verse 7b. But the parallelism and coherence of 8a and 8b speak against this; 8a and 8b have the parallel structure which is more likely in a saying. The words are in relation to one another in almost the same order throughout both statements:

ἡ γὰρ σωματικὴ γυμνασία πρὸς ὀλίγον ἐστὶν ὠφέλιμος
ἡ δέ εὐσεβεια πρὸς πάντα ὠφέλιμός ἐστιν...

ἡ εὐσέβεια is contrasted with ἡ σωματικὴ γυμνασία, πρὸς πάντα with πρὸς ὀλίγον, and in both we find ἐστὶν ὠφέλιμος. The order of ἐστὶν ὠφέλιμος or ὠφέλιμός ἐστιν may be explained by the desire to stress the ὠφέλιμος in connection with εὐσέβεια. Thus the antithetical parallelism between the two is virtually exact. The addition of ἐπαγγελίαν κ.τ.λ. to the saying at 8b is done with a view of elucidating the πρὸς πάντα for which the εὐσέβεια is ὠφέλιμος. This element is absent from 8a because there is no need to elucidate the πρὸς ὀλίγον. 8a is only included to serve as a contrast to 8b not to propound a philosophy about the subject there mentioned. Hence there is no need or desire to elaborate on its thoughts, whereas the contrary is the case with the main emphasis of 8b. The parallelism speaks for 8a as part of the saying.

Not only the formal parallelism but also the implied contrast between 8b and 8a points towards 8a as part of the saying. It is indeed possible to have a saying which says that "godliness is profitable for all things, having promise of the life which now is, and of that which is to come". However, within this part (8b), which is acknowledged as part of the saying by all those who recognize the saying as preceding verse 9, there is the πρὸς πάντα which implies, at least, the contrast which we find in 8a in πρὸς ὀλίγον.

The use of γάρ with σωματική γυμνασία in verse 8a would seem to indicate that Paul moves directly into the argument or basis for the statement of verse 7b, and would at the same time seem to rule verse 8a out as a parenthetical side comment by Paul. The γάρ would seem to introduce the totality of the thought, and thus the totality of the saying[12]. The γάρ, however, was not part of the saying itself but was added by the writer to connect it with his previous words γύμναζε κτλ[13].

The question then remains as to why the statement about bodily exercise (σωματική γυμνασία) being profitable for a little would ever be included in, or become part of, a faithful saying. Without discussing the possible origin of the saying at this point, certain conjectures, nevertheless, can be made. The first is that this part of the saying is included in view of the Greco-Roman stress on bodily training[14]. The second is that this is a self-conscious opposition to asceticism. Both, of course, assume a certain view of σωματική γυμνασία which must be discussed later. From the first viewpoint, the point of the inclusion of verse 8a in the saying is not so much to condemn bodily training, but to utilize the widespread concern and preoccupation with it as a foil or contrasting motif to emphasize the necessity for and the value of εὐσέβεια and the exercise unto εὐσέβεια. If σωματική γυμνασία is profitable for a little, and so much time and energy is devoted to it, then how much more should one exercise himself unto godliness which "is profitable for all things, having promise of the life which now is, and of that which is to come". The reference then to bodily training is incorporated as a slightly judgmental contrast which would point up the value of εὐσέβεια in a culture which esteemed the value of the former.

The saying referred to by the formula of 1 Tim. 4:9 is the entirety of verse 8: "bodily exercise is profitable for a little; but godliness is profitable for all things, having promise of the life which now is, and of that which is to come" (ἡ σωματική γυμνασία πρὸς ὀλίγον ἐστὶν ὠφέλιμος· ἡ δέ εὐσέβεια πρὸς πάντα ὠφέλιμός ἐστιν, ἐπαγγελίαν ἔχουσα ζωῆς τῆς νῦν καὶ τῆς μελλούσης).

This brings us to the point of considering the meaning of σωματική γυμνασία. Two views are held, one which takes the phrase to refer to

---

[12] Note how Ellicott himself says that "γάρ confirms the preceding clause by putting σωματική γυμνασία, the outward and visible, in contrast with γυμνασία πρὸς εὐσέβ., the internal and unseen".
[13] Rightly pointed out by Swete, op. cit., p. 4.
[14] See especially Excursus VII by C. Spicq, "Gymnastique et Morale", pp. 151-162; and his article "Gymnastique et Morale, d'après 1 Tim. IV, 7-8", Revue Biblique, 54 (1947), pp. 229-242.

some sort of asceticism[15], and the other which takes the phrase to refer to the training of the body, i.e., athletics[16]. Those who argue for the ascetical interpretation generally recognize the ordinary sense of the words in the phrase, but plead other considerations as meriting their interpretation[17]. Some, however, point out that "γυμνασία is not uncommonly used in less special references"[18]. Most plead a reference back to the ascetic practices dealt with in verse 3 and following[19]. They further argue that the idea of games or athletic exercise "is foreign to the context"[20], or at least that ascetic restrictions fit the contrast of the context better[21].

Against this interpretation in general it may be pointed out that it is very unlikely for the asceticism like that of verse 3 to be spoken of as profitable πρὸς ὀλίγον after the absolute negation which Paul gives in 4:1ff[22]. If the Apostle had meant ascetic exercises, such as those mentioned in verse 3, he would surely have said something sterner about them than that they were useful πρὸς ὀλίγον[23]. Further, it should be noticed that γυμνασία itself, and then the phrase, σωματικὴ γυμνασία, refers normally and naturally to the exercise for or in the games[24]. Moulton and Milligan state the matter thus: "There seems no very special reason why this normal meaning should not be recognized in 1 Tim. 4⁸: the exercises of the games, which are of service, but only to a limited degree, are contrasted in Pauline style with the spiritual training which 'has promise of life, here and hereafter'"[25]. Also, if verse 8a is part of the faithful

---

[15] Bernard, Calvin, Easton, Ellicott, Fausset, Jeremias, Lenski, Ridderbos, Schlatter, von Soden, Weiss. Also Thayer sub γυμνασία, and A. Oepke, TDNT, I, sub γυμνασία, p. 775.

[16] Alford, Bengel, Bouma, Chrysostom, Fairbairn, Falconer, Gealy, Guthrie, Hendriksen, Huther, Liddon, Lock, Parry, Spicq; also Moulton & Milligan sub γυμνασία.

[17] Cf., e.g., White: "σωματικὴ γυμνασία: The parallel cited by Lightfoot (Philippians, p. 290) from Seneca (Ep. Mor. xv. 2,5) renders it almost certain that the primary reference is to gymnastic exercises (as Chrys., etc., take it); but there is as certainly in σωματικὴ γυμνασία a connotation of ascetic practices as the outward expression of the theories underlying the fables of ver. 7".

[18] Ellicott.

[19] So A. Oepke, TDNT, I, sub γυμνασία, p. 775, Bernard, Easton, Ellicott. Lenski, however, objects to this and refers it back to 1:7.

[20] Bernard.

[21] Easton, Ellicott.

[22] Fairbairn, Gealy.

[23] Liddon.

[24] Arndt-Gingrich, sub γυμνασία, and Gealy.

[25] Moulton and Milligan, sub γυμνασία. For Paul's usage in this realm see especially the recent study by V. C. Pfitzner, Paul and the Agon Motif (Leiden: E. J. Brill, 1967).

saying it is much more likely that it refers to athletics, its normal significance, than to ascetism. It is highly unlikely that a saying would arise contrasting asceticism, and especially under this phrase, with εὐσέβεια[26]. The First Letter to Timothy itself, and 4:1—5 especially, show that the church was not sufficiently conscious of the need to eschew such asceticism. At least within that context it was improbable that a saying contrasting εὐσέβεια to asceticism would have arisen. And this is made more improbable by the use of words, and a phrase (σωματικὴ γυμνασία), which are normally and naturally associated with and used for athletics[27]. This view of σωματικὴ γυμνασία would also seem to fit in with the use of the verb γύμναζε in verse 7b and with the continuation of the figure of vigorous bodily exertion in verse 10 with the verbs labor (κοπιῶμεν) and strive (ἀγωνιζόμεθα). Thus the saying with the minor statement on athletic exercise fits in the context which begins by using the related verb (γύμναζε) drawn from athletic usage and comes to conclusion using the verbs that picture vigorous exertion (κοπιῶμεν καὶ ἀγωνιζόμεθα).

Πρὸς[28] ὀλίγον means "for a little"[29] and not "for little"[30]. The first indicates that the bodily exercise is profitable to some extent, even if that is very small. The second means that it is profitable in effect for nothing[31]. The meaning is evident by its contrast with πρὸς πάντα. "A little" is contrasted with "all". The contrast of the saying is not the "all things" for which εὐσέβεια is profitable over against the bodily exercise which is profitable "for little", but the contrast between the "for a little", of bodily exercise over against the "for all things" of εὐσέβεια. Bodily exercise is not mentioned to negate it by comparison and contrast, but to use its little profit as a foil for the "all things" for which εὐσέβεια is profitable. It must be remembered that in reference to bodily exercise the word ὠφέλιμος (useful, beneficial, advantageous τινί for someone or for something)[32] is used. This understanding is in

26 Gealy. Dibelius-Conzelmann, in view of their understanding of the origin of the expression in view, say: "Ursprünglich aber richtete er sich zweifellos gegen die körperliche ἄσκησις des Athleten".
27 For the references to Greek literature see Liddell & Scott, and Moulton and Milligan, sub γυμνασία; and also the excursus of Spicq (note 14). Cf., e.g., Aristotle, Politics, IV, X, 6 (1297a, 17).
28 See Arndt-Gingrich, sub πρός. III, 3, c, and Thayer, I, 3, a; also Turner, op. cit., Vol. III, p. 224.
29 So sub ὀλίγος Moulton and Milligan, and Arndt-Gingrich, who has "profitable for (a) little"; A.S.V. text; N.A.S.V., "only of little profit"; R.S.V., "of some value"; N.E.B., "limited benefit"; Alford, Ellicott, Huther, Liddon, Weiss.
30 So Thayer, sub ὀλίγος, "profitable for little" but gives in brackets "some, for a little ...".
31 So Easton: "'little value' in the sense of 'no value at all' ...".
32 Arndt-Gingrich, s.v.

accord with the way Paul has understood such exercise before. In 1 Cor. 9:25, Paul contrasts the "corruptible crown" which the victorious athlete receives with "an incorruptible" which the Christian receives. But they do receive a crown. Perhaps such a prize is one of the πρὸς ὀλίγον of which the saying here speaks. Although the contrast with πρὸς πάντα may indicate that the πρὸς ὀλίγον is not to be restricted to the meaning "for a little time" (James 4:14; πρὸς ὀλίγον), nevertheless, it may not be denied as part of the meaning, as most commentators do. The πρὸς πάντα is an absolute. Within the all embracive "all" may be included the profitableness not only for all things but also for all time. This possibility is made more plausible by the temporal explanation added, "having promise of. the life which now is, and of that which is to come". This is not to restrict πρὸς πάντα to a temporal significance. But just as πρὸς πάντα may have in view among others things a temporal, i.e., a temporal and eternal significance, so therefore by contrast πρὸς ὀλίγον may have in view among others the brevity of time for which the bodily exercise is profitable. This is not to restrict πρὸς ὀλίγον to this temporal significance. Of course at the same time it must be recognized that the πρὸς ὀλίγου need not refer by contrast to all that to which the πρὸς πάντα refers. The contrast between πρὸς ὀλίγον and πρὸς πάντα is essentially one of quantity. But the all embraciveness of the πρὸς πάντα inevitably brings the contrast also to one of quality. One might philosophize on the πρὸς ὀλίγον for which the bodily exercise is profitable, but since the saying does not do this, whereas it does enlarge on the πρὸς πάντα, it will be in keeping with the intent of the saying to use the first half primarily as a contrast and to honor its silence.

In concluding the evaluation of 8a it must be repeated that the saying is not primarily making an ethical or philosophical pronouncement on bodily exercise, but is using it as a foil for 8b. It does thereby inevitably recognize the limited benefit of bodily exercise but, however, not so much as to praise it but rather to point out the absolute value of εὐσέβεια in contrast to its little value.

The second part of the saying, the main part or contrast, begins, after the introductory conjunction δέ ("but"), with ἡ εὐσέβεια[33]. We might

[33] For articles on εὐσέβεια see Arndt-Gingrich, s.v.; W. Foerster, s.v., TWNT, VII, pp. 175 ff.; W. Foerster, "Eusebeia in den Pastoralbriefen", N.T.S. 5 (1958), pp. 213-18; W. Barclay, More New Testament Words, (New York: Harper, 1958), pp. 66-77; Falconer, section 7 of the introduction of his commentary, pp. 30-39; R. C. Trench, Synonyms of The New Testament, (London: Kegan Paul, 12th ed., 1894, reprinted by Eerdmans, 1953), section xlviii., pp. 172 ff.; Spicq, Excursus VI., pp. 125-134; also the commentaries ad 1 Tim. 2:2 and 3:16, especially Bernard, Ellicott and Dibelius; for further literature see Arndt-Gingrich, and Foerster, TWNT.

have expected the saying, in contrast to 8a, to say that exercise unto godliness is profitable, etc., but with a brachylogy[34] εὐσέβεια itself is immediately spoken of. That to which Timothy was urged to exercise (7b) is now set in contrast with bodily exercise. That towards which one exercises is compared with bodily exercise rather than the exercise itself πρὸς εὐσέβεια. Εὐσέβεια means "godliness"[35] and is best translated into English by that word. It may also be rendered "piety"[36] or "religion"[37], i.e., the Christian religion. Its etymology is that of right (ευ) reverence, worship or fear (the root — σεβ —), i.e., worship, reverence well and rightly given[38]. This etymological aspect continues, but it alone is not the determining factor in ascertaining its meaning. Neither must the meaning in the N.T. be determined solely by its Greek usage[39] or reflection in the Greek O.T.[40] or in 4 Maccabees[41]. The N.T. uses the word with the basic

---

[34] See Funk-Blass-Debrunner, Section 483.
[35] Thayer, Arndt-Gingrich, the A.S.V. usually; at 1 Tim. 4:7 and 8 the A.S.V., N.A.S.V. and R.S.V.
[36] W. Foerster, TWNT, VII, p. 182, "Frömmigkeit"; Falconer, p. 31; Alford ad Acts 3:12 speaks of "operative, cultic piety" which religious connotation Moulton and Milligan, s.v., say "comes out well in the inscr."; Thayer gives as the meanings "reverence, respect; in the Bible everywhere piety towards God, godliness"; Cremer, "piety, the good and careful cherishing of the fear of God".
[37] Moffatt translates εὐσέβεια either piety or religion, and the latter in the sense of the true religion; Arndt-Gingrich give as the meaning of the word "in our lit. and in the LXX only of the duty which man owes to God piety, godliness, religion"; Cremer (see note above).
[38] Spicq, p. 125 f.; Barclay, op. cit., p. 72 f.
[39] For the Greek usage see W. Foerster, TWNT., VII, pp. 175-178; also Spicq's excursus; Falconer, pp. 30 ff.; and Barclay, op. cit., pp. 66-69. Each brings the various definitions and the usage in regard to the gods, to parents and those in authority, to the ordinances of the gods and the state or religion, the relation to fellow men, and the Greek mean in regard to one's relation to the gods.
[40] Hatch and Redpath's Concordance of the Septuagint indicates that in the translation of the Hebraic canonical O.T. εὐσέβεια is only found 4 times and usually as a translation either of יִרְאַת or יְהֹוָה יִרְאַת: Prov. 1:7, εὐσέβεια (יִרְאָה) δὲ εἰς Θεὸν ἀρχὴ αἰσθήσεως. Prov. 13:11, ὁ δὲ συνάγων ἑαυτῷ μετ' εὐσεβείας πληθυνθήσεται. Isaiah 11:2, πνεῦμα γνώσεως καὶ εὐσεβείας (יְהֹוָה יִרְאַת). Isaiah 33:6, ἐκεῖ ... εὐσέβεια (יִרְאָה) πρὸς τὸν κύριον. W. Foerster, TWNT, VII, p. 180 f. makes the observation that the occurrence of the word group εὐσεβ- "im Neuen Testament sogar noch grösser als im Alten", and therefore evaluates, "Das hängt wohl auch damit zusammen, dass ein direkter sprachlicher Äquivalent für diese griechischen Bildungen im Hebräischen und in der Muttersprache der meisten Männer des Neuen Testaments nicht vorhanden war".
[41] Falconer, p. 32, notes that εὐσέβεια occurs in 4 Maccabees 47 times. Barclay, Falconer, Spicq and Foerster all note that therein εὐσέβεια is "pious reason", the controller of the passions, and that εὐσέβεια lies in obedience to the Law. None of these notes are evident in the N.T. usage or in that of the Pastorals in particular.

thrusts which are seen in its secular usage and in its few occurrences in the Greek O.T.[42]. There is the basic orientation toward God to which is related a sense of reverence and honor to those set in authority over one as well as a duty to one's fellow man which springs out of one's relation to God. But the εὐσέβεια is no longer, as in Greek thought, a general religious piety. It is now a εὐσέβεια which is rooted in the mystery of εὐσέβεια, Jesus Christ[43]. It is now a distinctly Christian εὐσέβεια, which is not just an external form, but which has an inner power (2 Tim. 3:5). That inner power is appropriated in Christ (cf. 2 Peter 1:3).

True εὐσέβεια is made known and manifested in Jesus Christ (1 Tim. 3:16)[44]. It is in and through Him that man may truly know God and be enabled to worship Him aright. God has "shined in our hearts, to give the light of the knowledge of the glory of God in the face of Jesus Christ" (2 Cor. 4:6). In the words of 2 Peter 1:3, God's "power has granted unto us all things that pertain unto life and godliness" (εὐσέβειαν). This concept of εὐσέβεια would seem to be strengthened in view of the fact that in two places where it is used the immediately following section stresses the fact that God is Savior (1 Tim. 2:22ff. and 4:7,8 and 10). In both cases the following verse(s) tie(s) in to the preceding comment about εὐσέβεια with τοῦτο. In the 1 Tim. 4:7ff. passage at least, εὐσέβεια and its attendant promise (ἐπαγγελίαν) is exercised unto and labored and striven unto just because one has already hoped in the living and saving God. To reflect again on 2 Peter 1:3, one enters into the εὐσέβεια through the power of the living and saving God wrought through Him who is the mystery of εὐσέβεια.

Εὐσέβεια in one's life comes about as a result of knowing God's will and obeying[45] it. The doctrine or teaching of the Christian Faith is that which produces εὐσέβεια. We read in 1 Tim. 6:3 of "the doctrine which is according to godliness" (τῇ κατ᾽ εὐσέβεια διδασκαλίᾳ). Titus 1:1 also speaks of "the knowledge of the truth which is according to godliness" (ἐπίγνωσιν ἀληθείας τῆς κατ᾽ εὐσέβειαν). And in Titus 1:1 it is not only

---

[42] Εὐσέβεια and the related words are found in the N.T. only in Acts, the Pastorals and 2 Peter. Εὐσέβεια is in Acts 3:12; 1 Tim. 2:2; 3:16; 4:7,8; 6:3, 5,6,11; 2 Tim. 3:5; Titus 1:1; 2 Peter 1:3,6,7; 3:11. Εὐσεβέω is in Acts 17:23 and 1 Tim. 5:4. Εὐσεβής is in Acts 10:2,7 and 2 Peter 2:9. Εὐσεβῶς is in 2 Tim. 3:12 and Titus 2:12.

[43] 1 Tim. 3:16. "It is worthy of remark", according to Cremer, s.v., "that when once it was shown what the μυστήριον τῆς εὐσεβείας is as contrasted with heathen views of the expression, the word came unmistakeably to be the distinctive title for the sum of Christian behaviour".

[44] Cf. Isaiah 11:2 which prophesies of Jesus Christ, according to the LXX version, that "the Spirit of the Lord shall rest upon him, ... the spirit of knowledge and of the fear of the Lord" (εὐσεβείας).

[45] Cf. Proverbs 1:7, "The fear (εὐσέβεια) of the Lord is the beginning of knowledge (wisdom)".

the knowledge of the truth but there is also joined with it the preceding statement "according to the faith of God's elect". Faith here is used in the subjective sense for saving faith[46]. That saving faith issues in a correct grasp of the apostolic message. So faith is in the purview of that which issues into godliness.

But although εὐσέβεια is made known in and through Jesus Christ, is the gift of the power of God, is appropriated by faith and the knowledge of the truth, one must also exercise oneself toward it. In 1 Tim. 4:7 Paul speaks of exercising (γύμναζε) oneself πρὸς εὐσέβεια, and then in 4:8 the saying contrasts that with σωματικὴ γυμνασία. In 1 Tim. 6:11 one is to flee (φεῦγε) the evil and follow after (δίωκε) righteousness, godliness (εὐσέβειαν), faith, love, patience and meekness". With this in view, verse 12 charges Timothy to "Fight (ἀγωνίζου) the good fight". This is the same verb as that found in 1 Tim. 4:10 which depicts the exertion which is made towards εὐσέβεια. A man is a Christian by God's grace, and has Christianity, but he is also charged by the Scriptures to grow in and develop his Christianity. One has true religion and one exercises toward true religion. So it is with εὐσέβεια, it is both the gift brought in Jesus Christ and it is that work which one follows after.

Εὐσέβεια is the mark of the Christian life[47]. Because the world sees that one is godly and one lives a godly life, one will inevitably draw persecution from the sinful world. "Yes, and all that would live godly (εὐσεβῶς) in Christ Jesus shall suffer persecution" (2 Tim. 3:12). Here the two previously noted elements are clearly combined. True εὐσέβεια is godly living. Both here and in Titus 2:12 "godly" is a characterization of one thing only, and that is living (ζῆν, ζήσωμεν). It is the expression of the Christian life. And at the same time it is in Christ Jesus. The godly life stems forth from Christ Jesus and is able to be lived out by the power of Christ Jesus within and working through one. Only the man in Christ Jesus has true εὐσέβεια or may exercise himself toward a fuller realization of it or may live a true εὐσέβεια.

Titus 2:12 makes abundantly clear that the godly (εὐσεβῶς) living which is to be done in this world is soteriologically grounded and also eschatologically orientated[48]. It is rooted in Christ's work and comes from God's grace. It is His salvation that has saved Christians, and His grace instructs them how to live godly. Verses 11 and 12 of Titus 2 speak of these things: "For the grace of God has appeared, bringing salvation to all men, instructing us, to the intent that, denying ungodliness and worldly lusts, we should live soberly and righteously and godly in this

[46] Kelly, *ad loc.*
[47] *Cf. Spicq,* p. 130.
[48] W. Foerster, *TWNT,* VII, p. 181 says that "εὐσέβεια bezeichnet in den Pastoralbriefen eine bestimmte Weise der Lebensführung".

present world". We live for God the Father and His Son our Savior in this world, as a result of His self-giving, His grace and instruction, and at the same time looking unto His appearing. The origin, the outworking and the goal of εὐσέβεια are all of God. Verses 13 and 14 of Titus 2 go on to say that we should live godly in this present world; "looking for the blessed hope and appearing of the glory of the great God and our Savior Jesus Christ; who gave himself for us, that he might redeem us from all iniquity, and purity unto himself a people for his own possession, zealous of good works". This aspect is quite similar to that of 2 Peter 3:11 and 12: "Seeing that these things are thus all to be dissolved, what manner of persons ought you to be in holy living and godliness (εὐσεβείας), looking for and earnestly desiring the coming of the day of God . . . ?".

Εὐσέβεια thus is profitable for here and now, indeed, in all things (1 Tim. 4:8). It has promise of the life which now is. But it is not "a way of gain" (1 Tim. 6:5). It does not automatically promise or produce material success or wealth. But it does provide the great gain, coupled with contentment, of being satisfied with the situation in which God places one (1 Tim. 6:6 ff.). It has within its scope that true and real life which one has even now on this earth in Christ.

Εὐσέβεια is not just one's inner and spiritual relationship to God, nor is it only a personal matter. As 2 Tim. 3:12 has already shown, it has an outer manifestation in one's life. True εὐσέβεια embraces the family relationships and governs one's concern for and attitude and practice towards the members of the family. "But if any widow has children or grandchildren, let them learn first to show piety (εὐσεβεῖν) towards their own family, and to requite their parents: for this is acceptable in the sight of God" (1 Tim. 5:4). Here care of parents is a true act of εὐσέβεια. This is the human element. But at the same time it is commended as "acceptable in the sight of God". Here εὐσέβεια would seem almost to combine within it the double aspect of loving God and one's neighbor[49].

It is with this rich background that εὐσέβεια must be understood at 1 Tim. 4:8. Εὐσέβεια there is godliness or true religion in the all embracing sense which this concept is seen to have[50].

Πρὸς πάντα is that for which εὐσέβεια is ὠφέλιμος (profitable)[51]. It

---

[49] Although in 2 Peter 1:7 one must add "in godliness brotherly kindness (φιλαδελφίαν); and in brotherly kindness love (ἀγάπην)".

[50] Falconer, p. 39, says, "To sum up, εὐσέβεια is a reverent, worshipful attitude of heart, expressed in constant and varied prayer, in adoration of the transcendent God and Saviour of all men through Jesus Christ, as well as in obedience to His will by personal virtue and loyalty to the family and the rulers". It seems only fitting that a man named Eusebius would have given a definition of εὐσέβεια (*Praep. Evang.* i. p. 3): ἡ πρὸς τὸν ἕνα καὶ μόνον ὡς ἀληθῶς ὁμολογούμενόν τε καὶ ὄντα Θεὸν ἀνάνευσις, καὶ ἡ κατὰ τοῦτον ζωή.

[51] Thayer gives *"profitable"*, as do most of the English translations; Arndt-

is profitable for all, "for all things"[52]. The Greek text sets forth without qualification the absolute value of εὐσέβεια. The contrast to σωματικὴ γυμνασία and πρὸς ὀλίγον is just this, that εὐσέβεια is not just profitable for much or for a larger amount or for much more, but its value is without limit in every way. Thus any attempt, on our part, to define or delimit the πάντα would be a misunderstanding and a partial negation at least of the universal scope of the text. The πάντα can best be illustrated by three other passages (1 Cor. 3:21-23[53]; Rom. 8:28[54]; Rom. 8:32).

The saying explicates the profitableness of εὐσέβεια by adding, "having promise of the life which now is, and of that which is to come". The statement introduced by ἐπαγγελίαν ἔχουσα[55] is an adverbial participle of cause, equivalent to a causal clause[56]. Everything in this participial qualification demonstrates how much greater, richer and superior εὐσέβεια is to bodily exercise[57].

The promise (ἐπαγγελίαν) is that which the εὐσέβεια has. The one that promised is God. It is this connection which gives significance to the addition of verse 10. One labors and strives[58] unto godliness because one has hoped on the God who as living and as Savior can and will keep this promise. 2 Timothy 1:1, the only other occurrence of ἐπαγγελία in the Pastorals, speaks of "the promise of life which is in Christ Jesus". Both godliness and the promise are in Christ Jesus. One lives godly in Christ Jesus (2 Tim. 3:12; Titus 2:12).

Gingrich give as the meaning "*useful, beneficial, advantageous* τινι *for someone, or for something*". The word occurs only in the Pastorals, *i.e.*, 1 Tim. 4:8; 2 Tim. 3:16; Titus 3:8.

52   The translation of *A.S.V., N.A.S.V.* The *R.S.V.* translates "godliness is of value in every way", and the *N.E.B.* has "The benefits of religion are without limit".

53   Referred to by von Soden *ad* 1 Tim. 4:8.

54   See J. Murray, *The Epistle to the Romans (N.I.C.N.T.), ad loc.* "'All things' may not be restricted, though undoubtedly the things contemplated are particularly those that fall within the compass of believers' experience...".

55   *Cf.,* H. Hanse, *TDNT*, II, p. 825.

56   E. DeWitt Burton, *Syntax of the Moods and Tenses in New Testament Greek* (Edinburgh: T. & T. Clark, 3rd ed., 1898), section 439; A. T. Robertson, *A Grammar of the Greek New Testament in the Light of Historical Research* (London: Hodder & Stoughton, 3rd ed., 1919), p. 1128. See also Col. 1:3,4; Mt. 2:3,10; Acts 9:26.

57   Thus Bouma.

58   For the textual question in regard to ἀγωνιζόμεθα ("strive"), found in the great uncial MSS and preferred by Nestle-Aland and the author, and ὀνειδιζόμεθα, see the textual apparatuses of the critical Greek New Testaments and the commentaries.

The ἐπαγγελίαν is ζωῆς τῆς νῦν καὶ τῆς μελλούσης. Is it a promise for[59] this life and that which is to come, or is it a promise of[60] the life which now is, and that which is to come? Alford points to Rom. 15:8 as an example of the use of the genitive with the meaning "for" and therefore as a proof not only of the possibility but of the rightness of that meaning for 1 Tim. 4:8. However, even though there is this passage with that meaning for the plural ἐπαγγελίας, not the singular ἐπαγγελία as in the saying, the word ἐπαγγελία in the singular is commonly used with the genitive to denote the content or purport of the promise[61] (cf. 2 Tim. 1:1, κατ᾽ ἐπ. ζωῆς τῆς ἐν Χ. 'Ι.; 2 Peter 3:4, ἡ ἐπ. τῆς παρουσίας αὐτοῦ; Heb. 9:15, ἐπ. τ. αἰωνίον κληρονομίας). To this list also add the following which, although not in the genitive construction with ἐπαγγελία. indicate that the content of the promise is indicated: Heb. 4:1, ἐπ. εἰσελθεῖν εἰς τὴν κατάπαυσιν αὐτοῦ; 1 Jn. 2:25, αὕτη ἐστὶν ἡ ἐπ. ἣν αὐτὸς ἐπηγγείλατο ἡμῖν, τὴν ζωὴν τὴν αἰώνιον; Rom. 4:13, ἡ ἐπ. ... τὸ κληρονόμον αὐτὸν εἶναι τοῦ κόσμου[62]. Where life (ζωή) is mentioned, twice above, it specifies the content or purport of the promise. And in no other case in the N.T. is ζωή in the genitive with ἐπαγγελία with the meaning "for". This brings us back to the only other place in the Pastorals where ἐπαγγελία is found, i.e., 2 Tim. 1:1, and there also it is qualified, as in 1 Tim. 4:8, by ζωή in the genitive case. The further qualification of ζωῆς by "which is in Christ Jesus" (τῆς ἐν Χριστῷ 'Ιησου) makes it patent that here the ζωή is the content of the promise, it is the promise of life not for life[63]. This identical structure is a strong presumptive argument at least for the same meaning in both places.

A further consideration in favor of construing ζωῆς as the content of the promise, i.e., as a qualitative or objective genitive, is the use of ζωή in the Pastorals and that especially in connection with those terms found in the context of 1 Tim. 4:8. 1 Tim. 4:8 and 10 speak of godliness (εὐσέβεια), promise (ἐπαγγελία), life (ζωή) and hope in God (ἠλπίκαμεν ἐπὶ θεῷ). In Titus 1:1 & 2 we find these same elements. Having mentioned god-

---

59 So, e.g., N.A.S.V., R.S.V., N.E.B., Alford, Lenski.
60 So, e.g., A.S.V.; Thayer, s.v., "with the gen. of the object, τῆς ζωῆς. 1 Tim. iv.8"; Cremer, s.v.; Arndt-Gingrich, s.v.; H. Hanse, TDNT, II, p. 825, sub ἔχω; G. Stählin, TWNT, IV, p. 1113, sub νῦν; Bouma, Bengel, Guthrie, Hendriksen, Kelly, Liddon, Lock, van Oosterzee, Parry, Scott.
61 Arndt-Gingrich state that "For var. reasons the gen. is used w. ε.: to denote the one fr. whom the promise comes (τ.) Θεοῦ ... ; to denote the things promised ... ἐ. τ. αἰωνίου κληρονομίας Hb. 9:15; τ. ζωῆς 1 Ti 4:8; τ. παρουσίας 2 Pt 3:4; to denote the one(s) for whom the promise is intended ... Ro 15:8 ...".
62 For the lists of passages see Cremer and Arndt-Gingrich sub ἐπαγγελία.
63 All those mentioned in note 59 espousing "for" in 1 Tim. 4:8 recognize the propriety of "of" for 2 Tim. 1:1.

liness in verse 1, Paul goes on to speak of "in hope (ἐλπίδι) of eternal life (ζωῆς), which God . . . promised" (ἐπηγγείλατο). That which is promised by God and which is the hope of believers is eternal life. Thus the only other occurrence of ἐπαγγελία (2 Tim. 1:1) and the only other occurrence of the verbal form (Tit. 1:1,2) with ζωή both point to ζωή as the content of the promise.

The consideration of the relationship of ζωῆς to ἐπαγγελίαν has had to impinge upon and assume a certain evaluation of ζωή itself. The sentence construction in part determines the meaning of ζωή and the meaning of ζωή helps to determine which construction is in view. *Life* is, of course, the general meaning of ζωή[64]. The ζωή is itself explained and defined in this passage by the very qualification that is added to it: ζωῆς τῆς νῦν καὶ τῆς μελλούσης. In this double addition qualifying the one word ζωῆς, the saying defines life in the fullest, most comprehensive, exhaustive and inclusive way[65]. Does this mean only that the promise is that one will exist now and in the future? In the light of the usage of ζωή elsewhere the meaning should not be restricted to this. This is more of the meaning of βίος in the N.T. However, just because the meaning is not to be restricted to this does not mean that this part of the concept is to be ruled out. Thus, the promise of Eph. 6:1-3 that those who obey their parents in the Lord will live long in the earth may not be excluded from the promise of life which now is, even if it is not all of that which is in view when that life is promised. Eph. 6:3 mentions one aspect of the reward of one part of εὐσέβεια, the obeying of parents in the Lord.

Although the N.T. is consciously thankful for life as existence and for longevity, and although it regards the former as from God, it never regards the former in itself as the promise of God. All men exist now, and in a sense will exist hereafter. Thus in this sense ζωή cannot be the promise which εὐσέβεια has, for all men do not have or practice εὐσέβεια. Ζωή when it is used in the N.T., and especially in the Pastoral Letters, has a fuller and richer significance.

2 Tim. 1:1 defines ζωή as "the life which is in Christ Jesus" (ζωῆς τῆς ἐν Χριστῷ 'Ιησοῦ). And it is this life which is promised (κατ' ἐπαγγελίαν ζωῆς). Thus, the ζωή as it is spoken of and known in the Pastorals is the life "which is in Christ Jesus", *i.e.*, it is the life which one has in union with Christ Jesus who is life. That εὐσέβεια should also have a ἐπαγγελία of such life is not strange when one remembers that Christ Jesus is the "mystery of godliness" (τῆς εὐσεβείας). The first chapter of 2 Timothy goes on to indicate that Christ Jesus has

---

[64] Cremer makes the excellent comment that ζωή, *life*, is that "which God *is*, and man *has* or *is said to have*".
[65] *Cf.* Bouma.

"abolished death (τὸν θάνατον) and brought life (ζωὴν) and immortality (ἀφθαρσίαν) to light through the gospel". The life which is in Christ is brought about by "our Savior Christ Jesus" in his abolishing death. The ζωή which is the promised possession of the believer is the opposite of the death in which he has lived, which indwelt him and which he would have reaped eternally. The life is then not a temporary possession but "a perfect and abiding antithesis to death"[66]. It is a life which he has in Christ Jesus and thus is a life which now is and which will be also. Those who are in Christ are united to him now and forever and have therefore by that union life beginning now and continuing then. Therefore the one word life may be used to refer to the believer now and hereafter because it is one life, not two, which is the promise[67]. Thus it can be sometimes characterized by the addition of αἰώνιος (1 Tim. 1:16; 6:12; Titus 1:2; 3:7) or by the qualification ὄντως (ἡ ὄντως ζωή, 1 Tim, 6:19)[68]. In this latter case it indicates the sense of "the very highest blessedness"[69]. When Jesus Christ describes the work which he has come to do, according to John 10:10, he says that he came "that they may have life (ζωή) and may have it abundantly" (περισσόν). So also in 1 Tim. 4:8, as in 6:19, the ζωή in view is the "abundant" life, that life which is life indeed.

The life which now is (ζωῆς τῆς νῦν) refers to this present age and this present earthly life. Here and now εὐσέβεια has promise of true ζωή[70]. The life which will be fully realized and enjoyed in the age to come is here and now already entered into. The ζωή which is now (νῦν) is explained and seen to be what it is in view of the fact that it is the same life which is to come (τῆς μελλούσης). And since it is the life which is to come it may be, and is, spoken of elsewhere in the Pastorals as eternal (αἰώνιος, 1 Tim. 1:16; 6:12; Titus 1:2; 3:7) and also as ἡ ὄντως ζωή (1 Tim. 6:19).

The closest parallel to this saying in the N.T. is to be found in the words of the Lord Jesus Christ in Lk. 18:29,30[71], "Verily I say unto you, There is no man that has left house, or wife, or brethren, or parents, or children, for the kingdom of God's sake, who shall not receive manifold more in this time, and in the world to come eternal life", and parallels in Mk. 10:29,30; Mt. 19:29. The similarity is not so much verbal as

---

[66] Cremer, sub ζωή.
[67] Parry, ad loc., says also "the distinction is not between two kinds of life, but the two conditions under which the one life is lived".
[68] Arndt-Gingrich, sub ὄντως, "real, true life 6:19".
[69] Moulton and Milligan, sub ζωή; Trench, Synonyms, p. 94.
[70] G. Stählin, TWNT, IV, p. 1113, sub νῦν B II 4 d, "göttliches Leben, an dem wir schon jetzt, in der Christusperiode, teilhaben und das in Fülle für dereinst in Aussicht steht".
[71] Among others suggested by Scott, Kelly, Parry.

conceptual. The particular parallel is found in the idea of blessing in this time and in the world to come eternal life. This is similar to the double reference of ζωῆς in 1 Tim. 4:8. The note of promise, although not the word itself, is evident in the dominical phrase, "Verily I say unto you" and in the stress of "There is no man ... who shall not receive manifold more ...". Scott points out that "the mention of a promise, in the New Testament, usually has reference to something promised in scripture..."[72]. Parry states that the catena of passages which refer to a promise usually of or from the Lord Jesus show that there is a definite reference to our Lord's utterances.[73] Scott and Parry are both saying in effect that a reference to a promise in the N.T. refers back to a known and authoritative source (scripture, Jesus)[74]. If Scott and Parry are correct in their thesis, and this would appear to be so, then it would strengthen the hypothesis that the saying is in part a reflection of Jesus' saying. The emphasis on a promise in the saying would then point to the authoritative source of Jesus. Thus it is Jesus who has made the promise that is here affirmed when he spoke the words of Lk. 18:29, 30. The other alternative, a possible O.T. background, seems less likely and a relevant parallel is not available. 1 Tim. 4:8 because of the parallel structure with τῆς νῦν speaks of the life as τῆς μελλουσῆς; Lk. 18:30 and the parallel accounts speak of ζωὴν αἰώνιον. It is possible that the Christian community in reflection on this saying of Jesus generalized it in terms of εὐσέβεια. Certainly the general concepts are alike, *i.e.*, the blessings for this life and the life to come in terms of faithfulness to God. "They seem to echo", as Kelly says, "words of our Lord recorded in the gospel tradition which offer precisely this reward to those who renounce all for his sake (Mt. xix.29; Mk. x.30; Lk. xviii.30)"[75].

Dibelius-Conzelmann and some others suggest that the saying was originally a proverb against athletics which came from a philosophical circle[76], possibly that of the Cynics-Stoics. On this point of view, the original contrast would have been the value of philosophy, etc., over against bodily training. The theory would then presume that the Christians took the saying over and made certain changes such as the

---

[72] Scott, *ad loc.* It must not be thought that Scott points only to the O.T. and rules out Jesus. As a matter of fact he posits the saying of Jesus as a possibility.

[73] Parry, *ad loc.*

[74] Arndt-Gingrich, *sub* ἐπαγγελία: "as a rule in our lit. of divine promises"; *cf.* also J. Schniewind/G. Friedrich, *sub* ἐπαγγελία, *TDNT*, II, pp. 581-585.

[75] Kelly, *ad loc.*; Lock, *ad loc.*, similarly states that "the saying may have been based on the Lord's own words".

[76] For the possibility and literature see Dibelius-Conzelmann, *ad* 1 Tim. 4:8, p. 55; *cf.* also Easton and Gealy. For the most extensive citing of the literature see however the Excursus VII of Spicq, esp. pp. 159 ff.

substitution of εὐσέβεια[77] and the addition of ἐπαγγελία κτλ. Although this is only an hypothesis or conjecture, it is not altogether unlikely. The Christians, as exampled in the N.T. by Paul's speech as recorded in Acts 17:28, have borrowed sayings and given them their own meaning and placed them in their own context. This could have been done with this saying.

Gealy and Lock both allow that the saying may have been as much Jewish as Christian in origin. They both cite Pirke Abboth 4:2, "Who is rich? He that is contented with his lot: for it is said, Happy art thou in this world, and it shall be well with thee in the world to come", which they assert is particularly relevant for the phrase ἐπαγγελίαν ἔχουσα κτλ.

Borrowing, as has been pointed out above, can not be ruled out completely as a possibility, although the stress on a promise (ἐπαγγελία) and the more probable reference of this to the tradition concerning Jesus' words are preferable. The saying as it was used and is now found is obviously distinctly Christian. It is as such that it can be referred to by the words πιστὸς ὁ λόγος καὶ πάσης ἀποδοχῆς ἄξιος.

Swete[78], Spicq and others bring out the special importance that γυμνασία had in the training of the youth of the city, as is further evidenced by entrusting it to an officer of high rank and also by the agonistic festivals which abounded in the Ephesian calendar[79]. Swete points out further that the εὐσέβεια family of words bears an almost technical sense in Ephesian inscriptions.

Thus the phrase φιλόπατρις καὶ φιλοσέβαστος, ἁγνός, εὐσεβής occurs...[80]; and other citizens are honoured ἀρετῆς ἕνεκεν καὶ τῆς πρὸς τὴν θεὸν (Artemis) εὐσεβείας...[81], or because the person was known as ἀποβλέπων εἰς τὴν εὐσεβείαν τῆς θεοῦ...[82]. Another Ephesian is described as νεωποιήσας εὐσεβῶς...[83], i.e. as having religiously discharged the office of temple-warden[84].

These sayings may reflect the view at the time of the Pastoral Letters, or earlier. If so, the *Sitz im Leben* for the saying is partially provided in Ephesus.

---

[77] Although εὐσέβεια is widely used among the Greeks (see Spicq, Excursus VI, pp. 125-134; and W. Foerster, *TWNT*, VII, pp. 175-178), it is not contrasted with bodily exercise as in 1 Tim. 4:8. Εὐσέβεια in the saying has the distinctively Christian sense found elsewhere in the Pastorals, as is demonstrated also by the words ἐπαγγελίαν ἔχουσα κτλ.

[78] Swete, *op. cit.*, p. 3 f.; Spicq, Excursus VII.

[79] Swete, *op. cit.*, p. 3 cites Hicks, *Ephesos* prolegg., pp. 79, 82.

[80] "in Hicks, pp. 127, 132 *bis*, where the inscriptions belong to the year A.D. 104".

[81] "*ibid.* p. 187, *circa* A.D. 106".

[82] "*ibid.* p. 143, A.D. 160".

[83] "*ibid.* p. 211".

[84] Swete, *op. cit.*, p. 3 f.

78

Thus it is possible that the original saying about or against athletic excesses, in the setting of a continual excessive accent on them, coupled with an emphasis or use of the εὐσέβεια words in the Artemis cult produced the saying which incorporated these elements in the setting of the promise of Jesus. Swete[85] aptly summarizes the possibility in these words, although without taking into account the promise of Jesus: "In the Christian at Ephesus, Christ had taken the place of Artemis and the Church that of the Artemision; and the self-control and self-sacrifice of the new life in Christ, which were good for both worlds, were the Christian substitute for the drill of the gymnasium, which was serviceable only for the life that now is".

---

[85]   Swete, *op. cit.*, p. 4.

CHAPTER V

TITUS 3:8 AND ITS SAYING

In Titus 3:1ff. the Apostle Paul instructs Titus to remind the Cretan Christians to conduct themselves as Christians in relation to governmental authorities in particular and non-Christians in general[1], regardless of how ungodly they may act or appear. Lest the Christians think that the attitudes and behavior of the non-Christians do not merit Christian conduct and speech on the part of the Christians to their unbelieving neighbors, Paul reminds them that they were once just like these fellow pagans and that in that condition God demonstrated love and kindness to them. By implication the Christians are called on to emulate God. Their salvation, not by any works done by themselves, but by the grace and mercy of God through Jesus Christ their Savior and the Holy Spirit, should make them not only ready but also careful to apply themselves to and engage in good deeds. Thus from an exhortation to Christian conduct on the part of Christians toward non-Christians the Apostle moves to the religious basis and motivation for that conduct, *i.e.*, God's goodness and lovingkindness to them as sinful men and their resultant salvation.

The citation-emphasis formula, "Faithful is the saying", is found in Titus 3:8 where it is followed by the words "and concerning these things I desire that you affirm confidently, to the end that they who have believed God may be careful to maintain good works" (καὶ περὶ τούτων βούλομαί σε διαβεβαιοῦσθαι, ἵνα φροντίζωσιν καλῶν ἔργων προΐστασθαι

---

[1] Similar exhortations are found in Romans 13 and 1 Peter 2:13-17. Some have questioned the quick transition from subjection to rulers (Titus 3:1) to the general concern to show "all meekness toward all men" (Titus 3:2) and related terms. But both in Romans 13 and 1 Peter 2:13-17 the same two elements are set in close juxtaposition to one another. Not only do admonitions similar to Titus 3:2 concerning conduct toward men precede Paul's discussion of the Christian's relation to government (Romans 13:1 ff.) in Romans 12:9-21 but also follow it in Romans 13:8-10. And in 1 Peter 2:13-17 Christians are not only instructed to be subject to civil authorities (verse 13) and honor the king, the Roman emperor (see Arndt-Gingrich, *sub* βασιλεύς), (verse 17) but also to honor all men (verse 17).

οἱ πεπιστευκότες θεῷ). Certainly the immediately conjoined words quoted here are not the λόγος. Nothing following the formula and this additional statement appears to be the saying to which it refers. Verses 8a through 10 all lack that which may properly be called a λόγος. The same holds for the remainder of the verses in the letter, verses 12—15, although the distance which they are removed from the formula would preclude them even if they were proverbial in character. Thus the negative evidence precludes the formula from referring to any of that which follows it. Joined to this is the positive evidence that the formula refers to that which precedes it, in that in the preceding verses are several statements which could well be referred to as a faithful saying.

As acknowledged by the virtually unanimous opinion of commentators on this passage, the evidence causes us to affirm that the formula refers to that which precedes it[2]. Then the question arises, which verses? With this question the unanimity ends, although a vast majority opinion still prevails. Dibelius-Conzelmann[3] stand virtually alone in positing that the saying consists of verses 3—7. The vast majority[4] of the exegetes opt for verses 4—7. A few scholars choose verses 5—7 or portions of them. Guthrie seems at one place[5] to select verses 5—7, Spicq[6] does so as a probability, and Swete[7] with more definiteness. Lock[8] says of verses 5—7,

---

[2]   The following scholars say that the saying refers to that which is before but fail to specify the verses: Bengel, Fairbairn, Falconer, Hanson and Lenski. The opinions of others who both hold the reference is to that which precedes verse 8 or some part thereof and also are specific will be given in the development of the survey. E. F. Scott, as an exception, surprisingly thinks it "best to look for the saying in the sentence following" (ad 3:8).

[3]   "Bei Tit 3₈ kann man fragen, welchen Umfangs der zitierte Text ist; aber dass in diesem Stück, das ganz der paränetischen Tradition entspricht, von 3₃ an (1. Pers. Plur. s.z. St.) ein Zitat enthalten ist, scheint glaublich", Dibelius-Conzelmann, ad 1 Tim. 1:15.

[4]   Alford, Barrett, Bernard, Bouma, Ellicott, Fausset, Hendriksen, Huther, Jeremias, Johnson, Kent, Van Oosterzee, Robertson, Simpson ("the foregoing sentence" which in his Greek text consists of verses 4-7), von Soden, Vine, White (who however says it is not a Saying that is referred to but the doctrinal statement as a single concept), Wohlenberg and Wuest. Guthrie at one point in his commentary appears to favor verses 4-7, at another verses 5-7. In his comments on verse 8 Guthrie says: "The faithful saying must relate to the previous theological statement (verses 4-7), which may be regarded as an epitome of Pauline theology". But at verse 5 he says: "The apostle next seems to quote from a Christian hymn as is suggested by the opening formula in verse 8".

[5]   See note 4.

[6]   Spicq ad Titus 3:8 speaks of the formula as especially underlining the character of the quotation of the preceding words and then adds, "probablement à partir de οὐκ ἐξ ἔργων du. v. 5".

[7]   Swete, op. cit., p. 5.

[8]   Lock, ad Titus 3:8.

"...either in whole or in part, *e.g.*, 5 only, 6 and 7 being the writer's own expansion". Easton selects verses 5b—7. Kelly narrows his choice to verses 5b—6, "i.e. the specifically baptismal section", but adds the sagacious note which all who tackle this problem must heed: "It is perhaps hazardous, however, to try to identify the *trustworthy saying* exactly, for Paul has clearly interwoven thought of his own with whatever traditional or liturgical material he has borrowed"[9]. Gealy, who presents most of these alternatives and who is apparently undecided, concludes his discussion with the same note of caution: "Obviously the problem of the extent and exact wording of the source cannot be solved with complete certainty"[10].

Dibelius-Conzelmann argues for the verses 3—7 because, as he says, the use of the first person plural from verse 3 on shows the extent of the saying[11]. But this is hardly an adequate criterion in view of the fact that the first person plural occurs elsewhere in this letter, and not always in citations. It is true that the first person plural gives a certain unity and continuity to the verses 3—7. But the use in verse 3, for example, may be influenced by the first person plural in the saying and adapted to it. And the inherent nature of the truth set forth in the saying may explain why the first person is used. This observation made by Dibelius is inadequate in itself to serve as a determinative norm[12]. Furthermore, as Gealy notes, "vs. 3 is less rhythmical in form and liturgical in phrasing than vss. 4—7 and may have been patterned by our author to be an effective introduction to vss. 4—7. Its list of vices would then ... serve as the dark shadow against which the light of the Christian gospel shines the more brilliantly"[13]. The obvious relationship of verse 3 to verse 2 both in the content evidenced by its nouns and also by the correlation given with the introductory words, *For we also once* (γὰρ ποτε καὶ), speaks against it being part of the saying viewed as verses 3—7. Further evidence against its inclusion is the fact that it stands as a separate sentence not necessarily or inherently related to verses 4 and following. All the other "faithful sayings" consist of a single sentence. Thus there is also the weight of the norm of the other sayings against the inclusion of verse 3. The cumulative effect of these considerations is the verdict that verse 3 was not part of the saying.

The remaining solutions are those of verse 4—7, or verses 5—7 with variations which select only parts of verses 5—7 for the saying. Lock

---

[9] Kelly, *ad* Titus 3:8.
[10] Gealy, *ad* Titus 3:8.
[11] See note 3. Also Dibelius-Conzelmann *ad* Titus 3:3-7 the following: "Aus dem Schematismus der Redeweise erklärt sich auch die 1. Pers-Plur.".
[12] The pronoun ἡμεῖς occurs 397 times in all of Paul's letters, 15 times in Titus itself.
[13] Gealy, *ad* Titus 3:8.

simply throws out the possibility that the saying is that of verses 5—7 or portions of it, and then cites merely as an example of this latter possibility "*e.g.* 5 only, 6 and 7 being the writer's own expansion"[14]. But no argumentation or reasons are given for this example or possibility. And there is not evidence in the vocabulary and style to demand the solution that verse 5 alone is the saying and that verses 6 and 7 are not. Kelly has opted for verses 5b—6. He eliminates verse 4 but with the qualification that it "probably" should be excluded from the citation. His argument for the deletion of verse 4 is "since both *was manifested* and *God our Saviour* are in the idiom of the Pastorals" they can not be part of a saying quoted. Then he says, "Since both 5a and 7 have a strongly Pauline tang, the extract may well be limited to 5b—6, i.e. the specifically baptismal section"[15]. The appeal to the "idiom of the Pastorals" and "a strongly Pauline tang" is indeed legitimate. In fact, this is one of the best gauges to be used in ascertaining what is and what is not the citation, if it truly and clearly distinguishes one part from another. However, this cannot be so definitely done with these verses. For in the verses 5b—6 which Kelly suggests as probably the citation, these same two elements are also found. For example, the words within 5b "according to his mercy he saved us" (κατὰ τὸ αὐτοῦ ἔλεος ἔσωσεν ἡμᾶς) have within them both the "idiom of the Pastorals" and "a strongly Pauline tang". Ἔλεος which is found 27 times in the N.T., is found 10 times in Paul (including the Pastorals where it is found 5 times inclusive of Titus 3:5). Thus the note of God's mercy is common to both the Pastorals and the other Pauline letters[16]. The same may be said of σῴζειν[17]. If it be argued that the close combination of ἔλεος and σῴζειν seem to be lacking elsewhere in the other two areas (Paul in general, the Pastorals in particular), then it may be said with equal validity that this is also true of the combination ἔργων τῶν ἐν δικαιοσύνη in 5a or the combination of ἡ χρηστότης καὶ ἡ φιλανθρωπία in 4. Admittedly παλιγγενεσίας in 5b does not occur anywhere in Paul and only one other place in the N.T.

14 Lock, *ad* Titus 3:8.
15 Kelly, *ad* Titus 3:8.
16 This is not to say that ἔλεος is exclusively Pauline but only to say that it is Pauline. The usage of ἔλεος in the N.T. is not particularly conclusive in view of the fact that it is found in eight authors but in only two does it occur more than three times (Luke and Paul). In the other six it occurs three times (Mark, James) or less (2 times, Hebrews; 1, 1 Peter; 1, 2 John; 2, Jude). The word occurs six times in Luke's Gospel but not at all in Acts. And five of these occurrences are in the first chapter in the speeches (of those five one is actually in the context) and are probably influenced by the O.T. The linguistic rootage for all the N.T. may well be the LXX where the word is found with frequency, expecially in the Psalms. See Hatch and Redpath, *A Concordance to the Septuagint, sub* ἔλεος, and R. Bultmann, ἔλεος κτλ., *TDNT*, II, pp. 477-487. But of the N.T. authors the word is most typically Pauline.
17 29 times in Paul of which 7 are in the Pastorals.

(Mt. 19:28). But the same is true of φιλανθρωπία in verse 4, being only found elsewhere in Acts 28:2 and then with men, not God, as the subject in view.

Thus a consideration of Kelly's view, which declares the saying to be 5b—6, not only has shown us that his criterion itself cannot with certainty so delimit the saying, but also has the merit of pointing up the fact that the criteria which he suggests, as valuable as they might rightly be, do not serve to delineate the saying with certainty. The unique vocabulary, whether it be designated as "idiom" or "tang", does not allow us the confidence to say within verses 4—7 only these particuar verses, *e.g.*, 5b—6, are the saying.

Two other objections must be entered against Kelly's position and others like his. The first is concerning the elimination of verse 7. Although it is not a conclusive objection, it does have the force of removing the formula "faithful is the saying" from the position of complete juxtaposition to the saying by the intervention of one verse, *i.e.*, verse 7, which is not part of the saying. There would be something strange about the author's saying "faithful is the saying" (ὁ λόγος) when he is not as a matter of fact referring to the words of the statement that immediately precede. Would not the reader assume, as so many commentators have naturally done in like fashion, that the author refers by his emphasis-citation formula to that which he had just written? The evidence being lacking that verse 7 is excluded it would naturally be included.

The second objection to both Kelly's view (verses 5b—6) and Easton's view (verses 5b—7) is that both exclude the first part of verse 5. Easton's translation and use of quotation marks in that translation indicate that he regards the saying as beginning with the words "By a washing that gave us a new birth ..."[18] (διὰ λουτροῦ ...). His notes, however, seem to include ἔσωσεν[19]. Kelly does not say where the line of demarcation comes, but his comments seem to suggest Easton's division. The division is so abrupt and arbitrary that it seems to rend that which belongs together. Both commentators, Easton and Kelly, seem to be motivated by the assumption that the saying is connected with a baptismal setting and therefore should begin with or be restricted to that which relates to baptism. Kelly admits, as does Easton in his translation, that the words "he saved us" and even the rest of verse 5 and even perhaps verse 4 are needed to complete the words and thought pattern they claim begins with διὰ λουτροῦ. Would the words of verse 5a or even verse 4 be inappropriate even to a baptismal setting or liturgy? Are they not in fact appropriate and fitting, indeed necessary? Since both implicitly

[18] Easton, p. 97.
[19] Easton, p. 100.

84

admit that some words preceded the saying as they see it (5b, etc.), why not the words of 5a and perhaps also verse 4? Easton's objection that the theological statement of 5a "would be out of place in the hymn that follows" is certainly as questionably out of place in his argument as a convincing part of it. The very fact that both men seem to include ἔσωσεν with 5a but then treat it as necessarily introducing and virtually part of 5b shows the difficulty of dividing this verse. Admittedly it may show Paul's skillful blending of his argument and the saying, as Kelly has in principle allowed for. But it may more convincingly show that the two parts of the verse are inherently and intrinsically one with ἔσωσεν as the verbal focal point and cement that bind them together. Both parts need ἔσωσεν. Both together constitute one coherent thought.

The decision thus reduces to a choice between verses 4—7 or verses 5—7. Swete is "disposed to think that it begins at οὐκ ἐξ ἔργων [verse 5], and ὅτε δὲ... θεοῦ [verse 4] is the writer's note of transition from ἦμεν γάρ ποτε κτλ. to the quotation"[20]. This is a plausible statement of the case and cannot be absolutely negated as impossible and untenable. But neither does it conclusively make the case. On the other hand there are considerations which may be plead on behalf of verses 4—7 as the saying. Verses 4—7 constitute a unit both as a sentence and also in regard to the thought content. It is verse 4 which gives the comparison and contrast to verses 3 and preceding and makes for the significance of the quotation of this saying in this context. The ὅτε of verse 4 speaks to the Ἦμεν... ποτε of verse 3, while ἡ χρηστότης καὶ ἡ φιλανθρωπία coupled with τὸ αὐτοῦ ἔλεος is set in contrast to the ἡμεῖς ἀνόητοι, ἀπειθεῖς κτλ. The force of the saying comes in the affirmation that God our Savior saved us (ἡμᾶς verse 5, compare καὶ ἡμεῖς of verse 3) when (ὅτε verse 4) we were once also foolish, etc. (Ἦμεν γάρ ποτε καὶ ἡμεῖς, verse 3). Hence it is the saying as a whole (including necessarily verse 4) which provides the reason for the admonition in verses 1 and 2 by showing what God our Saviour has done to and for us who were once sinful (verse 3) in His salvation (verses 4—7). The bridge for the saying is the added δέ which sets forth immediately the contrast and carries one from verse 3 to the saying beginning with verse 4. It must be further emphasized that verses 4—7 do constitute a unit both in form and in content, and may aptly be designated a saying. There must be conclusive reasons for exscinding or excluding verse 4 from this evident unit before this may be done. And those conclusive reasons are lacking. Further bespeaking the inclusion of verse 4 in the saying is the presence of the word φιλανθρωπία. This word occurs only twice in the N.T., here and in Acts 28:2. In Acts 28:2 it is used with men as the subject. Its occurrence

[20] Swete, *op. cit.*, p. 5.

here, predicated of God, may be more readily explained as the result of its being in a saying which Paul included rather than as an heretofore unused word of his vocabulary. An early understanding of the extent of the saying as embracing verses 4—7 may be seen in the form of the uncial, Codex Sinaiticus, in separating verse 4 from verse 3 and joining verses 4—7[21]. The given factors upon which one may decide between verses 5—7 or 4—7 are not extensive or intensive. While choosing verses 4—7 on the basis of the arguments here adduced, we do so however aware of the fact that the dictum of Gealy must still stand: "Obviously the problem of the extent and exact wording of the source cannot be solved with complete certainty"[22].

The saying, Titus 3:4—7, is as follows:
"When the kindness of God our Savior,
and his love toward man, appeared,
not by works done in righteousness which we did ourselves,
but according to his mercy he saved us,
through the washing of regeneration and renewing of the Holy Spirit,
which he poured out upon us richly, through Jesus Christ our Savior;
that, being justified by his grace,
we might be made heirs according to the hope of eternal life"[23].

A question which must be immediately asked is that of the time reference in verse 4, "But when (ὅτε) the kindness of God our Savior, and his love toward man, appeared" (ἐπεφάνη). But this question cannot be answered until one ascertains what has appeared, i.e., ἡ χρηστότης καὶ ἡ φιλανθρωπία. Χρηστότης occurs ten times in the N.T. and all of these are in Paul[24]. It is used both of men[25] and of God[26]. In both cases the general meaning is that of goodness, kindness, generosity. Since it is the χρηστότης "of God our Savior" that is in view in Titus 3:4, it is

---

[21] Noted by Ellicott and Simpson, *ad* Titus 3:8. See the manuscript itself.
[22] Gealy, *ad* Titus 3:8.
[23] The saying is quoted in the form in which it is rendered in the *American Standard Version* with the exception of the omission of the initial connective "but" (δέ). The Greek text of the saying is as follows:
ὅτε ἡ χρηστότης καὶ ἡ φιλανθρωπία ἐπεφάνη τοῦ σωτῆρος ἡμῶν Θεοῦ,
οὐκ ἐξ ἔργων τῶν ἐν δικαιοσύνῃ ἃ ἐποιήσαμεν ἡμεῖς
ἀλλὰ κατὰ τὸ αὐτοῦ ἔλεος ἔσωσεν ἡμᾶς
διὰ λουτροῦ παλιγγενεσίας καὶ ἀνακαινώσεως πνεύματος ἁγίου,
οὗ ἐξέχεεν ἐφ' ἡμᾶς πλουσίως διὰ Ἰησοῦ Χριστοῦ τοῦ σωτῆρος ἡμῶν,
ἵνα δικαιωθέντες τῇ ἐκείνου χάριτι
κληρονόμοι γενηθῶμεν κατ' ἐλπίδα ζωῆς αἰωνίου.
[24] Rom. 2:4, 3:12, 11:22 (3 times); 2 Cor. 6:6; Gal. 5:22; Eph. 2:7; Col. 3:12; Titus 3:4.
[25] Rom. 3:12; 2 Cor. 6:6; Gal. 5:22; Col. 3:12.
[26] Rom. 2:4, 11:22; Eph. 2:7; Titus 3:4.

to the usages with God that we are drawn. In all the passages where God is the subject (Rom. 2:4, 11:22; Eph. 2:7; Titus 3:4) the context shows that it has a soteriological meaning. In Rom. 2:4 χρηστότης leads to repentance[27]. In Eph. 2:7, "God's grace is manifested through his kindness [χρηστότης] towards us, and that kindness is exercised through Christ and for his sake"[28]. Χρηστότης is the "experienced embodiment"[29] of God's grace to us in Christ Jesus. Likewise in Titus 3:4 χρηστότης is that of God as our Savior (τοῦ σωτῆρος ἡμῶν θεοῦ), it is that which has appeared (ἐπεφάνη), and it is that which leads to our salvation. When (ὅτε) God's *kindness* appeared, he saved us (Titus 3:4 and 5). In Rom. 11:22 the term is contrasted with severity and it is the χρηστότης which caused the believing Gentiles to be grafted into the people of God. Χρηστότης is thus the opposite of severity. In two of these passages in which God is the subject χρηστότης has joined to it one or more similar words as is done in Titus 3:4, *i.e.*, in Rom. 2:4 it is combined with ἀνοχή and μακροθυμία, and in Ephesians 2:7 with χάρις αὐτοῦ. Thus it is not surprising to find χρηστότης joined with φιλανθρωπία in Titus 3:4.

Φιλανθρωπία is found only twice in the N.T., Acts 28:2 and Titus 3:4. In Acts 28:2 the term is used of men, while in Titus 3:4 of God. Field asserts "that *philanthropy* as felt and exercised by a human being towards mankind in general is a novel use of the word; but this does not apply to beings of a superior nature"[30]. Outside the N.T. it is frequently used of the virtue of rulers and of their gods in their relations to their subjects. Here in Titus 3:4 it means God's love for mankind as man. Hence this saying was an apt one to cite because it presents the answer of God to the hatefulness of man (verse 3) and thus demonstrates what the Christian's attitude should be toward hateful men (verse 2), indeed toward all men. It is not love in the abstract but love that focuses upon man as man, and comes to him (ἐπιφάνη)[31]. Nor is it love in general but rather the love

---

[27] "Or do you despise the riches of his goodness (χρηστότητος) and forbearance and longsuffering, not knowing that the goodness (χρηστὸν) of God leads you to repentance?" Actually the second occurrence of "goodness" is the related word χρηστός used as a substantive, but it obviously is used to repeat the former concept.

[28] C. Hodge, *A Commentary on the Epistle to the Ephesians* (Grand Rapids: Eerdmans, reprint, n.d.), *ad loc.*

[29] J. Eadie, *Commentary on the Epistle to the Ephesians* (Grand Rapids: Zondervan, reprint of 1883 edition), *ad* Eph. 2:7. *Cf.* further R. C. Trench, *Synonyms of the New Testament* (Grand Rapids: Eerdmans, reprint of the 9th ed., 1880), pp. 232 ff., and G. Holtz, *Die Pastoralbriefe, ad* Titus 3:4, p. 232 f.

[30] Field, *Notes*, p. 222; *cf.* also *ad* Acts 28:2 in Field.

[31] C. Spicq, *ad* Titus 3:4 gives an able survey of φιλανθρωπία. *Cf.* further his "La Philanthropie hellénistique, vertu divine et royale (à propos de Tit. III, 4)", *Studia Theologica* 12 (1958), pp. 169-191.

of God as Savior, love that manifests itself in the salvation of men who embrace him as their Savior (τοῦ σωτῆρος ἡμῶν θεοῦ).

The terms χρηστότης and φιλανθρωπία must not be considered just individually but also as one unified expression. They occur together frequently in extra-biblical Greek[32]. The verb ἐπεφάνη in the singular demonstrates that the expression "the kindness and the love toward man" is regarded as one concept[33]. It is "the-kindness-and-the-love-toward-man" of God our Savior that has appeared. And this composite expression is comparable to the expression "the grace of God has appeared" ('Επεφάνη γὰρ ἡ χάρις τοῦ θεοῦ) in Titus 2:11 but is a more Hellenistic way of expressing virtually the same thought. The parallel is demonstrated further by the fact that the appearing of both brings salvation (Titus 2:11 and 3:4 and 5). Such a parallel will be of help later in our attempt to understand the specific meaning of ἐπεφάνη in Titus 3:4. The saying thus embodies and uses a well-known Hellenistic expression[34]. But in the saying this expression has a rich soteriological import because it expresses the attitude of God as Savior. Christians can be exhorted "to be gentle, showing all meekness toward all men" (verse 2), because God our Savior showed to us his "kindness and love toward man" when we were as they now are[35].

This kindness and love toward man of God our Savior has already appeared (ἐπεφάνη, aorist) at a particular time (ὅτε). What was the appearance and when was it? To answer this most important and pressing question we must give consideration to the verb used (ἐπεφάνη)[36]. The verb ἐπιφαίνω occurs only four times in the N.T. (Lk. 1:79; Acts 27:20; Titus 2:11; 3:4). In Acts 27:20 it is used with reference to the sun and stars. For many days "neither sun nor stars shone" (ἐπιφαινόντων). Luke 1:78, 79 speak "of the tender mercy of our God, whereby the dayspring from on high shall visit us, to shine (ἐπιφᾶναι) upon them that sit in darkness and the shadow of death". In the context of Zacharias' "Benedictus" (Luke 1:68-79) it is clear that "the dayspring from on high" is a person that shall visit the people and it is he that shall shine upon those sitting in darkness. This reference to the "dayspring from on high" is an allusion to the Messiah, i.e., Jesus Christ[37].

---

[32] See Arndt-Gingrich, sub φιλανθρωπία, and for a rather extended list of citations, Field, Notes, p. 222 f.

[33] Hendriksen, ad Titus 3:4, also Lenski, and Lock, ad loc.

[34] For a discussion of a possible courtly style (Hofstil) used here, and perhaps self-consciously, see Dibelius-Conzelmann, pp. 108-110, Easton, p. 99, and Jeremias, Gealy, and Ridderbos, ad loc. An answer to this style "problem" here would seem to reside in recognizing this passage as a saying.

[35] Fairbairn, ad loc., and Huther, ad loc.

[36] A second aorist passive, third person singular of ἐπιφαίνω.

[37] See H. A. W. Meyer, Commentary on Mark and Luke, Vol. I, ad loc., and Greijdanus, Lucas (K.N.T.), Vol. I, ad loc.

Thus we have the combination of the usage of the verb ἐπιφαίνω in reference to the sun and stars with the figurative application of it to "the dayspring from on high" shining upon them that sit in darkness. This is also exampled in the O.T. "The Lord ... rose from Seir upon them; he shined forth from mount Paran" (Dt. 33:2; cf. also Ps. 118:27; 31:16). Here in Luke 1:78, 79, we have the mercy of God manifesting itself in the visit of "the dayspring from on high" and that to accomplish a soteriological act for and in the people, i.e., "to shine upon them that sit in darkness and the shadow of death; and to guide our feet into the way of peace". Since Titus 2:11 and context is so much like Titus 3:5, these two passages will be considered together later.

In addition to the verb, note should be taken of the noun form, ἐπιφά-νεια. "As a religious technical term it means a visible manifestation of a hidden divinity, either in the form of a personal appearance, or by some deed of power by which its presence is made known"[38]. In the New Testament it is used only of Christ's appearing on earth[39]. Hence the conceptual usage would point in the direction of the appearance of Christ as the meaning for the verbal forms in Titus 3:5 and 2:11.

The semantic key to our question how and when did "the kindness of God our Savior and his love toward man" appear is to be found in 2 Timothy 1:9 and 10. And we get to that key over the bridge afforded by Titus 2:11 which says that "the grace of God has appeared, bringing salvation to all men". We have seen before that this expression is virtually synonymous with the expression of Titus 3:4 taken in connection with verse 5. Both speak of an appearance (ἐπεφάνη, the exact same word and in the same form) of an attitude and inclination of God in respect of man which brings salvation or causes men to be saved. Thus if we ask how and when did the grace (χάρις) of God appear we are also asking how and when did his kindness and love toward man appear. 2 Timothy 1:9, 10 speak of the grace (χάρις) of God and specifically of its appearance. Verse 9 says that God's grace "was given us in Christ Jesus". That grace appears or is manifested "by the appearing (ἐπιφανείας) of our Savior Christ Jesus, who abolished death, and brought life and immortality to light through the gospel" (verse 10). Therefore we may say that the grace, kindness and love toward man of God our Savior appeared (ἐπε-φάνη) in the first coming or appearance (ἐπιφάνεια) of Christ Jesus[40].

Ephesians 2:7 also substantiates the teaching of 2 Timothy 1:9 and 10 that the grace of God appeared in Christ and it ties together grace

---

[38] Arndt-Gingrich, s.v. ἐπιφάνεια.
[39] All the occurrences are found in Paul, and all but one in the Pastorals; 2 Thess. 2:8; 1 Tim. 6:14; 2 Tim. 1:10; 4:1,8; Titus 2:13.
[40] Cf. also John 1:14,16,17, especially the latter: "...grace and truth came through Jesus Christ".

(χάρις) and kindness (χρηστότης). God made us alive together with Christ and raised us up with him (verses 5 & 6). And that act of saving us sinners who were dead in sins (verse 1) and once (ποτε) lived in the lusts of flesh and were like the rest (verse 2 & 3) came about in Christ Jesus, and by God's soteriological action in Christ in time and history. He did this to us "when we were" (καὶ ὄντας, verse 5) sinners, and he made us who were dead in sins alive in Christ (verses 5 & 6). And in the ages to come God will show "the exceeding riches of his grace (χάριτος αὐτοῦ) in kindness (χρηστότητι) toward us in (ἐν) Christ Jesus" (verse 7).

Hence the account of Titus 3:4 ff. has in view first of all the great event that has taken place in the history of salvation by the appearance of Christ Jesus[41]. When Christ appeared, then the kindness and love of God toward man appeared. It is only through Jesus Christ (διὰ 'Ιησοῦ Χριστοῦ) as our Savior (τοῦ σωτῆρος ἡμῶν) that the Holy Spirit is poured out richly so that we may be renewed and thus saved ("according to his mercy he saved us through the . . . renewing of the Holy Spirit which he poured out upon us richly, through Jesus Christ our Savior"; Titus 3:5, 6). Likewise in Titus 2:11-14, the grace of God which brings salvation has been wrought in "our Savior Jesus Christ who gave himself for us, that he might redeem us from all iniquity" (verses 13 & 14). It is in the person and work of Jesus Christ that God's grace truly appears and accomplishes salvation. So the "when" (ὅτε) and the "appeared" (ἐπεφάνη) refer first of all to Christ's first earthly appearance.

However, it would be a mistake to assume that the time references in view in Titus 3:4-7 are only to Christ's first earthly appearance and that there is not also a time reference which relates Christ's accomplishment of salvation to its application to those in the purview of these verses. Although it is true that the time reference in view in "he saved us" (verse 5) is encompassed by the time reference of the "when" (ὅτε) and the "appeared" (ἐπεφάνη) of verse 4, it is also true that "he saved us" is further delineated by the time reference involved in the specific act in which they were saved, i.e. "through the washing of regeneration and renewing of the Holy Spirit" (verse 5). And further, the other time references of the context must not be forgotten. Above all the time reference is personal. "We (ἡμεῖς) also once (ποτε) were (ἤμεν) foolish . . ." (verse 3). Upon their horizon has burst forth the love of God in Christ, and this great eschatological event has now made them personally those who are saved, washed, regenerated and renewed. This contrast between "before and after" is a recurring theme in the N.T.[42]; and as in Titus 3

---

[41] For an able discussion of the history of salvation or the eschatological perspective in Paul's theology see H. N. Ridderbos, *Paulus. Ontwerp van zijn Theologie* (Kampen: Kok, 1966), especially pp. 23 ff., 40 ff.

[42] See Rom. 6:17-23; 1 Cor. 6:9-11; Eph. 2:2 ff.; Col. 3:7 ff.

it relates both to what has happened in Christ and also to what therefore has happened in believers. The existential, that which happens to the believer and in him, comes to pass because of the great eschatological event of Christ's appearing.

Again 2 Timothy 1:9 provides a correlation between the eschatological event of Christ's appearing and the personal event in the believer's life by which his life is transformed by what Christ has done. 2 Tim. 1 : 10 not only speaks of Christ manifesting the grace of God by his appearance and thereby abolishing death and bringing life and immortality to light but it also reminds us that this is done by Christ "through the gospel" (διὰ τοῦ εὐαγγελίου; see also Titus 1:2,3). It is only when men hear and respond to that gospel that they are saved (Rom. 10:13,14; 2 Cor. 4:4-6) by the work of God's Spirit (Titus 3:5). Thus 2 Tim. 1:9 ff. speaks of redemption from eternity, in history in Christ, and existentially through the gospel. Just as the blessed personal and existential hope of believers that they might be heirs of eternal life is bound up particularly with the great eschatological second appearing of Christ Jesus (Titus 2:13), so also the personal salvation through the renewing of the Holy Spirit is bound up with and dependent upon the great eschatological first appearing of Christ. The time reference of "saved" (verse 5) is thus, in terms of the history of salvation, the eschatological appearing of God's kindness and love in Christ, but in terms of the people involved, that is existentially, it is when they experience the "washing of regeneration and renewing of the Holy Spirit". The term "saved" is thus qualified from two sides. The salvation is accomplished in the appearing of God's kindness and love toward man in Christ, it is applied when the Holy Spirit is actually poured out upon those who are thereby renewed.

If the appearance of the kindness of God our Savior and his love toward man was accomplished in the first appearance of Christ Jesus, why is this not stated more explicitly? Why is the truth expressed in terms of attitudes and attributes of God?[43] It may well be to throw in sharp relief the action and concern of God the Father and provide at the same time a Trinitarian statement[44]. It is manifest in the N.T. that Christ Jesus has come. By speaking of God's kindness and love, the work of the Father in the appearance of Jesus becomes more evident. And more particularly in the saying of Titus 3 by having God the Father as the main subject of the opening clause enables the saying to continue

[43] Likewise in Titus 2:11.

[44] For a discussion of Trinitarian or Binitarian in relation to the form in which a statement is couched see J. N. D. Kelly, *Early Christian Creeds* (London, New York & Toronto: Longmans, Green & Co.), pp. 13-29. Kelly contends, and rightly so, that Binitarian and Trinitarian forms are not just a result of the process of development which only manifests itself quite late in the early Christian church but are already evident in the N.T.

smoothly with the Father as the subject. Thus the subject of the verbs "saved" and "poured" is the Father, and the pronouns in "his mercy" and probably also in "his grace" also refer to God the Father. The focus of the saying is not so much on what God is in and of himself but on what God has done for man. Thus all the verbs and verbal forms focus on man and how God has saved and changed him. It is the kindness of God and his love toward *man* that has *"appeared"* (verse 4). It is God who *"saved us"* (verse 5) and this he did by that which man experiences, *i.e.*, "through the washing of regeneration and renewing of the Holy Spirit" (verse 5). God *poured out* his Spirit upon *us*. We are *justified* and *made heirs* by God (verse 7). The movement within the saying is chronological in the perspective of redemption accomplished and particularly applied to man. It begins with God's love and kindness appearing, it continues with the inner transformation of men by God's Spirit and through Christ, and it concludes with the affirmation of our standing by justification and our hope as heirs in eternity. Neither the accomplishment of salvation in Christ, what he did in life and death, nor the needed response of men is in the purview and emphasis of this saying[45]. Rather what is in view is what God the Father has done for us and in us according to his mercy. Thus the saving transformation accomplished apart from any works of ours by God's love and mercy serves as the motivating example for us men and thus for verses 1-3. This thrust of the saying explains why Paul uses it here.

The saying continues with a strong negation: "not by works (done) in righteousness, which we did ourselves ... he saved us"[46] (οὐκ ἐξ ἔργων τῶν ἐν δικαιοσύνῃ ἃ ἐποιήσαμεν ἡμεῖς ... ἔσωσεν ἡμᾶς, verse 5). That which is negated is that God has saved us because of works which we have done. The repudiation of works as a basis or grounds for God's saving men is a dominant theme in Paul[47]. It removes any cause for boasting. No one may claim that God's mercy or salvation falls upon them because of anything they have done which merits salvation or demands that God must save them. This negation particularly underscores the fact that salvation is purely of God and of his mercy, and makes abundantly plain that it is not of man at all. Paul usually uses either the term ἔργα by itself or in the form ἔργα νόμου[48]. In the places where the term is used elsewhere it is apparent that Paul is opposing the false Jewish idea of salvation by works, and especially works of the Law[49]. Here in

[45]   An awareness of the purpose and thrust of this saying will remove much of the criticism of its failure to mention faith and other items.

[46]   Translation of the *A.S.V.*

[47]   Rom. 3:27,28; 4:2-6; 9:11; Gal. 2:16; Eph. 2:9; 2 Tim. 1:9.

[48]   Ἔργα by itself: Rom. 2:6; 3:27; 4:2,6; 9:11,32; 11:6; Eph. 2:9; 2 Tim. 1:9; with νόμου: Rom. 3:20; Gal. 2:16; 3:2,5,10.

[49]   *Cf.* G. Bertram, *TDNT*, II, pp. 645 ff.

Titus 3:5 the term is qualified in a way that does not appear in Paul's writings, i.e., τῶν ἐν δικαιοσύνῃ⁵⁰. The ἔργα are not now qualified as νόμου (ἔργα νόμου) but as ἔργων τῶν ἐν δικαιοσύνῃ. It is indeed admittedly difficult to translate this phrase into an English idiom, and especially attempting to do justice to the ἐν. But it is evident from the Greek, nevertheless, that the saying is depicting the works or deeds as being righteous, that is, (up)right and good in a moral sense⁵¹. Thus what is denied is salvation from God (and also justification by God, verse 7) for those who did righteous or good deeds and who thus merited that response of God. The qualification of τῶν ἐν δικαιοσύνῃ is probably used here because the sayings arose over against a general heathen situation rather than a special Jewish situation. This would make it especially significant for the Cretan situation in view in this letter to Titus⁵². This usage, ἐν δικαιοσύνῃ, would admittedly not apply any less to the false Jewish view of works of the law, but by using δικαιοσύνῃ rather than the more restrictive νόμος it would probably be chosen to apply to a wider situation which would include particularly the heathen.

The statement under consideration is completed by the words "which we did ourselves" so that the entire expression is negated, not just the first half. God did not save us because of or by the righteous works which we did. The saying is not affirming that we have as a matter of fact done righteous works but that God has not saved us on the basis of some righteous works. This would be contrary to the Pauline evaluation of our works in the eyes of God (cf., e.g., Rom. 3:10-12,19,23, etc.). And

---

⁵⁰ Ἐν δικαιοσύνῃ occurs 8 times in the N.T., of which 4 are in Paul (Lk. 1:75; Acts 17:31; Eph. 4:24; 5:9; 2 Tim. 3:16; Titus 3:5; 2 Peter 1:1; Rev. 19:11). Only once is it found in direct connection with faith (2 Peter 1:1). The one occurrence each in Luke's Gospel and Acts are both in speeches, and the latter a speech of Paul. When used in reference to God it characterizes how he will judge (κρίνω, Acts 17:31; Rev. 19:11). It is twice associated with holiness (ὁσιότης, Lk. 1:75; Eph. 4:24) and twice with truth (ἀλήθεια, Eph. 4:24; 5:9). In reference to man δικαιοσύνη in the phrase ἐν δικαιοσύνῃ, leaving aside 2 Peter 1:1 and Titus 3:5 for the moment, is an ethical response engendered by God in man, taught by His Word (2 Tim. 3:16), which is a fruit (Eph. 5:9) acceptable to God (Lk. 1:75, ἐνώπιον αὐτοῦ). Thus these passages in distinction from Titus 3:5 speak of δικαιοσύνη in the phrase under consideration as a result of God's salvation. On the other hand Titus 3:5 is in the same spirit as these passages and others in the N.T. when it negates righteousness as a basis or ground for salvation. Titus 3:5 (οὐκ ἐξ ἔργων τῶν ἐν δικαιοσύνῃ ἃ ἐποιήσαμεν ἡμεῖς) is saying in more general terms what Paul says in Philip. 3:6,9 in more Hebraistic terms, viz., that our salvation is not accomplished by human attainment (G. Schrenk, δίκη, . . . , δικαιοσύνη κτλ., TDNT, II, p. 202). Therefore the use of the expression in the context of Titus 3:5 is rather unusual for the N.T. in terms of form but not in terms of material emphasis.

⁵¹ Arndt-Gingrich, sub δικαιοσύνη 2 b.

⁵² Cf. Ridderbos, ad loc.

this repudiation of our own righteousness is also apparent from the preceding context. Verse 3 speaks of us as disobedient, serving various lusts, etc. The saying has used the words "which we did" to focus attention on us. Not by things which we have done and which we considered righteous did God save us. This negation is not an exposition of our pre-Christian state and the value of our works in that condition as such, but rather a denial of any work righteousness as a foil for the emphasis on the free mercy and grace of God. Actually the saying is not discussing whether our deeds were righteous and not accepted, or whether we lacked righteous deeds. It is using the language and attitude of the day and of men in general that God should accept us and "save" us because we have done "good" things. This entire looking unto man and what he has done as a basis for his salvation is absolutely denied (οὐκ). And this denial is made more abundantly plain by the use of that which is diametrically the opposite of works, i.e., mercy (ἔλεος). The reason for our salvation does not rest in us or in anything that we have done but solely in God, in his[53] mercy. The attributive position of "his" (αὐτοῦ) in the phrase τὸ αὐτοῦ ἔλεος emphasizes the fact that it is *his* mercy. Thus his mercy (αὐτοῦ) is contrasted with our works (ἡμεῖς). Not by our works, not even by the works which we think we have done and which we and other men might consider good, but by God's mercy he saved us.

To men who are unable by what they do to save themselves God in Christ comes in mercy, compassion and pity to save them. The entire thrust of this saying in its context is fully exemplified in Ephesians 2:3—5. There in the midst of the stark contrast the meaning of mercy is set forth in sharp relief:

> ". . . we also all once (ποτε) lived in the lusts of our flesh, doing the desires of the flesh and of the mind, and were by nature children of wrath, even as the rest (ὡς καὶ οἱ λοιποί): — but God (ὁ δὲ θεός), being rich in mercy (ἐλέει), for his great love wherewith he loved us, even when we were dead through our trespasses, made us alive together with Christ (by grace have you been saved) (σεσῳσμένοι)".

This passage exemplifies the various facets of mercy. The mercy of God is extended to man in his dire condition of spiritual death through his own trespasses and in his state of lust and rebellion. God's mercy pities our miserable condition and removes us from it. His mercy is the expression of the freeness and unconditionalness of his love. Because he is rich in mercy, God made us alive together with Christ and saved us by his grace. That which is explicit in this Ephesian passage is inherent in the word mercy and the Titus 3 context as it is used therein.

[53] Blass-Debrunner-Funk, section 284,3.

94

On the basis of his mercy, not our righteous works, God saved us. Particular attention should be paid to the fact that the verb is in the aorist tense (ἔσωσεν). Those who originally utilized the saying, as well as Paul in his utilization, were speaking of a once for all past action or event that had occurred in the life of Christians: he saved us (ἔσωσεν ἡμᾶς). The saying does not say that the appearance of God's love and kindness in Christ in the history of salvation saves, or is saving, or will save us, but that διὰ λουτροῦ κτλ, God has saved us. Although the verb looks back to and is based upon God's mercy, and particularly looks back to the when (ὅτε) of the manifestation (ἐπεφάνη) of God's love and grace in Christ, it is immediately conditioned in reference to us by the addition of the means, διὰ λουτροῦ. Thus our salvation may not only be spoken of as accomplished in Christ but also as applied in time and history in our own lives. We are saved through the means of (διά)[54] or when we have experienced the λουτρόν, the work of the Holy Spirit, poured out upon us richly (ἐξέχεεν ἐφ' ἡμᾶς). Not only does the qualification of διὰ λουτροῦ κτλ but also the specific reference to the pouring out of the Holy Spirit upon us (ἐφ' ἡμᾶς) point to the experience within the person of the Christian. That this is indeed the application of salvation accomplished in Christ is made more pointed by the words conjoined to the Holy Spirit: "through Jesus Christ our Savior" (διὰ Ἰησοῦ Χριστοῦ τοῦ σωτῆρος ἡμῶν). Thus because Jesus Christ is Savior (σωτῆρος) and particularly because he is our (ἡμῶν) Savior the Holy Spirit applies our salvation διὰ λουτροῦ.

The word λουτρόν here means "bath" or "washing"[55], not "laver"[56]. Although "bath" is acceptable as a translation just because it is ambiguous, the term "washing" is clearer in meaning and more accurate[57]. Salvation is wrought through this washing which cleanses the sinner of his sins. The compound verbal from (ἀπολούω) is used in a similar

---

[54] Blass-Debrunner-Funk, section 223,3.

[55] *Cf.* Arndt-Gingrich, Liddell and Scott, Moulton and Milligan, *s.v.* λουτρόν and A. Oepke, *TDNT*, IV, *s.v.* λούω, pp. 295-307. λουτρόν is found in the LXX only at Song of Solomon (Cant.) 4:2, 6:6, and Sirach 34:25, and in the N.T. only twice, at Eph. 5:26 and here in Titus 3:5. In Song of Solomon 4:2, 6:6 it is used of the washing of animals, and at Sirach 34:25 of purification after contact with the dead, and that figuratively of cleansing from sin by fasting. *Cf.* also J. A. Robinson, *St. Paul's Epistle to the Ephesians* (London: Macmillan, 2nd ed., 1928), *ad* 5:26.

[56] As Alford, Fairbairn and Fausset, also R.V. mg. Simpson shows that τὸ λουτρόν does not mean "laver" (as does the LXX term ὁ λουτήρ) and gives abundant evidence from throughout Greek literature *ad* Titus 3:5.

[57] Chosen by most modern English translators, *e.g.*, A.V., R.V., A.S.V., R.S.V., and by most modern English commentators, *e.g.*, Barrett, Guthrie, Hendriksen, Lock and Simpson.

context in 1 Cor. 6:9—11 as λουτρόν is used in Titus 3. The sinfulness, the defilement of the Christians is first sketched ("and such were some of you", verse 11 referring to the preceding verses). And then Paul says: "but you were washed" (ἀπελούσασθε). It is clear that the verb "washed" is here used of cleansing from sin[58]. Likewise, the only other N.T. occurrence of ἀπολούω (Acts 22:16) says: "be baptized, and wash away your sins (βάπτισαι καὶ ἀπόλουσαι τὰς ἁμαρτίας σου), calling on his name". And not only do these passages point to λουτρόν as meaning a cleansing or washing away of sins, but also the latter shows the strong tie with baptism[59]. Many commentators think that the only other occurrence of λουτρόν in the N.T., in Eph. 5:26, refers to baptism because of the specific qualification by the words "of water". The discussion of the fuller significance of λουτρόν must await the consideration of the larger context.

The question that next presses upon us is the relationship of the genitives that follow λουτροῦ: παλιγγενεσίας καὶ ἀνακαινώσεως πνεύματος ἁγίου. There is no doubt that παλιγγενεσίας is dependent upon λουτροῦ. The question comes to focus in the relationship of ἀνακαινώσεως to what precedes. Is it also dependent upon and a further definition of λουτροῦ?[60] Or is ἀνακαινώσεως dependent upon διά?[61] The question is not easily resolved in view of the fact that the givens can be taken plausibly in either construction. There are, however, indications that point at least in the direction of ἀνακαινώσεως as dependent upon λουτροῦ. The first is the fact that διά is not repeated before ἀνακαινώσεως. This is cited by Barrett and others as an indication that ἀνακαινώσεως is not dependent upon διά but upon λουτροῦ. Second, that ἀνακαινώσεως is dependent upon λουτροῦ is a proper understanding of the Greek language is underscored by the fact that the Greek exegetes of old have so understood this verse in that way[62]. And finally, one's decision rests upon the understanding of the words themselves and their inter-

---

[58] Note also the textual variant at Rev. 1:5 in the *textus receptus*: λούσαντι ἡμᾶς ἐκ τῶν ἁμαρτιῶν ἡμῶν ἐν τῷ αἵματι αὐτοῦ. The better attested reading is λύσαντι.

[59] *Cf.* also Heb. 10:22: "let us draw near with a true heart in fulness of faith, having our hearts sprinkled from an evil conscience, and having our body washed (λελουσμένοι) with pure water".

[60] The following commentators hold that ἀνακαινώσεως is dependent on λουτροῦ: Barrett, Bouma, Ellicott, Gealy, Hanson, Hendriksen, Huther, Kelly, Lock, Parry, Ridderbos, Spicq, Weiss, Wohlenberg.

[61] The following commentators hold that ἀνακαινώσεως is dependent on διά: Bengel, Bernard, Fairbairn, Fausset, Guthrie, Lenski, White, Wuest. Most of these commentators regard ἀνακαινώσεως as progressive sanctification.

[62] The Greek Fathers or old Greek exegetes are brought forth by Bernard and Ridderbos, among others. K. Staab, *Pauluskommentare aus der griechischen Kirche* (Münster, 1933), does not, unfortunately, cite any authorities for this passage.

relationships[63]. This is seen by the fact that those who consider ἀνακαινώσεως as a progressive sanctification take it as dependent upon διά and on the other hand by the fact that those who take ἀνακαινώσεως as the initial change in man see it as dependent upon λουτροῦ. And it is the latter understanding of ἀνακαινώσεως which seems to fit its usage in the context. And therefore these cumulative considerations lend their weight to be construction of ἀνακαινώσεως as dependent upon λουτροῦ.

Λουτροῦ is qualified first of all by παλιγγενεσίας[64]. This word is found only twice in the N.T., here in Titus 3:5 and in Mt. 19:28. Büchsel[65] states that "the word derives from πάλιν and γένεσις and thus means 'new genesis'". The meaning can be best rendered in English by the terms "rebirth" or "regeneration"[66]. At first it may seem strange for παλιγγενεσίας which here applies to individuals in this present life to be found elsewhere in the N.T. only at Mt. 19:28 where it refers to the future and end time, "in the regeneration (ἐν τῇ παλιγγενεσίᾳ) when the Son of man shall sit on the throne of his glory, you also shall sit upon twelve thrones, judging the twelve tribes of Israel". This is the regeneration, the transformation, the renewing of all things in the coming kingdom of God in the age to come[67]. What relationship can these two have? It is indeed one of the unusual aspects of this saying that must be examined later that παλιγγενεσίας is used in this way. However, the apparent dif-

---

[63] J. Ysebaert makes the significant point that "in the general language παλιγγενεσία in a non-technical sense repeatedly appeared connected by hendiadys with a noun which conveyed its meaning more precisely. For this reason alone we shall have to keep to the, for the rest, most current opinion that in Tit. 3.5 both nouns, παλιγγενεσία and ἀνακαίνωσις depend upon λουτρόν" (Greek Baptismal Terminology: Its Origins and Early Development, 1962), p. 134.

[64] Cf. Arndt-Gingrich, Moulton and ˙ Milligan, s.v. παλιγγενεσία and F. Büchsel, TDNT, I, pp. 686-689. For a very fruitful study see also J. Dey, Παλιγγενεσία. Ein Beitrag zur Klärung der religionsgeschichtlichen Bedeutung von Tit 3,5 (Neutestamentliche Abhandlungen, xvii. Band 5. Heft), (Münster i. W., 1937), who shows rather conclusively that the concept is not rooted in the Mystery religions. See finally the excursus by Dibelius-Conzelmann, ad loc., who with a clear insight comes to a similar judgment as that of Dey, even though he is always looking for parallels: "Zwischen der Wiedergeburtsvorstellung der Mysterien und dem Bedanken unserer Stelle besteht also in zwei Punkten ein Unterschied: Tit 3,5 weiss nichts von Ektase, sondern nur von dauernder Kraftwirkung eines neuen Lebens; die Wiedergeburt ist dementsprechend nicht nur dem einzelnen Mysten möglich; sie ist vielmehr das grundlegende Ereignis für alle Christen".

[65] F. Büchsel, TDNT, I, p. 686.

[66] So Arndt-Gingrich, s.v. Most modern English translations use "regeneration", e.g., R.V., A.S.V., R.S.V. and N.A.S.V. The N.E.B. utilizes "rebirth".

[67] F. Büchsel, TDNT, I, p. 688: "The parallel saying in Lk. 22:20 has ἐν τῇ βασιλείᾳ μου. In Mk. 10:30 and Lk. 18:30 the phrase ἐν τῷ αἰῶνι τῷ ἐρχομένῳ has the same meaning".

ferences are not as great as they may seem. In fact they refer to different aspects of the same great event, the παλιγγενεσία wrought by the Son of man, the Savior Jesus Christ. We see the lines of connection encompassing both the individual and the cosmic in Mt. 19:28 itself. The conversation between Jesus and his disciples concerns the entrance of individuals into the kingdom of God (Mt. 19:23ff.) and thus of their individual salvation (19:25). Sitting on thrones as judges is Jesus' way of promising to them future salvation, i.e., eternal life (19:29). And this individual entrance into the kingdom, this salvation and eternal life, finds its full consummation "in the regeneration". Thus in Mt. 19:28 the individual's salvation is seen in the scope of the history of salvation which is there denoted by παλιγγενεσία. Likewise in Titus 3:5 the παλιγγενεσία which there focuses more narrowly on individuals (ἡμᾶς) is seen in the scope of the first appearance of the Son of man, Jesus Christ the Savior, and has as its final perspective nothing else than the final παλιγγενεσία and its concommitant eternal life(ζωῆς αἰωνίου). Those who are saved by the washing of regeneration are "heirs (κληρονόμοι) according to the hope of eternal life" just as Jesus said the disciples "shall inherit (κληρονομήσει) eternal life" (Mt. 19:29). Thus παλιγγενεσία in Titus 3:5 refers to a "new birth", "a new beginning" which causes a man to be transformed here and now, just as the cosmos will be transformed in the future[68]. And the transformation or rebirth for the individual finds its full consummation in the inheritance of eternal life. The saying has used a word common in the Greek world, with little or no O.T. and Jewish rootage, although some usage[69], to express in that society in a term with which it was familiar the radical transformation accomplished in the salvation which Christians experienced and of which they spoke.

The concept of a new birth or rebirth is found in the N.T. using the related word γεννάω or its compound ἀναγεννάω. James is the one exception using the word ἀποκυέω. In the Johannine writings γεννάω is used with some qualification; "born anew" or "born from above" (γεννάω ἄνωθεν, John 3:3 and 7), "born by the Spirit" (John 3:5,6 and 8, γεννάω qualified by ἐκ πνεύματος and also once by ἐξ ὕδατος), "begotten of God" (γεννάω ἐκ τοῦ Θεοῦ, 1 John 3:9; 4:7; 5:1, 4, 18) or "begotten of him" (γεννάω ἐξ αὐτοῦ, 1 John 2:29; 5:1(?)). In 1 Peter 1:3, 23 we find "God ... begat us again" and "having been begotten again" (ἀναγεννάω). Finally in James 1:18 we read that "he brought us forth" (ἀποκυέω). Admittedly the concept in Titus 3:5 is the same as the one found in the passages above which use a form of γεννάω or its compound

---

[68] Paul in particular and the N.T. in general draw these relationships together. Cf., e.g., Paul's statement in 2 Cor. 5:17 that "any man in Christ is a new creature" (or "creation", καινὴ κτίσις), and that of him as of the total creation in that day of παλιγγενεσία it may be said, "the old things are passed away; behold, they are become new".

[69] Cf. F. Büchsel, TDNT, I, pp. 686 ff.

ἀναγεννάω. The question inevitably arises when one sees the connection between these concepts and usages why some form of γεννάω or ἀναγεννάω was not used here, particularly the latter, which it would seem could express *rebirth* and *regeneration*. The answer would seem to lie in the facts that a noun form of ἀναγεννάω is virtually lacking in the common vocabulary of the day[70], and when it does occur it refers to the regeneration of the world, and further that παλιγγενεσία was widely used and recognized and moreover expressed the thought in view[71]. Further, the noun form of γεννάω is not fully appropriate to express the concept because without a prefix or some qualification such as a prepositional phrase[72] it would not convey the thougt of a *rebirth* or a *new* birth. The question then arises why the term παλιγγενεσία is found here and not more widely in the N.T. A partial answer to this double sided question may be found in the setting and form of the discourses where the verbal form of γεννάω and ἀναγεννάω are found and where the noun παλιγγενεσία is found. In the Johannine writings and in 1 Peter the writers there want to lay stress on the action of God. Hence to emphasize God's action they use the more activistic verbal forms and the attendant qualifications which focus upon God[73]. Here in the saying the people of God are seeking to express their faith tersely and, in a sense, in a more objective "creedal" way. Note the dominant use of nouns

[70] Liddell and Scott give just one reference to the noun form of ἀναγεννάω, ἀναγέννησις, and that in Philo in respect of the κόσμου. F. Büchsel, *TDNT*, I, p. 673, says that ἀναγέννησις "was a current word" but cites only Philo with the statement "that Philo employs this for the Stoic doctrine of the regeneration of the world".

[71] Although it is true that παλιγγενεσία has a similar usage as the occurrence of ἀναγέννησις in Philo, *i.e.*, the regeneration of the world, it is also clear that its usage is much wider, its meanings more varied, including that which is comparable to the usage in Titus 3:5. "It seems quite early to have come into use outside the Stoic schools and to have become part of the heritage of the educated world, thus acquiring a more general sense", Büchsel, *TDNT*, I, p. 687. For a further substantiation of the hypothesis that is being presented in the main body of the text I am indebted to Professor Jay E. Adams of Westminster Theological Seminary who has brought to my attention, as a result of the presentation of the hypothesis to him for consideration, the usage in "A secret discourse of Hermes Trismegistus to his son Tat, concerning Rebirth". In this discourse Hermes uses (ἀνα)γεννάω consistently in verbal forms and just as consistently uses the noun παλιγγενεσία when he desires to speak of rebirth as a noun (*Hermetica*, Vol. I., edited by Walter Scott [Oxford: Clarendon Press, 1924], pp. 238-255, Libellus XIII). Although this writing is later in time than the N.T. it would still seem to reflect the common Greek usage.

[72] Wherever γεννάω is used in the N.T. to express the spiritual change that is wrought in a man it is qualified by some term (*e.g.*, ἄνωθεν, ἐκ πνεύματος, ἐκ τοῦ θεοῦ, ἐξ αὐτοῦ) to make abundantly clear that God has accomplished this change and that what is in view is not a natural birth but a spiritual birth.

[73] See note 72.

tied together with the pivotal verbs "appeared", "saved", "poured out", "justified" and "be made heirs". Hence in this new creedal situation the noun usage is more preferable than the more cumbersome and round about way via the verbal construction. Further, the qualifications pointing to God would be redundant here since the clause already refers to God as saving us through the washing of regeneration, and this is further amplified by the words "of the Holy Spirit". With παλιγγενεσία appearing as a qualification of the previous noun λουτρόν the concept is thereby objectified. In Titus 3 the concept expressed by παλιγγενεσία particularly focuses upon what is done in us more than upon how God accomplishes it, and it specifies more particularly what the λουτρόν is which we experience and through which we are saved. Therefore a noun which expresses what happens in the person is more apt than a verbal form which speaks more particularly of God's action[74]. This is not to say that the saying considered regeneration any less to be the direct and personal work of God in the life of the person. What was needed was a noun to express the fact that Christians are born again by God. Παλιγγενεσία was used as the currently available and most apt expression. In using that expression it is abundantly plain that God has saved us and not our works, and further that we were so corrupt that we must have a new beginning. When παλιγγενεσία qualifies λουτρόν it expresses the truth that an inner transformation has washed away our sins which were so evident and which evidenced themselves by appearing in our external actions.

Λουτροῦ is further specified by the words "and renewing" (καὶ ἀνακαινώσεως). Ἀνακαινώσεως occurs only here in Titus 3:5 and in Romans 12:2. And it is apparently "not quotable outside Christian literature"[75]. The verbal form to which it is most closely related, ἀνακαινόω, is found only in Paul and then in the passive (2 Cor. 4:16; Col. 3:10)[76]. (The other related verbal form, ἀνακαινίζω, is found only in Hebrews 6:6 in the N.T.)

As that which qualifies or defines λουτροῦ as that through which God

---

[74] Perhaps an analogy may be found in the modern church situation which will convey the thought expressed above. In preaching, in evangelism and in pastoral work one usually speaks of "being born again", and that by God, with the verb being used. In the more objective statement of creeds, confessions and the like, even liturgy, one is more apt to refer to the same truth under the rubric "regeneration", using the noun. May not this same tendency have been inherent in the situation of the early church?

[75] Arndt-Gingrich, s.v. ἀνακαίνωσις.

[76] 2 Cor. 4:16, "but though our outward man is decaying, yet our inward man is renewed (ἀνακαινοῦται) day by day". Col. 3:10, "and have put on the new man, that is being renewed (τὸν ἀνακαινούμενον) unto knowledge after the image of him that created him".

has saved us, it is evident that ἀνακαινώσεως in this context refers to the initial spiritual rebirth of man accomplished by the Holy Spirit (so the addition, πνεύματος ἁγίου). The Holy Spirit is the author of the renewal[77]. It is accomplished by God's Spirit, the *Holy* (ἁγίου) Spirit. Ἀνακαίνωσις may therefore be rendered best by the words "renewal" or "renewing"[78].

It must indeed be noticed that the verbal form ἀνακαινόω when it is used in the N.T. is used in the sense of the continual and progressive renewal. In 2 Cor. 4:16 this thought is evident: "yet our inward man is renewed day by day" (ἀνακαινοῦται ἡμέρᾳ καὶ ἡμέρᾳ). Likewise in Col. 3:10 we read of the "new man, that is being renewed (τὸν ἀνακαινούμενον) unto knowledge after the image of him that created him"[79]. And Romans 12:2 in its exhortation to Christians, "be transformed by the renewing (ἀνακαινώσει) of your minds", would seem to emphasize the continual work of God's Spirit. This thought of the continual process is not shut out of ἀνακαίνωσις in Titus 3, but is included in the basic initial action of God's Spirit who continues His work. The same thought of the once for all transformation is in view in Col. 3:10. It is because "we have put off the old man with his doings and have put on the new man" that "that new man is being renewed". The continual renewing is but a continuation of the beginning of renewal. The change is so decisive that the word created is used. The new man which is renewed is created. And not only created but created in God's image. There is a completely new beginning, a new creation. This is the renewal. Two aspects may be ascertained in the ἀνακαινόω-ἀνακαίνωσις family. The first is that the transformation is a change from the old to the new, both temporally and qualitatively. We have emphasized already the decisive break. Now note the moral aspect. Col. 3:9 speaks of putting off the old man "with his doings" which are more fully described in verse 8 in terms of sins which are similar to Titus 3:3. Likewise in Romans 12:2, the other use of ἀνακαίνωσις in the N.T., the process is described in the exhortation "be not fashioned according to this world: but be transformed by the renewing of your mind". Also in Titus 3:5 the washing of ἀνακαινώσεως is that which makes a radical once for all change, a change which is also moral, and which has its continuing effect in the life of the one renewed and being renewed by the Holy Spirit. Secondly, the renewal is definitely an inner action with a noetic emphasis as well as a moral one.

---

[77] The genitive of πνεύματος ἁγίου is a subjective genitive. Πνεύματος ἁγίου probably is related syntactically only to ἀνακαινώσεως, although it may be said that the Holy Spirit also accomplishes the παλιγγενεσίας.

[78] Arndt-Gingrich, J. Behm, *TDNT*, III, *s.v.* ἀνακαίνωσις, likewise the English translations of the *A.S.V.*, *R.S.V.* and *N.A.S.V.*

[79] Compare the parallel in Eph. 4:23, "and that you be renewed (ἀνανεοῦσθαι) in the spirit of your mind".

Or rather, the noetic aspect in the N.T. is always also religious and moral. This aspect can be seen in 2 Cor. 4:16 ("our inward man") and most clearly in Col. 3:10 ("renewed unto knowledge [εἰς ἐπίγνωσιν] after the image of him that created him")[80]. Similarly in Romans 12:2 the stress on the inward and noetic ("be transformed by the renewing of your mind, so that you may prove what is the good and acceptable and perfect will of God") is seen as the only way not to be fashioned according to this world and the only way positively to give our bodies as a living and holy sacrifice.

In fine, ἀνακαίνωσις in Titus 3:5, in the light of N.T. usage, bespeaks the completely new transformation which the Holy Spirit effects in our life. It is a creative or recreative act that makes one a new man, and puts off his old man and its evil doings, by changing his inner being into the image of Christ. This renewal continues in his life day by day and enables him to ascertain aright God's will so that he is not fashioned according to this world but presents his body a living sacrifice unto God.

The saying places alongside of παλιγγενεσία the complementary concept ἀνακαίνωσις. In so doing it not only enriches the statement but also provides for the direct reference to the Holy Spirit which qualifies ἀνακαινώσεως[81].

The saying next unfolds with the words "which he poured out upon us richly, through Jesus Christ our Savior" (οὗ ἐξέχεεν ἐφ᾽ ἡμᾶς πλουσίως διὰ Ἰησοῦ Χριστοῦ τοῦ σωτῆρος ἡμῶν). "Which" (οὗ) refers undoubtedly to its nearest antecedent "the Holy Spirit" (πνεύματος ἁγίου), not back to λουτροῦ. This is further substantiated by the verb "poured out" (ἐξέχεεν). It is true that the verb is used of liquids and could be used in reference to the "washing" (λουτρόν). But its use with the Spirit in Acts (2:17,18,33, in dependence upon Joel 2:28 ff.) would seem definitely to establish its usage with the Holy Spirit. The adverb "richly" (πλουσίως) makes the application to the Holy Spirit rather than the washing seem almost beyond doubt. To speak of the washing poured out richly makes far less sense than to speak of the Holy Spirit poured out richly. Finally, the fact that that which is poured forth is "through Jesus Christ our Savior" again points to the Holy Spirit. The Scriptures reflect the understanding of the early church that it is Christ who is the one who pours forth the Holy Spirit. Compare, e.g., Acts 2:33: "Being therefore by the right hand of God exalted, and

---

[80] Note the parallel in Eph. 4:23: "renewed in the spirit of your mind" (τῷ πνεύματι τοῦ νοὸς ὑμῶν). The interrelation of righteousness, holiness and truth is seen clearly in Eph. 4:23 where Paul speaks of the new man created "in righteousness and holiness of the truth".

[81] See note 77.

having received of the Father the promise of the Holy Spirit, he (Jesus) has poured forth (ἐξέχεεν) this, which you see and hear".

The question must now be asked as to what occasion this pouring out of the Spirit refers. There are some commentators who argue that the reference in view is Pentecost[82]. And it is argued that the use of the same verb here and in Acts 2 leads to that conclusion. But this is not necessarily the case at all.

The O.T. prophets speak of the inner renewal by the Spirit and especially of a promise for God's people in the Messianic age (Joel 2:28 f.; with which compare Ezekiel 36:26 f.; 39:29; Isaiah 44:3 ff.; Zechariah 12:10)[83]. The passage in which the concept and word "poured out" is most evident is Joel 2:28 ff. (LXX 3:1 ff.). It is this passage that is cited by Peter in Acts 2:16 as being fulfilled at Pentecost. But we must not assume that the promise was only fulfilled at Pentecost and is not also being fulfilled in rich outpouring upon Christians in an individual way since then. It may be readily admitted that the linguistic background for the phrase to pour out the Spirit is found in Joel 2:28 ff. and the Acts-Pentecost experience. But the Acts account can show that the early church understood and applied the Joel passage and its language to the occasion of the giving of the Spirit in this eschatological and messianic age with all its soteriological accomplishments (*cf.* Acts 2:21 = Joel 2:32). We see Paul using the same verb[84] "poured out" (ἐκκέχυται) in Romans 5:5: "... the love of God has been shed abroad (poured out) in our hearts through the Holy Spirit which was given unto us". Here the pouring out of God's love in our hearts is a result of Christ's redeeming work (*cf.* Rom. 5:1 & 6) through the Holy Spirit which has been given particularly to us Christians as individuals. The reference to our hearts (ἐν ταῖς καρδίαις ἡμῶν) and to the Spirit as given unto us (πνεύματος ἁγίου τοῦ δοθέντος ἡμῖν) makes this direct and personal aspect clearly evident.

The same direct and personal aspect is evident concerning the pouring out of the Holy Spirit in Titus 3:5 ff. It is specified as personal; God pours the Holy Spirit upon us (ἐφ' ἡμᾶς). It is through that particular

---

[82]   *E.g.*, Bouma, Hendriksen, Robertson.

[83]   J. Behm, *TDNT*, II, s.v. ἐκχέω, p. 468 f.

[84]   Moulton and Geden's *Concordance* lists ἐκχέω and ἐκχύννομαι separately and gives two separate lists for occurrences as if they were two entirely different words. However, once one goes to the lexicons and grammars, one finds that they all take the two as variant forms of the one verb, *i.e.*, that ἐκχύν(ν)ω is a form of ἐκχέω (see Arndt-Gingrich, Thayer, Liddell & Scott). They treat the various occurrences in the N.T. as one word and indicate as much in their introductory comments. And they too bring together Rom. 5:5 and Titus 3:6. Blass-Debrunner-Funk deals with the variant forms as one stem or word in sections 73 and 101.

pouring out (ἐξέχεεν, past action, aorist)[85] of the Spirit that we are saved. And the Spirit is poured out upon those who are thus brought to know and regard Jesus Christ as "our Savior" (τοῦ σωτῆρος ἡμῶν). None of these specific elements may be left out of consideration. Therefore using the language of Joel, which may have become known and used in the early church in connection with the gift of the Holy Spirit and salvation, the saying speaks of the abundant outpouring of the Holy Spirit which they had experienced as individuals.

The Holy Spirit has been poured out upon us richly "through Jesus Christ our Savior" (διὰ 'Ιησοῦ Χριστοῦ τοῦ σωτῆρος ἡμῶν). The giver of the Holy Spirit, the one who pours out the Holy Spirit, i.e., the subject of the verb ἐξέχεεν, is God the Father, but he pours out the Holy Spirit διὰ Jesus Christ. The Holy Spirit is given through Jesus Christ because he is the Savior (τοῦ σωτῆρος). Through this one word, σωτήρ, in relation to Jesus Christ, the entirety of his life, death and resurrection is brought into the heart of the saying. That Jesus Christ is the one who gives the Holy Spirit as part of his prerogative as the exalted Lord and Savior is a uniform teaching of Scripture. Acts 2:33 enunciates this so clearly, "Being therefore by the right hand of God exalted, and having received of the Father the promise of the Holy Spirit, he has poured forth this ..." (cf. also Lk. 24:49, "And behold, I send forth the promise of my Father upon you")[86].

The saying confesses and acknowledges that this Jesus Christ is our (ἡμῶν) Savior[87]. There is connoted thereby the intimate personal relationship which is elsewhere denoted by faith in Christ or union with Christ.

The saying moves on to its conclusion with the words, "that, being justified by his grace, we might be made heirs according to the hope of eternal life" (verse 7, ἵνα δικαιωθέντες τῇ ἐκείνου χάριτι κληρονόμοι γενηθῶμεν κατ' ἐλπίδα ζωῆς αἰωνίου). This part of the saying focuses on our future hope and privilege ("heirs according to the hope of eternal life"), but it points to this hope and privilege through the present position effected by "being justified by his grace".

We must ask immediately about the connection set forth in the word "that" (ἵνα). The balance and thrust of the whole sentence would seem to demand that the ἵνα refer back particularly to ἔσωσεν, although it

---

[85] The verb refers to a past action which they had experienced and which had accomplished their salvation, viz., "through the washing of regeneration and renewing of the Holy Spirit".

[86] See also the sayings in John's Gospel such as John 15:26; 16:7.

[87] Note that this is a stress made already at the beginning of the saying and thus a pervasive note in the saying. In verse 4 God is described as "our Savior" (τοῦ σωτῆρος ἡμῶν Θεοῦ).

104

must also be acknowledged that it takes into its purview the words intervening. The purpose[88] of God's saving us, which includes the pouring out of the Holy Spirit through Jesus Christ our Savior, is to make us heirs, being justified by his grace.

"Justified" (δικαιωθέντες) is qualified by the phrase, "by his grace" (τῇ ἐκείνου χάριτι). The grace in view here is God's favor to us in Christ. It should not be seen as an either/or as many commentators take it, *viz.*, either the grace of God the Father or of Christ. One is cautioned about such sharp disjunctions in view of the combination expressed so clearly in 2 Tim. 1:9: God "saved us ... not according to our works, but according to his own purpose and grace (χάριν), which was given us in Christ Jesus". The only other occurrence of the phrase[89] "justified (freely) by his grace" (δικαιούμενοι δωρεὰν τῇ αὐτοῦ χάριτι, Rom. 3:24) also makes it clear that the grace is God's grace in or through Christ Jesus by adding the words, "through the redemption that is in Christ Jesus". In Titus 3:7 for the first time ἐκεῖνος is used to make that combined point. It is that particular grace of his, *i.e.*, God's favor to us throught Jesus Christ our Savior. Justified is virtually a technical term in Paul and it is used in a Pauline sense here. In reference to man, the full-orbed sense of the concept declares that the person's sins are forgiven and that he is considered innocent and righteous in God's sight[90]. It is thus a forensic term and as such it is used in the saying. The declaration is one that is made during the lifetime of the one who is justified and it is not just some future action, although as can be seen from this passage it has a future reference. The judicial nature of the action is underscored by the fact that it is done τῇ ἐκείνου χάριτι. And the present and forensic character is further connoted by the fact that it causes the one so justified to be made an heir. However, the inner work of the Holy Spirit, the washing of regeneration and renewal, should not be thereby shut out. Although the justification is based on God's grace, not on the new inner status, nevertheless, the one who is justified by God's grace is also transformed by his Spirit. These aspects are concomitant and must not be set in any opposition to one another. The sinner is both renewed by God's Spirit and declared to be righteous by his grace in Christ. God saves sinners by an inner transformation and also by a decisive declaration. The one who is declared righteous is always also made new by God. That these elements are drawn close together is evident from Paul's statement in 1 Cor. 6:11: "... But you were washed,

---

88 Robertson, *ad loc.*, also Blass-Debrunner-Funk, section 369.

89 Even this occurrence is different in some respects from the phrase in Titus 3:7, *e.g.*, the addition of δωρεάν, and αὐτοῦ instead of ἐκείνου.

90 Justification is treated extensively by J. Murray, *The Epistle to the Romans* (*N.I.C.N.T.*; Grand Rapids: Eerdmans, 1959), Vol. I, pp. 336-362, Appendix A. Titus 3:5-7 is discussed on page 350.

but you were sanctified, but you were justified in the name of the Lord Jesus Christ, and in the Spirit of our God" (ἀλλὰ ἀπελούσασθε, ἀλλὰ ἡγιάσθητε, ἀλλὰ ἐδικαιώθητε ἐν τῷ ὀνόματι τοῦ κυρίου Ἰησοῦ Χριστοῦ καὶ ἐν τῷ πνεύματι τοῦ θεοῦ ἡμῶν).

The justification, and indeed the salvation, is not just for here and now, but has as its purpose that "we might be made heirs according to the hope of eternal life" (κληρονόμοι γενηθῶμεν κατ' ἐλπίδα ζωῆς αἰωνίου). The word κληρονόμος is used 15 times in the N.T.[91] In the synoptic gospels it is used once each in a parallel account to designate the heir of the husbandman in Jesus' parable (Mt. 21:38; Mk. 12:7; Lk. 20:14). Also in Hebrew 1:2 the heir is God's Son, Jesus Christ. Elsewhere in the N.T. the heirs are those redeemed[92]. Because of our standing before God through justification and our renewal by his Holy Spirit we have been made those who will inherit his promise and his provision. That of which we are heirs is eternal life (ζωῆς αἰωνίου). And our heirdom is one "according to hope" (κατ' ἐλπίδα). A problem arises as to the connection of ζωῆς αἰωνίου. Does it qualify κληρονόμοι or ἐλπίδα? The decision is not at all simple. On the former view the inheritance of the heirs is eternal life and this heirdom is qualified almost parenthetically by hope. They are heirs of eternal life not by sight but by hope. On the latter view the word heirs stands alone almost absolutely, but then that position is immediately qualified by saying that they are heirs according to the hope of eternal life. This latter view is favored by some because of the proximity of ἐλπίδα and ζωῆς αἰωνίου and also by the fact that κληρονόμοι is removed from ζωῆς αἰωνίου by the intervention not only of κατ' ἐλπίδα but also of γενηθῶμεν. The choice is difficult to decide and the sense is not materially changed by either view. For on either view the goal of the heirs is eternal life, and that goal and their position of heirs expecting it is always in the attitude of hope[93]. The fact that hope is characteristic of the eschatological perspective of Christians is seen in Titus 2:13 ("looking for the blessed hope,

[91] Mt. 21:38; Mk. 12:7; Lk. 20:14; Rom. 4:13,14; 8:17(bis); Gal. 3:20; 4:1,7; Titus 3:7; Heb. 1:2; 6:17; 11:7; James 2:5.

[92] There seem to be two strong and not mutually exclusive strands in the N.T. that give the background of the word and concept. The one is the promise of inheritance and of heirs to Abraham and his great significance in the history of salvation and in the N.T. economy (cf., e.g., Rom. 4:13,14; Heb. 6:17). The other is the wider and more common family usage with its correlation of sonship (which the believer has in Christ) and of being an heir. This latter usage is also tied in with the work of the Holy Spirit (cf., e.g., Rom. 8:17). Both elements are tied together in Gal. 3:29 and also in a lesser degree in Gal. 4:1 and 7. Hebrews 11:7 (Noah) and James 2:5 do not appear to fall directly into either pattern.

[93] See R. Bultmann, *TDNT*, II, *s.v.* ἐλπίς, especially p. 531 f.

τὴν μακαρίαν ἐλπίδα, and appearing of the glory of the great God and our Savior Jesus Christ"). The note of hope is connected with that of being heirs in Rom. 8:16,17,24,25. This hope does not make anything less real or sure, but says that it is not seen but looked for (Rom. 8:24). Hope is not an unrealistic dream but it is marked by patient and expectant waiting on God and the inheritance (Rom. 8:25). Hope is the manward response to the Godward promise of the inheritance. Hope answers to the promise of God, for we are heirs according to God's promise (Gal. 3:29; see also Heb. 6:17; James 2:5). Hope, trustful expectation, is the earnest anticipation of God's promise·of eternal life.

The author of the Pastorals draws attention to the fact that this is a saying and gives the attendant emphasis to it by the formula of verse 8, "Faithful is the saying" (Πιστὸς ὁ λόγος). Rather than adding the addition used elsewhere, "and worthy of all acceptance", he adds his own words: "and concerning these things I desire that you affirm confidently, to the end that they may be careful to maintain good works".

The first reason for this variation is the desire of Paul to have the entire preceding account "affirmed confidently", i.e., verses 1-8, and not just the saying (verses 4-8) which is quoted to undergird the ethics of verses 1 and 2. The phrase "these things" (τούτων) refers to the entirety of the preceding pericope. In the first part of verse 8 with the words "Faithful is the saying" he points with emphasis to the saying as such. But then in the latter part of verse 8 he exhorts Titus to insist on the ethical response already demanded in verses 1 and 2 substantiated by the truth of the saying.

That the foregoing interpretation is correct is validated by the remaining words of verse 8: "to the end that they who have believed God may be careful to maintain good works" (ἵνα φροντίζωσιν καλῶν ἔργων προΐστασθαι οἱ πεπιστευκότες θεῷ). The point of Titus' insisting on these things ("and concerning these things I desire that you affirm confidently") is that (ἵνα) the Christians "may be careful to maintain good works". The apparent thrust of this entire second half of verse 8 is on the ethical realm, on "good works".

A second reason for this extended variation would seem to be the apparent desire of Paul to lay stress on man's response of faith: "they who have believed God" (οἱ πεπιστευκότες θεῷ). This response is not mentioned in the saying, although implied, and Paul in characteristic manner is determined to set it forth explicitly. The enlarged statement of emphasis by its enlargement carries with it those two distinctives of Pauline theology which were absent from the saying itself, i.e., faith in God and the resultant good works.

What is the origin of the saying? When one analyses the saying from the point of view of vocabulary one is struck by the fact that almost all of it is used by Paul and may well be called Pauline (χρηστότης[94], ἐπιφαίνω[95], σωτήρ[96], ἔργον[97], δικαιοσύνη[98], ἔλεος[99], σώζω[100], λουτρόν[101], ἀνακαινώσις[102], πνεῦμα ἅγιον[103], πλουσίως[104], δικαιόω[105], χάρις[106], κληρονόμος[107], ἐλπις[108], ζωὴ αἰώνιος[109]). Of course many of these words are not exclusively Pauline. However, it needs to be noticed that even in the use of some of these words there is that which appears less than Pauline. The "works" of men are never characterized by "righteousness". Ἀνακαίνωσις in its only other occurrence in the N.T. and in Paul (Rom. 12:2) seems to have a somewhat different emphasis. Added to this is the occurrence of several words that are not known in Paul's other letters (φιλανθρωπία and παλιγγενεσίας), and the fact of the

[94] Χρηστότης occurs only in Paul in the N.T. and that 10 times. For the statistics in this note and those immediately following I am indebted to R. Morgenthaler, *Statistik des neutestamentlichen Wortschatzes* (Zürich: Gotthelf, 1958) and to Moulton and Geden, *Concordance to the Greek Testament* (Edinburgh: T. & T. Clark, 3rd ed. 1926, reprinted 1957).

[95] Four times in the N.T. (Lk. 1:79; Acts 27:20; Titus 2:11; 3:4). The noun form ἐπιφάνεια occurs 6 times in the N.T. and all are in Paul (see note 39).

[96] Twenty times in the N.T. (2 in Lk., 1 in Jn., 2 in Acts, 12 in Paul of which 10 are in the Pastorals, 5 in 2 Peter, 1 in the Johannine letters, 1 in Jude). In Paul in reference to God the Father only in the Pastorals (also 1 in Lk. and the 1 in Jude). The occurrences in 1 Tim. all refer to God the Father, but the 1 in 2 Tim. to Jesus. In Titus itself there seems to be a pattern of referring first to God the Father and then to Jesus Christ (Titus 1:3 God, 1:4 Jesus; 2:10 God, 2:13 Jesus; 3:4 God, 3:6 Jesus).

[97] Of the 169 times in the N.T. 68 times in Paul. See also note 48.

[98] Fifty seven times in Paul out of 91 in the N.T. But δικαιοσύνη is never used by Paul or any other N.T. writer to characterize man's works. For ἐν δικαιοσύνη see note 50.

[99] Although not as typically Pauline as one might expect, it is used 10 times by Paul out of 27 times in the N.T. See note 16.

[100] Out of 106 times in the N.T. it is found 29 times in Paul.

[101] Two times only in the N.T. and both in Paul (Eph. 5:26 and Titus 3:5).

[102] Twice only in the N.T. and both in Paul (Rom. 12:2 and Titus 3:5). The verb form ἀνακαινόω is also only twice in the N.T. and again only in Paul (2 Cor. 4:16; Col. 3:10).

[103] See Moulton and Geden *s.v.* ἅγιος.

[104] Four times in the N.T. and 3 of these in Paul (Col. 3:16; 1 Tim. 6:17; Titus 3:6; also 2 Peter 1:11).

[105] Twenty seven times in Paul out of 39 times in the N.T.

[106] Out of 155 occurrences in the N.T. 100 are found in Paul.

[107] The N.T. totals 15 occurrences and of these 8 belong to Paul. See previously in the text for the study of this word.

[108] Of the 53 times in the N.T. Paul accounts for 36.

[109] See the Moulton and Geden *Concordance*: 43 times in N.T., 9 in Paul.

virtual non-existence of ἐκχέω. In addition, attention must be drawn to the omission of the Pauline reference to faith in this summary of Christian soteriology. The evidence of many words which although Pauline are not exclusively Pauline, of several "Pauline" words or combinations thereof which are used differently than they are elsewhere in Paul, of some words not found at all in Paul, and of the absence of the Pauline concept of faith (added after the saying) combine to question the direct Pauline authorship of the saying itself. But although this evidence would appear to point to a saying rather than to something Paul himself had written in the course of his letter, it is less than adequate to determine the influences of any other known N.T. author. Παλιγγενεσίας is found elsewhere only in Matthew 19:28 but then with a somewhat different perspective. The concept itself is expressed with some frequency in the Johannine writings (and in 1 Peter) but then not with this word but rather with the verbal form of γεννάω and ἀναγεννάω. The only other N.T. writer that seems to share several terms is Luke with φιλανθρωπία (Acts 28:2), ἐπιφαινέω (Lk. 1:79; Acts 27:20), ἐκχέω (Acts 2:17, 18, 33) and ἔλεος (6 times in Luke). But this similarity is not impressive when examined more closely. Both φιλανθρωπία and ἐπιφαινέω, are used in somewhat different ways. Ἐκχέω seems only to reflect a common dependence on Joel. And ἔλεος is restricted in Luke to virtually one place (Luke 1:50-78, the Magnificat of Mary and the Benedictus of Zacharias, with one exception, Lk. 10:37). Hence the latter three words may possibly be explained by a common dependence on the O.T. or utilization of the language of the LXX O.T. Although Titus 3:4-7 has enough elements to disclose its non-Pauline origin and to enable one to recognize that it is a saying, on the other hand those elements are insufficient to ascertain any particular influence of any other N.T. author. Because of the presence of certain Pauline elements, the saying would seem to have arisen in an area influenced by Paul. And as indicated much earlier in this study, certain elements may have been added or inserted by Paul (e.g., verse 4) in his incorporation of this saying in the position it now stands in his letter.

There remains also one other fruitful field of inquiry which may yet open up the origin of the saying. And that is the focus on "washing" (λουτρόν) and other similar aspects. In what setting would there be a tendency to utilize the concept of washing? At baptism, as a considerable number of commentators have pointed out. This hypothesis is strengthened by several other considerations. The first is the concomitant focus on the Holy Spirit. In the Book of Acts, but also elsewhere in the N.T., baptism and the gift of the Holy Spirit are related. Second, the saying lays particular stress on the initial inner change, ("the washing of regeneration and renewal of the Holy Spirit") which is appropriate at the time of the reception of the initial rite of Christianity which signifies such an inner change. Third, the saying is a terse creedal/

liturgical statement that would be appropriate at Christian baptism[110]. This is exemplified in its Trinitarian elements (God, the Holy Spirit, Jesus Christ) which is fitting at the time and occasion when one is baptized into the name of the Trinity (*cf.* Mt. 28:19). Further, its fitness for a baptismal situation is reflected by the fact that the saying does not deviate from its stress on God's work within the Christian by elaborating on the work of Christ or the response of the believer.

The corporate or public nature of the utilization of the saying can be seen in the use of the plural pronouns ("we", "us", in each of the verses 5-7). The setting is not one in which a single believer is involved but rather where the believers together make this affirmation.

Some have suggested a "hymn" or a direct expression of praise. Against this is the indirect, rather than the direct, reference to God. God is referred to in the third person ("he" saved us, "he" poured out the Holy Spirit) rather than in the direct second person ("you"). This factor would point in the direction of a creedal or confessional usage at baptism rather than to usage as a "hymn". Perhaps it was the affirmation spoken by those who were receiving baptism, or perhaps it was spoken by them and the congregation together.

This probable *Sitz im Leben* helps to unfold the meaning of the phrase "he saved us, through the washing of regeneration and renewing of the Holy Spirit" (ἔσωσεν ἡμᾶς διὰ λουτροῦ παλιγγενεσίας καὶ ἀνακαινώσεως πνεύματος ἁγίου). We have noted earlier that λουτρόν can be best explained as a reference to baptism. Now we need to note however with equal force that the saying has self-consciously used "washing" (λουτρόν) and not "baptism" (βάπτισμα). There is no doubt

---

[110] For the question of *vestigia* of baptismal liturgy elsewhere in the N.T. and especially in 1 Peter see the following: W. Bornemann, "Der I Pet. – eine Taufrede des Silvanus?", *Z.N.W.* 19 (1919-20) pp. 143 ff.; A. M. Hunter, *Paul and his Predecessors* (1940), pp. 44 ff., (1961 ed., pp. 38 ff.); P. Carrington, *The Primitive Christian Catechism* (1940), esp. pp. 12 ff.; E. G. Selwyn, *The First Epistle of St. Peter* (1947), esp. pp. 369 ff.; R. Bultmann, "Bekenntnis- und Liedfragmente im I Pet.", *Coniectanea Neotestamentica XI in honorem A. Fridrichsen* (1947), pp. 1 ff.; O. Cullmann, *Baptism in the New Testament* (1950), esp. the appendix; C. F. D. Moule, "The Nature and Purpose of I Peter", *N.T.S.* 3 (1956-57), pp. 1 ff., and *Worship in the New Testament* (1961), esp. p. 69, and *The Birth of the New Testament* (1962), esp. pp. 25 ff.; R. P. Martin, "The Composition of I Peter in Recent Study", *Vox Evangelica* (1962), pp. 29-42; "Aspects of Worship in the New Testament Church", *Vox Evangelica* II (1963), pp. 6-32, and "A Footnote to Pliny's Account of Christian Worship", *V.E.* III (1964), pp. 51-57, and also *Worship in the Early Church* (1964), esp. chapters 4 & 5. M.-E. Boismard in his article "Une liturgie baptismale dans la Prima Petri", *Revue Biblique* 63 (1956), pp. 182 ff., says that parallel themes and terms are found in 1 Peter 1:3-5 and Titus 3:5-7 and that these similarities may be due to dependence upon a common, written source: a baptismal hymn (esp. p. 186).

that βάπτισμα was well-known and could have been utilized. But the Christian community chose rather to use a term that could point to both the external symbol and the inner spiritual reality rather than "baptism" which would seem to point only to the external rite. This perspective is strengthened by attention to the form of the verb "saved" (ἔσωσεν), as well as by the fact that the related verb "poured out" (ἐξέχεεν) is in the same past tense. In the saying the Christians speak of the fact that they have been saved, in the past tense, not of the fact that they are being saved, using the present tense. Hence in the baptismal setting they confess that God has already saved them through the radical inner washing wrought by the Holy Spirit, a washing that may be spoken of as regeneration and renewal. And they do so at the time when they receive that which signifies that washing, even baptism. They are not then speaking of the sacrament as saving them or being the means of salvation but rather of a past action wrought by the inner work of the Holy Spirit which baptism symbolizes and represents. In this sacramental setting they thus utilize, similar to the usage of the N.T. elsewhere[111], the forceful and picturesque sacramental language which speaks of the reality of the work of the Holy Spirit under a designation which may also depict the sacrament[112].

[111]   Rom. 6:1 ff.; Col. 2:11 f.; 1 Peter 3:18 ff., esp. verses 20 and 21.
[112]   Compare the good Biblical-theological insight of *The Westminster Confession of Faith*, Chapter XXVII, Section II: "There is in every sacrament a spiritual relation, or sacramental union, between the sign and the thing signified; whence it comes to pass, that the names and effects of the one are attributed to the other".

CHAPTER VI

2 TIMOTHY 2:11 AND ITS SAYING

Does the formula "Faithful is the saying" of 2 Timothy 2:11 refer to that which precedes or to that which follows? Some commentators refer the reference to something in the preceding verses[1]. Most of these seem also to take the general viewpoint that πιστὸς ὁ λόγος does not refer to a saying as such[2]. But even of these who think that πιστὸς ὁ λογος refers to that which precedes it, a goodly number acknowledge that verses 11ff. are a "saying"[3], although not all[4]. In addition to the general argument that πιστὸς ὁ λόγος does not refer to a saying, others maintain that the formula always refers to a statement about salvation and thus point to the soteriological references in that which precedes the formula[5]. But the evidence of 1 Timothy 3:1 would seem to have removed this latter principle as an absolute and infallible criterion. The formula in 1 Timothy 3:1 refers to that which follows which does not have to do with salvation.

Among the verses chosen by those that think the formula refers to that which precedes are verse 8[6] or verse 10[7], although White says the entirety of verses 4—11. There is, as can be seen by this indication, by no means unanimity among those who find the reference in that which precedes the formula. Furthermore, a reference to verse 8 would have the difficulty of separating the formula from that to which it refers, unexampled at least in the other occurrences of the formula and thus questionable. One may ask also how the reader was to know that the formula in verse 11 referred back over verses 10 and 9 to verse 8 when verse 8 is not particularly unique in the setting.

Perhaps the most forceful objection that is offered by those who think

---

[1] Ellicott, Fausset, Holtz, Ridderbos, Schlatter, von Soden, Weiss, White.
[2] Ridderbos is an outstanding recent example.
[3] *E.g.*, Fausset, Holtz, Ridderbos (perhaps), von Soden. Lock is not sure whether the formula refers to that which precedes or follows, but is sure that verses 11-13 are a hymn.
[4] White for example.
[5] Schlatter for example.
[6] Weiss (and also verse 9). Ridderbos says either verse 8 or 10.
[7] Fausset. See also the preceding note.

112

the λόγος is in that which precedes to finding it in that which follows is the word "for" (γάρ)[8] which is found between the formula and the beginning of that which most recognize as same sort of saying. The argument states that this "for" is out of place if the formula refers to verses 11ff. It is explained then as the bridge which connects verses 11ff. to the preceding as a further demonstration that that which precedes verse 11 is indeed a "faithful saying". Thus, to paraphrase, one may say that verse 10, for example, is a faithful saying "for" and then verses 11 ff.

The proponents of verses 11 ff. as that to which the formula refers[9] give the following answers to the problematics of the γάρ. Some[10] take γάρ as meaning "namely", and thus as emphasizing that which follows in the saying. Most[11] take the γάρ as referring to something which preceded in the original hymn and that verses 11 ff. are only a fragment of that hymn. It is this latter understanding of γάρ which seems by far to be preferable. The former suggestion is somewhat unnatural and forced and not in accord with the usual usage of γάρ. The latter fits in place when one recognizes that the verses 11 ff. are a fragment of a "hymn" and did refer to something which preceded in its original form[12]. The recurring συν- in the first two and fourth verbs (συναπεθάνομεν, συζήσομεν, συμβασιλεύσομεν) are evidence for some preceding antecedent, that is, some reference to Jesus Christ. The saying of verses 11 ff. as it is used in its present context gives evidence for the statements in verses 10 and preceding. It is likely that these verses (11 ff.) provided a similar concluding statement in a fuller context in their original setting. The "for" (γάρ) does not present an insurmountable obstacle to "faithful is the saying" referring to verses 11 ff. Rather the γάρ bespeaks the fact that verses 11 ff. were part of some faithful saying. And may not Paul have left the γάρ in the saying to provide, in part, a transition from verse 10 to this saying? Are verses 11 ff., or at least parts thereof, not cited to give the undergirding of what precedes? The γάρ would, even after the interposition of the formula πιστὸς ὁ λόγος,

---

[8] So Ellicott and Weiss, as is so with most protagonists against referring the formula to verses 11 ff. and who favor some part of the preceding.

[9] Those who indicate verses 11 ff. either in entirety or in part as that to which the formula refers are as follows: Alford, Barrett, Bernard, Bouma, Dibelius-Conzelmann, Easton, Falconer, Gealy, Guthrie, Hanson, Hendriksen, Holtzmann, Huther, Jeremias, Jones, Kelly, Kent, De Kruijf, Lenski, van Oosterzee, Robertson, Scott, Simpson, Smelik, Spicq, Wohlenberg.

[10] Huther, Lenski, van Oosterzee, Wohlenberg.

[11] Bernard, Bouma, Easton, Gealy, Guthrie, Hendriksen, Kelly, Scott.

[12] We shall consider at a later and more appropriate point in this study the idea proposed by Spicq and others that Paul paraphrases the first part of the hymn in verses 8-10 and intermingles his own thought and words. On such a view the words about Jesus Christ in verse 8 could have been part of the original hymn and the γάρ could have referred to this.

serve to make that transition and provide that link. The occurrence of γάρ does not rule out verses 11 ff. as the saying.

Further consideration, however, must be given to other arguments pro and con. Against referring the πιστὸς ὁ λόγος to that which precedes is the strongly personal note that dominates verses 8—10. Every verse has some pronominal reference to Paul (verse 8, *"my* gospel", verse 9, *"I* suffer hardship", verse 10, *"I* endure"). And this personal note is seen not only in this vocabulary but also in the pervasive reference to his own particular situation as one in bonds. That Paul would refer to something so entirely personal with the words "Faithful is the saying" seems to be highly unlikely, particularly in view of the fact that the other sayings have not had any personal reference. This means in reference to verse 8, in addition to the objection that arises from its distance from the formula, that the statement "according to *my* gospel" brings in this personal note and makes it less likely to be a saying. Likewise the deeply soteriological and eschatological verse 10 is nevertheless hinged on the first part of that verse with its reference to Paul ("Therefore *I* endure all things for the elect's sake, that they also may obtain the salvation which is in Christ Jesus with eternal glory"). This inherent personal note thus raises serious doubts about verse 10 being the saying.

There is within the verses that follow a completely different situation. In verses 11 ff. the references in the verbal forms is to "we" ("if we"). This corporate reference lends itself to a saying situation (compare Titus 3:5 ff. with its reference to "us" and "our"). Further, there is nothing strictly personal in these verses. Not only is there nothing strictly personal in these verses, but also their content is something that could readily be designated as a faithful saying. The form of verses 11 ff. is so striking that it compels almost all commentators to recognize that here is indeed a "hymn" or "saying". This form is evidenced by various characteristics. The first is the evident symmetry signalled by the fact that each of the four lines begins with εἰ. This balance is exampled further in the first two and last two lines respectively. In the first two lines the protasis begins with εἰ and the apodosis begins with καί. Both in the apodosis and protasis the verb form is first person plural ("we"). In the last two lines the protasis begins with εἰ, the apodosis begins with κάκεῖνος and ἐκεῖνος. In the last two lines in the protasis the verb form is first person plural again ("we"), and in the apodosis the verb form is third person singuar ("he"). The almost poetical nature of the saying can be readily seen as it appears before one in printed form:

εἰ γὰρ συναπεθάνομεν, καὶ συζήσομεν·
εἰ ὑπομένομεν, καὶ συμβασιλεύσομεν·
εἰ ἀρνησόμεθα, κάκεῖνος ἀρνήσεται ἡμᾶς·
εἰ ἀπιστοῦμεν, ἐκεῖνος πιστὸς μένει,
    ἀρνήσασθαι γὰρ ἑαυτὸν οὐ δύναται.

And not only is the form striking but also the content. The correlation throughout is between "we" and "he" (Christ). In the first two lines this correlation is manifested by the use three out of four times of συν- in the verb forms. The συν- drives home the truth that that which is being spoken of is a relationship of Christians ("we") with (συν-) Christ. A very similar note is manifested in the last two verses by the "we" contrasted and compared by means of the strong word for "he" (ἐκεῖνος).

The content and arrangement is noteworthy also in regard to the parallelism evident in the protases of the first two lines and of the last two lines respectively. The first two lines speak in positive terms of our relationship to Christ. They are words of commendation ("if we died with him", "if we endure"). The protases of the last two lines speak in negative terms of one's relation to Christ ("if we deny him", "if we are faithless").

The schematic and chronological progress within the saying presents itself in a movement from past (aorist, συναπεθάνομεν) to present (ὑπομένομεν) to future (ἀρνησόμεθα) and then back to a strongly contrasting and self-consciously chosen present (ἀπιστοῦμεν).

The cumulative weight of these considerations points definitely in the direction of verses 11 ff. as the λόγος in view in the formula "faithful is the saying". The question still remains as to which portion of verses 11 ff. is the saying. In addition to the view that ascribes the whole statement to Paul as one he composed for the occasion[13], there are three positions taken on these verses as a saying. There are those who regard all but 13b ("for he cannot deny himself") as the saying and 13b as an addition of the author of 2 Timothy[14]. Others regard the first two lines only as the saying[15]. A number of commentators regard the entirety of verses 11—13 as the saying[16]. The saying now stands as a whole made up of verses 11—13, and we will consider it in its present form, at this stage of the study. The origin of the particular elements will be considered when the question of the possible origin of the saying arises at the end of this chapter.

The relationship of the saying to its present context and the reason why it is cited must be considered at this point. There are those who view the immediately preceding context in the light of this last letter of the

---

[13] E.g., Lenski, White.

[14] Bouma(?), Gealy(?), Hanson, Hendriksen, Lock, von Soden, Spicq(?), cf. p. 348, "la dernière formula constitue une conclusion, peut-être ajoutée par Paul lui-même".

[15] Above all Easton. Ridderbos, if this is a saying, would hold that the last two lines are probably Pauline. Jeremias takes the first two lines from Paul and the last two from Jesus.

[16] Barrett, Bernard, Bouma(?), Falconer, Guthrie, Scott.

Apostle Paul as a stress upon martyrdom, especially those who take verses 11—13 as a song of martyrdom[17]. Therefore the saying of verse 11 is quoted first of all because it speaks of dying with Christ, *i.e.* martyrdom. The basic explanation is found is this motif.

However, it must be realized that the connection between the saying and its preceding context does not lie in martyrdom and a martyr's death with Christ. This is seen first of all in the fact that the preceding context does not speak of a martyr's death at all. It does speak of suffering hardship and of bonds (verse 9) and of enduring all things (verse 10), but not of death as such.

It is true that the statement "I endure all things" may well some day encompass death for Paul (compare 4:6), but it is a stress on enduring (ὑπομένω) as such, and not on death as such, that is in Paul's purview. And it is this stress on "enduring" that forms both the semantic and ideological bridge to the saying. The saying is quoted because one of its leading and early motifs is "if we endure (ὑπομένομεν), we shall also reign with him". Paul quotes the saying at the natural transition point (note the γάρ again) in its original setting. In so doing he includes the saying in its unity as a compact whole. Therefore the other lines must not be artificially interpreted just to fit into this context but must be viewed in their normal interrelationships to one another. The saying is quoted because it commends enduring and warns against its negative opposite, denial.

The first question we must raise is that of the reference of the συν- in the verbs συναπεθάνομεν, συζήσομεν and συμβασιλεύσομεν. The answer is agreed upon by all that the συν- has in view and refers to Jesus Christ. Of whom else may it be said that we die, shall live and shall reign "with" him? Surely this corporate way of speaking in reference to the Christian and Jesus Christ is a refrain of the N.T. The ἐκεῖνος serves to strengthen this identification as well as conversely the συν- helps to identify the one in view in the ἐκεῖνος. The ἐκεῖνος is the one in view in the συν- of the preceding verbs and with the συν- in those verbs refers to a common antecedent referred to in the original setting by the γάρ. The N.T. speaks of no one else as denying us than Jesus Christ, that is, no one else of whom it may also be said that we died, we shall live and we shall reign with him. Both in terms of particular vocabulary and in terms of the ideas expressed the one in view in both the συν- and the ἐκεῖνος can be none other than Jesus Christ.

Συναπεθάνομεν has been interpreted by certain commentators[18] as indicating a martyr's death. The main argument cited on behalf of this

---

[17]   Bernard, Bouma, Holtzmann, Huther, von Soden.
[18]   See note preceding.

view consists of an appeal to the context as having in view a martyr's death, and that this can only be explained in that way. We have already shown above that this is not, in fact, the case. We may even question whether a martyr song would have arisen at this time in the history of the church. There are other considerations which may be pointed out against this interpretation and in favor of the view that understands συναπεθάνομεν as a reference to the spiritual death of Christians when they are united by faith to Christ. The first consideration is the fact that the verb is in the past tense (συναπεθάνομεν, aorist). It does not refer to something that is happening or that will happen, but to something that has already happened. It seems most unlikely to speak of a martyr's death as a past action rather than as a present or future occurrence. But it is quite in keeping with the N.T. usage and the phenomenon itself to speak of the Christian's spiritual death with Christ as a past action. Further, the order of tenses in the saying speaks against a reference to a martyr's death. They are past, present, future and then present again. The chronological progression is shattered by a reference to a martyr's death. Thus, if a martyr's death was in view the first two lines should be in a different order. Enduring (or remaining) comes before death, not vice versa. Dying *with* him (συν-) is also somewhat inept as a way of describing a martyr's death. There is no example in the N.T. of such a usage. And on the other hand the N.T. speaks of dying with Christ uniformly in reference to the spiritual death of Christians who have been crucified with Christ (Gal. 2:20) and who have therefore died with Christ to sin (*cf., e.g.,* Rom. 6:3 ff., also Col. 2:12). Thus we may say that the death referred to is that decisive event that has taken place already in the lives of those who utilize these words: "we died with him".

The thought and the words are almost exactly paralleled in Romans 6:8: "But if we died with Christ, we believe that we shall also live with him" (εἰ δὲ ἀπεθάνομεν σὺν Χριστῷ, πιστεύομεν ὅτι καὶ συζήσομεν αὐτῷ). The saying is obviously much more compressed than Rom. 6:8, but as the spacing indicates the vocabulary, tenses and order are almost identical. In the saying, the reference to Christ in that which originally preceded removes the need for Χριστῷ and αὐτῷ and causes the σύν to become part of the first verb form. Since it is already part of a faithful (πιστός) saying, there is no need to say "we believe that" (πιστεύομεν ὅτι). The δέ and ὅτι fit their respective contexts. This analysis demonstrates that Rom. 6:8 and 2 Tim. 2:11 are even more identical than it may have first seemed to be the case. Thus συναπεθάνομεν in the saying may be explicated in the light of Romans 6:8 and context[19]. Death with Christ is death unto sin (verse 11)

---

19 Συναποθνῄσκω occurs at two other places in the N.T., Mk. 14:31 and 2 Cor. 7:3, but neither one provides an adequate parallel.

even as Christ died unto sin once (verse 10). It is the crucifixion of our old man, the doing away of the body of sin, our removal from the bondage of sin in our crucifixion with Christ (all in verse 6). It is in Christ's death (verse 5) that we died with him. And because we have been united with Christ (verse 5) we have died with him in his death which wrought an inner death for our old man. And that union and death with Christ is described as being baptized into Christ Jesus. To die with Christ means to be so united with him that our inner sinful self ("our old man", "the body of sin") is destroyed as a result of his death on the cross. Thus we are no longer in bondage to sin (verse 6), and are justified from sin. With this death comes the concomitant life. In the words of Gal. 2:20 (in the Greek, 2:19,20) which uses crucified rather than died but expresses the exact same thought: "I have been crucified with Christ (Χριστῷ συνεσταύρωμαι); and it is no longer I that live, but Christ lives in me" (ζῶ δὲ οὐκετι ἐγώ, ζῇ δὲ ἐν ἐμοὶ Χριστός).

Likewise συζήσομεν[20] is to be interpreted in the light of Romans 6:8 and context. What does "we shall also live with him" mean? Christ is now living (verses 9 & 10) and living unto God. Paul therefore draws the conclusion "even so reckon you also yourselves to be dead unto sin, but alive unto God in Christ Jesus" (verse 11). This reckoning (λογίζεσθε) encompasses the present life of the believer. They are to reckon themselves to be dead unto sin here and now in the life they now live. And they are likewise here and now to reckon themselves alive (ζῶντας) unto God in Christ Jesus. As Christ Jesus now lives and that unto God, so they live with him now unto God. The life they are to live is a present "walk in newness of life" because they have been united to Christ in his death (verse 4). Thus they are not now to live any longer in sin (verse 2), and this because they have been united with Christ in the likeness of his death and thus they shall also be in the likeness of his resurrection (verse 5). They are now "alive from the dead" (verse 13). It may be objected that συζήσομεν in 2 Tim. 2:11 and in Rom. 6:8 is in the future tense and thus that it must refer exclusively to a future time[21], i.e., life after death[22] or the resurrection life[23]. But this view misses the whole thrust of Romans 6. Romans 6 is concerned with the

---

[20] Συ(ν)ζάω is found only 3 times in the N.T. and these are all in Paul. In addition to 2 Tim. 2:11 and Rom. 6:8 it occurs in 2 Cor. 7:3. 2 Cor. 7:3, where συναποθνήσκω also occurs, presents no helpful parallel because of its particular use there. "... you are in our hearts to die together and live together" (ἐν ταῖς καρδίαις ἡμῶν ἐστε εἰς τὸ συναποθανεῖν καὶ συζῆν).

[21] E.g., von Soden.

[22] E.g., Huther, Wohlenberg.

[23] E.g., Ellicott, Weiss.

present effect within one's life of one's union with Christ. It is concerned with how one lives now, as is seen by the introductory question of verse 2: "We who died to sin, how shall we any longer live (ζήσομεν) therein?" There also the future tense is used, but evidently to refer to the life here and now. The use of the future with reference to the present life is evident elsewhere in Romans 6. In addition to verse 2, there is also the statement in verse 5 ("we shall be [ἐσόμεθα] also in the likeness of his resurrection") which means that we here and now walk in newness of life. And Romans 6:8 is saying exactly the same thing. Hence, that we shall live with him (Christ) has in view the life with Christ which proceeds from our death with him and is manifested in our life here and now. Galatians 2:20 again expresses the thought for us in supremely wonderful and clear words: "I have been crucified with Christ; and it is no longer I that live, but Christ lives in me: and that life which I now live in the flesh ..." (ζῶ δὲ οὐκέτι ἐγώ, ζῇ δὲ ἐν ἐμοὶ Χριστός· ὃ δὲ νῦν ζῶ ἐν σαρκί ...). Likewise in 2 Timothy 2:11 the death with Christ as a past event carries with it also (καί) the fact that we shall (certainly) live with him. The union that accomplished our death in his death has also accomplished at the same time our life in his life with him. The future utilized is what which denotes the immediate future and following, indeed, the time which flows forth from our death with Christ in immediate life. The believer who has died with Christ shall also from that time on live with him.

It should not be thought however that this understanding of συζήσομεν excludes the life eternal. Not at all. Rather it encompasses the entirety of the new life with Christ, now and in eternity, without excluding the present reference. We have now received the life with Christ that never ends. There is a continuousness to our life with Christ. Paul speaks of this very same relation in the concluding verses of Romans 6. "But now (νυνὶ) being made free from sin and become servants to God, you have your fruit unto sanctification, and the end eternal life" (τὸ δὲ τέλος ζωὴν αἰώνιον, Rom. 6:22). By using the future συζήσομεν Rom. 6:8 and 2 Tim. 2:11 encompasses the entirety of our life with Christ all of which is future from the perspective of our past death with Christ[24]. If we have truly died with Christ, we shall also (καί, surely as a result) live with him.

[24] Cf. R. Bultmann, TDNT, II, p. 869: "In virtue of this twofold nature of the ζωή concept, the Pauline statements have a twofold reference. Sometimes (αἰώνιος) ζωή means the future blessing, sometimes it means the present life (R. 6:4,11,13; 8:2-10), and often it means both in an inseparable relationship". In note 316 attached to the end of this statement just quoted he refers first of all to Romans 6.

"If we endure, we shall also reign with him" (εἰ ὑπομένομεν, καὶ συμβασιλεύσομεν; 2 Tim. 2:12). Ὑπομένω[25] means essentially to remain or stay behind and thus comes to mean remain instead of fleeing, stand one's ground, hold out, endure in trouble, affliction, persecution[26]. This last meaning, to endure, is rather uniform in the occurrences of ὑπομένω in the N.T., except for a few statements in which a more general meaning of stay behind is demanded by the context[27]. Believers endure hatred of all men for Christ's sake[28] (καὶ ἔσεσθε μισούμενοι ὑπὸ πάντων διὰ τὸ ὄνομά μου· ὁ δὲ ὑπομείνας εἰς τέλος, οὗτος σωθήσεται.); "in tribulation" (τῇ θλίψει ὑπομένοντες) they are patient[29]; they endured "a great conflict of sufferings"[30] (πολλὴν ἄθλησιν ὑπεμείνατε παθημάτων), and "temptation"[31] (ὑπομένει πειρασμόν); and they suffer for doing good[32]. The great conflict of sufferings which Christians endure are further explained in Hebrews 10:33 by these words: "partly, being made a gazing-stock both by reproaches and afflictions; and partly, becoming partakers with them that were so used". They endure these things because of their position as Christians ("for my name's sake", Mt. 10:22, Mk. 13:13; suffer for "doing good", 1 Peter 2:20). And they endure them continuously throughout their life[33]. Christ presents the great example for them (Heb. 12:1,2,3 ff., cf. also 1 Peter 2:20,21) in their running the race with patience (δι' ὑπομονῆς). They are to look unto Jesus who endured (ὑπέμεινεν) the cross and "consider him that has endured (ὑπομεμενηκότα) such gainsaying of sinners against himself, that you wax not weary, fainting in your souls" (Heb. 12:2 & 3).

The eschatological perspective of endurance is always in view. Jesus endured the cross "for the joy that was set before him" and "has sat down at the right hand of the throne of God" (Heb. 12:2). Those who

[25] Used 17 times in the N.T.; in the books that follow the number of times is indicated: Mt. 2, Mk. 1, Lk. 1, Acts 1, (Paul 4 times as follows), Rom. 1, 1 Cor. 1, 2 Tim. 2, Heb. 4, James 2, 1 Peter 2. A textual variant at Rom. 8:24 would increase the number for Paul and in Romans.

[26] Liddell and Scott, Arndt-Gingrich, s.v. Cf. also F. Hauck, TDNT, IV, p. 581 ff.

[27] Lk. 2:24; Acts 17:24.

[28] Parallel passages Mt. 10:22; Mk. 13:13; cf. Mt. 24:13 with a stress on the iniquity which impinges on the disciples.

[29] Romans 12:12.

[30] Hebrews 10:32.

[31] James 1:12.

[32] 1 Peter 2:20.

[33] Note the recurring use of the present tense: Rom. 12:12; 2 Tim. 2:10; Heb. 12:7; James 1:12; 1 Peter 2:20. The past tenses can be explained by noting that they refer to Jesus (Heb. 12:2,3), the prophets (James 5:11), or the past action of the recipients of the letter called Hebrews (10:32). And these are being encouraged by the letter to resume their faithful endurance. In the Gospels (Mt. 10:22, 24:13; Mk. 13:13) the enduring (ὁ ὑπομείνας) is εἰς τέλος.

endure unto the end (εἰς τέλος), the same shall be saved (οὗτος σωθήσεται, Mt. 10:22, 24:13; Mk. 13:13). Believers endured joyfully the spoiling of their possessions, "knowing that you have for yourselves a better possession and an abiding one" (Heb. 10:32). The Christians of Hebrews are encouraged to patience (ὑπομονή) "that, having done the will of God, you may receive the promise" (Heb. 10:36). And that is seen not only in "the saving of the soul" (Heb. 10:39), but also in the eschatological coming of God (Heb. 10:37). Likewise the man who truly endures temptation "shall receive the crown of life" (James 1:12), for endurance is a proof of love to God and this crown is promised to all them that love the Lord.

In the saying, ὑπομένομεν in the present tense refers to the continually faithful standing for Christ by the Christians over against the attacks of the sinful world, the hatred of all for those who bear Christ's name, the afflictions, tribulations and temptations that press upon them as Christians[34]. In positive terms, "Here is the patience (ἡ ὑπομονή) of the saints, they that keep the commandments of God, and the faith of Jesus" (Rev. 14:12). Although one must remain under and suffer, the idea is not that of hopeless submission but rather of hopeful perseverance that endures with faithfulness to God with an eye on the future. This note is seen in the context of the saying in that very phrase which elicits this saying, i.e., 2 Tim. 2:10: "Therefore I endure (ὑπομένω) all things for the elect's sake, that they also may obtain the salvation which is in Christ Jesus with eternal glory". This expectant note, found throughout the N.T. references to enduring, is also here in the saying: "If we endure, we shall also reign with him" (εἰ ὑπομένομεν, καὶ συμβασιλεύσομεν).

As we have seen above, the expectation at the end of endurance is that of the end time situation. For those who endure and are thereby faithful to Christ there is also (καί) a reigning with Christ (συμβασιλεύσομεν). Συμβασιλεύσομεν means to rule or reign together with someone. In 2 Timothy 2:12, Christians, viz., those who have died with Christ and have remained stedfast for him, shall reign with Christ. Two emphases are present in the verb. The συμ- points to the fact that the ruling is with Christ, and the plural "we" to the fact that it is the ruling together of Christians with Christ. This ruling has no other qualifications and thus it may be presumed to be a continuous ruling in the future.

Συμβασιλεύσομεν occurs only twice in the N.T. (2 Tim. 2:12 and 1 Cor. 4:8). The latter passage, even though written in irony, throws further light on the concept in view[35]. The Apostle Paul therein scores

[34] "In most of the NT passages ὑπομένειν refers to the stedfast endurance of the Christian under the difficulties and tests of the present evil age", F. Hauck, *TDNT*, IV, p. 586.

[35] *Cf.* A. Robertson and A. Plummer, *The First Epistle of St Paul to the Corinthians (I.C.C.)* (Edinburgh: T. & T. Clark, 1911), *ad* 1 Cor. 4:8.

the pride and self-esteem of the Corinthian Christians. In doing so he says that they act and think as if they are already reigning (ἐβασι- λεύσατε) in the Kingdom of God, the Messianic Kingdom. And they are supposedly reigning while the Apostles are still laboring and suffering. Paul speaks of them reigning "without us" (χωρὶς ἡμῶν ἐβασιλεύσατε). He then says that he would they did reign "that we also might reign with you" (ἵνα καὶ ἡμεῖς ὑμῖν συμβασιλεύσωμεν). Two facets are to be noted. The first is that Paul in his irony rules out any reference to a present reign. The call to the Christian now is to serve and remain stedfast, not to reign. This is the same note as that of the saying of 2 Tim. 2:12 which stresses that our present task is to remain stedfast (ὑπομένομεν). The second note is that Christians are going to reign together and the reigning will be at the same time. Paul ironically says that he would that they were reigning here and now for (ἵνα) then Paul and his co-laborers (ἡμεῖς) would be reigning with them. And this note is also evident in 2 Tim. 2:12; the reigning with Christ is a reigning together of all with Christ.

Furthermore, the corporate reigning with Christ in 2 Tim. 2:12 is future (συμβασιλεύσομεν) from the perspective of their remaining stedfast, and that is a continuous and lifelong activity (ὑπομένομεν). Hence any reference to a present earthly or spiritual rule with Christ is completely out of the question.

The theme of ruling with Christ recurs elsewhere in Paul and the N.T. In 1 Cor. 6:2 Paul says that "the saints shall judge the world". This refers to the eschatological judgment. Jesus promised the disciples that they "shall sit on thrones judging the twelve tribes of Israel" as his appointment of their place in his kingdom (Luke 22:29,30). This appointment is given to them that continued (διαμεμενηκότες) with him in his temptation (verse 28). Here their stedfastness is spoken of not as ὑπομένω but as διαμένω, as continuing, remaining or standing by someone. The kingdom in which they‾ have their place and in which they judge or rule is Christ's kingdom, the kingdom of the consummation. Matthew 25:34 ff. speaks of those inheriting that kingdom who have manifested their relation to Christ by their faithful and stedfast concern and care for others. The kingdom which they inherit is then described as "eternal life" (Mt. 25:46). According to Rev. 22:5, the servants of God "shall reign for ever and ever" (βασιλεύουσιν εἰς τοὺς αἰῶνας τῶν αἰώνων). Likewise, the promised ruling with Christ in view in 2 Timothy 2:12 is a ruling of Christians together with him in his eschatological consummation kingdom which shall never end[36].

---

[36] For a comprehensive view of the teaching of the N.T. on the kingdom see H. Ridderbos, *The Coming of the Kingdom* (Philadelphia: Presbyterian and Reformed, 1962), and K. L. Schmidt, *TDNT*, I, pp. 564-593.

Since the Christian has died with Christ so he shall also live with Christ. He bears up under the oppression and dominion of others because he knows that he shall rule and reign with Christ. The contrasts are striking and are chosen because of their seemingly diametrically opposite aspects. The saying speaks of death unto life, and from being under domination to a place of dominion. In each of these aspects the role of Christ and the Christian's relation to Christ is dominant. We died with Christ, we shall also live with him and shall reign with him. And our enduring is a stedfast remaining with and for him. Indeed we are empowered to endure[37] by living with Christ and Christ living in us. And this presupposes and is based upon the fact that we have died with Christ.

"If we shall deny him, he also will deny us" (εἰ ἀρνησόμεθα, κἀκεῖνος ἀρνήσεται ἡμᾶς). The saying now turns from the aspects of comfort and encouragement to one of a stern warning. It turns from continuous stedfast endurance (ὑπομένομεν) to a contrary action of continuous denial (ἀρνησόμεθα). The tense of the verb changes again and this time to the future (ἀρνησόμεθα). And with the future tense the verb presents as a possibility in the future that we shall deny Christ. That the action in view focuses upon Christ is evident in the second half of the statement, "he also well deny us" (κἀκεῖνος ἀρνήσεται ἡμᾶς). The κἀκεῖνος κτλ. indicates a resultant reciprocal action. It definitely implies that he (ἐκεῖνος), Jesus Christ, will also (the κἀ of κἀκεῖνος being a contraction of καί) deny us as we have denied him. The stress in the verb ἀρνησόμεθα is not upon some vague or general action but upon that which relates to Christ.

Ἀρνέομαι is a word used thirty-two times in the N.T.[38] Its basic meaning is to say no, to deny, in description of a negative attitude towards a question or a demand[39]. In the N.T. the meaning to deny

---

[37] Col. 1:11, "strengthened with all power, according to the might of his glory, unto all patience (ὑπομονήν) and longsuffering with joy". F. F. Bruce, *Commentary on the Epistles to the Ephesians and the Colossians* (*N.I.C.N.T.*; Grand Rapids: Eerdmans, 1957), p. 187 shows the connection with the following words: "Such an endowment with divine power will enable them to stand firm in the face of trial and opposition and everything else that will test their faith in Christ".

[38] It occurs in the following books the number of times indicated: Mt. 4, Mk. 2, Jn. 4, Acts 4, in Paul 6, 1 Tim. 1, 2 Tim. 3, Titus 2, Heb. 1, 2 Peter 1, Johannine letters 3, Jude 1, Rev. 2. It is noteworthy that the verb is used in Paul only in the Pastoral Letters. The compound form ἀπαρνέομαι is found only in the synoptic gospels in the N.T., although there it is used interchangeably with ἀρνέομαι (Mt. 4, Mk. 4, Lk. 3).

[39] See the helpful articles by H. Schlier, *TDNT*, I, pp. 409-71, and by H. Riesenfeld, "The Meaning of the Verb ἀρνεῖσθαι", *Coniectanea Neotestamentica*, XI, (Lund: Gleerup, 1947), pp. 207-219.

receives its emphasis from the fact that the object whose claim is resisted and denied is supremely a person[40]. This has been noticed already in 2 Tim. 2 : 12. The most illustrative use of ἀρνέομαι elsewhere in the N.T. is the saying of our Lord in Mt. 10:33 (and Luke 12:9)[41], a passage which may well be the source behind 2 Tim. 2:12. "But whosoever shall deny me before men, him will I also deny before my Father who is in heaven" (ὅστις δ' ἂν ἀρνήσηταί με ἔμπροσθεν τῶν ἀνθρώπων, ἀρνήσομαι κἀγὼ αὐτὸν ἔμπροσθεν τοῦ πατρός μου τοῦ ἐν [τοῖς] οὐρανοῖς). Here the denial is specified as being a denial of Christ (με) and more particularly as before men (ἔμπροσθεν τῶν ἀνθρώπων). By the contrast to the preceding verse, "Every one therefore who shall confess (ὁμολογήσει) me before men, him will I also confess before my Father who is in heaven", we see that "deny" (ἀρνήσηται) is the opposite of "confess". The particularities involved in denying come to light in the denial of Peter (Mt. 26:69 ff.; Mk. 14:66 ff.; Lk. 22:54 ff.; Jn. 18:15 ff.)[42]. The denial on Peter's part is not only a repudiation of the truth of the statements of the maid and others ("I know not what you say", Mt. 26:70; Mk. 14:68; Lk. 22:60), but it is particularly a repudiation of knowledge of ("I know not him", Mt. 26:72,74; Mk. 14:71; Lk. 22:56) and fellowship and relationship with Jesus Christ ("you also were with Jesus . . .", Mt. 22:69, 71; Mk. 14:67; Lk. 22:56,59; Jn. 18:26; "you also are of them", Mt. 26:73; Mk. 14:70; Jn. 18:25; "this is one of them. But he again denied it", Mk. 14:69,70; Lk. 22:58; Jn. 18:26,27). The denial as a personal act of unfaithfulness to his Lord, rather than a mere act of untruthfulness, is underscored by the poignant words of Lk. 22:61,62: "And the Lord turned, and looked upon Peter. And Peter remembered the word of the Lord, how that he said unto him, Before the cock crow this day you shall deny me thrice. And he went out, and wept bitterly".

The personal element in denial presents itself also in 2 Peter 2:1 ("denying even the Master that bought them"; cf. Jude 4). Denial assumes in Peter's case for example and also in other cases a knowledge of and some sort of prior relationship to Christ. For only under these terms can one be said to deny a person. To deny Christ manifests itself in various ways. It may consist in denying Christ's name (Rev. 3:8) or His faith (Rev. 2:13). The positive counterparts of denial in these two passages are keeping Christ's word (Rev. 3:8) and holding fast his name (Rev. 2:8). Denial is the failure to do this.

Denial can thus take the form of forsaking or repudiating the Christian faith and its truths, particularly the truth concerning Jesus. In doing

---

[40] H. Schlier, *TDNT*, I, p. 469.
[41] See K. Aland, *Synopsis Quattuor Evangeliorum* (Stuttgart: Württembergische Bibelanstalt, 2nd ed., 1965), p. 146.
[42] *Cf.* also the passages where Jesus predicts this denial, Mt. 26:34 f.; Mk. 14:30 f.; Lk. 22:34; Jn. 13:38.

so one personally denies Christ (and the Father). "Who is the liar but he that denies (ὁ ἀρνούμενος) that Jesus is the Christ? This is the anti-christ, he that denies (ὁ ἀρνούμενος) the Father and the Son. Whosoever denies (ὁ ἀρνούμενος) the Son, the same has not the Father: he that confesses (ὁ ὁμολογῶν) the Son has the Father also" (1 John 2:22,23).

And denial can manifest itself by one's activity in the moral realm. Men may "profess that they know God; but by their works they deny him" (Titus 1:16). Thus because they love pleasure rather than God, even though they appear to have a form of godliness, they have denied the power of godliness (2 Tim. 3:5). To fail to provide for one's own household is an evidence of denying the faith (1 Tim. 5:8).

One of the main motives involved in denial is shame and its attendant fear. "For whosoever shall be ashamed of me and of my words in this adulterous and sinful generation, the Son of man also shall be ashamed of him, when he comes in the glory of his Father with the holy angels" (Mk. 8:38; cf. Lk. 9:26). The context is that of losing one's life for Christ's sake and the gospel. When one is ashamed of Christ and denies him, it is because one is afraid, as was Peter, to take the consequences for his life. Amid a sinful generation one seeks to gain and maintain a good relationship over against this world by denying his relationship to Christ, or by failing to confess it. Thus in such a situation one does not deny oneself (ἀπαρνησάσθω ἑαυτόν, verse 34), but rather one denies Christ by being ashamed of him. This is also the difference between enduring and denying in the saying.

Because ἀρνέομαι expresses primarily a denial of Christ and because that denial may manifest itself in various forms, the verb can be used almost absolutely and without qualification, as in 2 Tim. 2:12 except for the apodosis which makes it evident that the denial has to do with Christ and that it elicits from him necessarily the same response. In the terse language of the saying of 2 Tim. 2:12 the fulness of Mt. 10:33 has been completely compacted to εἰ ἀρνησόμεθα. But in that terseness is compacted all the terrible significance of ὅστις δ᾽ ἂν ἀρνήσηταί με ἔμπροσθεν τῶν ἀνθρώπων.

The dire consequence of our denial is that "he also will deny us" (κἀκεῖνος ἀρνήσεται). Ἐκεῖνος, as is evident in the reference implicit in the συν- verbs in the saying and also on the assumed background of Mt. 10:33, refers to Jesus Christ. The denial in view on Christ's part is that future (ἀρνήσεται) evaluation which he will make of us unto His Father ("him will I also deny before my Father who is in heaven", Mt. 10:33) and in the presence of the angels of God (Lk. 12:9) at Christ's coming ("when he comes in his own glory, and of the Father, and of the holy angels", Lk. 9:26; also Mk. 8:38). The words of Jesus in Mt. 10:33 (& 32) are spoken to give force to the words of Mt. 10:28, "And be not afraid of them that kill the body, but are not able to kill the soul: but rather fear him who is able to destroy both soul and body in hell". These words speak of God's judgment in being "able to destroy both soul and body in hell". However, those who confess Christ need not fear this destruction by God for Christ will confess them so that they will not be destroyed in hell. On the other hand, those who deny Christ will be denied by him and will therefore reap such a destruction. The context of the words "him will I also deny before my Father who is in heaven" are therefore obviously eschatological.

The denial on Jesus' part is the denial of an abiding relationship to Him which is the same denial that they have made. It is a repudiation of them who have repudiated him. In the pregnant use of the word "know" in Scripture, Jesus will profess concerning them that he never knew them (see Mt. 7:23). A final and complete disavowal of Christ in this life means that Christ will finally and completely disavow those in the life to come.

The statement in the saying that we are now considering does not mean that Christ is not faithful to his promise to us, nor does it mean that our fall into a denial even as grave as Peter's is unforgivable or that it from that time henceforth forever and ever seals our doom. The denial in view in the saying which calls forth Christ's denial is not like that of Peter's who later sought forgiveness but rather is a situation of hardness and permanence.

There is yet another possibility to faithfulness (ὑπομένομεν) or complete denial (ἀρνησόμεθα), and it is that of unfaithfulness (ἀπιστοῦμεν). What of the day in and day out (present tense, ἀπιστοῦμεν) unfaithfulness on our part? Does that unfaithfulness mean that Christ will deny us? The saying appropriately comes to a close with our propensity to sin and with Christ's faithfulness (ἐκεῖνος πιστὸς μένει).

What does the ἀπιστοῦμεν in εἰ ἀπιστοῦμεν mean? Does it refer to unbelief[43] or unfaithfulness[44]? Ellicott insisted that ἀπιστεῖν always means unbelief and not unfaithfulness in the N.T. It is true that of the six (eight) occurrences of ἀπιστέω in the N.T. at least four (six) of them do mean unbelief[45]. However, it should be noted that the number of occurrences are so limited that it is precarious to insist, as did

---

[43] So Alford, Bernard, Chrysostum, Ellicott, and Fausset.

[44] So Bouma, Guthrie, Hendriksen, Huther, Kelly, Kent, Lenski, Ridderbos, von Soden, Weiss, White and Wohlenberg.

[45] The statistics are as follows: Lk. 24:11,41; Acts 28:24; 1 Peter 2:7, mean unbelief (also Mk. 16:11,16). Rom. 3:3 and 2 Tim. 2:13 can be interpreted either as unbelief or unfaithfulness. The location of the occurrences are also of interest. Excluding the late Marcan ending, the word is found only in Luke, 1 Peter and Paul.

Ellicott, that ἀπιστέω must always mean unbelief. And particularly is this so with a word which may inherently have several meanings, as is the case with ἀπιστέω. When this is the case, even though the predominant usage in the N.T. is in one direction, the word must finally be understood in its context. And here in 2 Tim. 2:13 ἀπιστοῦμεν is definitely contrasted with ἐκεῖνος πιστὸς μένει. And obviously that which is in view in this πιστός is not God's faith or belief, but his faithfulness. That which is contrasted to God's faithfulness is our unfaithfulness (εἰ ἀπιστοῦμεν). And the contrast is not merely a linguistic one but also is inherent in the relationship in view. "If we are faithless" presumes (as did the previous protasis clause) a faithlesness in regard to Christ, viz., if we are faithless to him. The apodosis, "he remains faithful", also presupposes a faithfulness in relation to us (even as the other three apodoses have set forth a relation between Christ and the one in view in the protasis). Thus we may paraphrase "he remains faithful to us"[46]. This relationship determines in large measure the meaning of the word faithful here in its reference to God. To remain faithful to us means that God holds on to us and sustains us in his promises. To understand faithfulness here as punishment and rejection would be quite out of accord with the fact that the apodosis contrasts God's faithfulness with our unfaithfulness. The fact of contrast rather than of result is noticeable too in the omission of "also" (καί) from this apodosis only of the entire saying. All the other apodoses, i.e., the first three, have that resultant "also" (καί), because each of the first three apodoses follow from the truth or action of its protasis. But in this apodosis there is no "also", just because the apodosis does not inherently follow from the protasis but is in marked contrast to it. Therefore only the positive note of God's faithfulness adequately contrasts and compares with our faithlessness in this tightly knit statement. Just because the apodosis does not "also" follow from the protasis, the negative faithfulness to punish, which might be asserted as also following from the protasis, is not the faithfulness in view. That God's positive faithfulness is in view is further underlined by the use of the word μένει. The apodosis does not say that he is faithful, but rather that "he remains (μένει) faithful". The word remains indicates a continuing and abiding relationship. He who calls on us to remain stedfast (ὑπομένομεν) remains (μένει) faithful to us. This means that God will not change in his faithfulness to us because we fail in our faithfulness to him. Our unfaithfulness does not remove his abiding and unchanging faithfulness.

---

[46] The omission of the personal references "to him" and "to us" are to be explained by the terseness of the saying and by similar terseness in other statements of the saying, e.g., the omission of a reference for the συν- verbs and of "him" after the verb "deny". The saying apparently restricts the protasis to εἰ plus the verb.

It is this basic and all important consideration that has caused the great majority of commentators[47] and also lexicographers[48] to regard ἀπιστοῦμεν in this statement as meaning faithless or unfaithful. This does not mean that the element of a weak and wavering faith, *i.e.*, a temporary unbelief or lack of trust, is not also present in unfaithfulness[49]. But the emphasis would seem to fall on being unfaithful.

The understanding of ἀπιστοῦμεν is inextricably bound up with one's whole understanding of this last statement of the saying in its entirety, and that in two ways. First, is the saying now giving another, and perhaps worse, expression of denial, or is it giving an expression of the frailty of the believer which is less than a hardened and final denial? Second, what is the response of Christ delineated in the words ἐκεῖνος πιστὸς μένει, ἀρνήσασθαι γὰρ ἑαυτὸν οὐ δύναται? Is Christ faithful to punish and repudiate, or is he faithful to hold us in faithfulness to his being and promise? One's understanding of these words in reference to Christ also color one's understanding of the words in reference to men, εἰ ἀπιστοῦμεν, because the statement manifestly has an inner and correlative relationship and coherence, as we have seen in part already. We must therefore now turn more specifically to the second half of verse 13.

"He abides faithful, for he cannot deny himself" (ἐκεῖνος πιστὸς μένει, ἀρνήσασθαι γὰρ ἑαυτὸν οὐ δύναται). Christ (ἐκεῖνος) remains faithful (πιστός). In what sense does the N.T. speak of the faithfulness of God and of Christ? The usage in Paul is particularly striking and is uniform throughout. In Paul, God's faithfulness is set in the positive context of man's salvation and of faithfulness on God's part to his promises. A survey of the passages[50] will display this remarkable feature. In 1 Cor. 1:9, God who is faithful has called believers into the fellowship of Jesus Christ and because of his faithfulness Christians shall be confirmed "unto the end" and be unreproveable in the day of the Lord Jesus Christ[51]. The faithfulness of God is intimately related

---

[47] See note 44.

[48] *E.g.*, Arndt-Gingrich, *s.v.*, "be *unfaithful*"; and R. Bultmann, *TWNT*, VI, pages 205 and 208.

[49] This aspect may in part explain why English Bible translation committees have chosen the word "faithless", *e.g.*, A.S.V., N.A.S.V., R.S.V. and N.E.B., because it includes both elements. It may also have been chosen because of its ambiguity so that the translators could leave the matter of interpretation open. "Faithless" can be understood either as unbelief or unfaithfulness, or both together.

[50] 1 Cor. 1:9; 10:13; 2 Cor. 1:18; 1 Thess. 5:24; 2 Thess. 3:3 (and also 2 Tim. 2:13).

[51] 1 Cor. 1:8,9: "who shall also confirm you unto the end, that you be

to the final salvation of believers, indeed it is the assurance that God will confirm them to that end. In 1 Cor. 10:13 God's faithfulness is that which enables Christians to endure temptation and to escape from it[52]. Likewise in 2 Cor. 1:18-20, the fact that God is faithful assures that the preaching of Christ and the gospel is not a yes and/or no proposition, but rather the faithfulness of God assures that the promises (ἐπαγγελίαι) of God in Christ are "yes" and "amen"[53]. In similar fashion in 1 Thess. 5:23,24 God who is faithful will indeed ("who will also do it", ὃς καὶ ποιήσει) sanctify believers wholly and preserve them entire and without blame at the coming of Jesus Christ[54]. Finally, in a similar vein in 2 Thess. 3:3 we read: "But the Lord is faithful (πιστὸς δέ ἐστιν ὁ κύριος) who shall establish you, and guard you from the evil (one)". In each of these occurrences the fact that God is faithful is related not as the basis for the certainty of punishment to those who are faithless but as the guarantee that his people shall be kept from falling into temptations, from the evil one, and that they shall be kept unto the end, unreproveable in the coming and day of the Lord Jesus Christ according to the promises in Christ[55].

unreproveable in the day of our Lord Jesus Christ. God is faithful (πιστός), through whom you were called into the fellowship of his Son Jesus Christ". C. Hodge comments on this passage as follows: *"God is faithful,* one in whom we may confide; one who will fulfil all his promises. The apostle's confidence in the steadfastness and final perseverance of believers was founded neither on the strength of their purpose to persevere, nor on any assumption that the principle of religion in their hearts was indestructible, but simply on the fidelity of God", *An Exposition of the First Epistle to the Corinthians* (Grand Rapids: Eerdmans, reprint 1956), p. 10.

[52] "There has no temptation taken you but such as man can bear: but God is faithful (πιστός), who will not suffer you to be tempted above that you are able; but will with the temptation make also the way of escape, that you may be able to endure it" (1 Cor. 10:13).

[53] "But as God is faithful (πιστός), our word toward you is not yes and no. For the Son of God, Jesus Christ, who was preached among you by us . . . was not yes and no, but in him is yes. For how many soever be the promises (ἐπαγγελίαι) of God, in him is the yes: wherefore also through him is the Amen, unto the glory of God through us" (2 Cor. 1:18-20).

[54] "And the God of peace himself sanctify you wholly; and may your spirit and soul and body be preserved entire, without blame at the coming of our Lord Jesus Christ. Faithful (πιστός) is he that calls you, who will also do it" (ὃς καὶ ποιήσει) (1 Thess. 5:23,24).

[55] The conclusion reached above is not nullified by Rom. 3:3 f.: "For what if some were without faith? shall their want of faith make of none effect the faithfulness of God? God forbid" (μὴ ἡ ἀπιστία αὐτῶν τὴν πίστιν τοῦ θεοῦ καταργήσει; μὴ γένοιτο, note πίστις not πιστός as above). God's faithfulness in Rom. 3:3 is his truth (Rom. 3:4). The truth and faithfulness in view are his promises which are not nullified by the "want of faith". It is true that unrighteousness is visited by the righteous God with wrath (Rom. 3:5). But

129

The Pauline emphasis on the relation of God's faithfulness to the believer and his security in that faithfulness is also exemplified in the other N.T. writings[56]. The admonition to "hold fast the confession of our hope that it waver not" is undergirded with the reason "for he is faithful that promised" (πιστὸς γὰρ ὁ ἐπαγγειλάμενος, Heb. 10:23). 1 Peter 4:19 summons those that suffer according to the will of God to "commit their souls in well-doing unto a faithful (πιστῷ) Creator". The usage of faithful in connection with God by Paul and elsewhere in the N.T. gives us every reason to think that God's remaining faithful in 2 Tim. 2:13 also refers to his stedfastness to his promises to his people so that they are held by his faithfulness.

The explanation or reason given that "he abides faithful" is "for he cannot deny himself" (ἀρνήσασθαι γὰρ ἑαυτὸν οὐ δύναται). The connecting "for" (γάρ) introduces the concluding clause as the substantiation of the preceding clause: "he abides faithful, because (γάρ) he cannot deny himself". The final cause of Christ's faithfulness does not reside in our faithfulness, no quite the contrary, but in his own nature. He cannot (οὐ δύναται) deny himself (ἑαυτόν). He is not able, it is an impossibility for Him who is faithful and true to be unfaithful. This would be to say no, to belie, or to be untrue (ἀρνήσασθαι)[57] to his own being. The impossibility (οὐ δύναται; ἀδύνατον) of Christ (God) lying or denying himself and his truth stands out in Heb. 6:17 ff.: "Wherein God, being minded to show more abundantly unto the heirs of the promise the immutability of his counsel, interposed with an oath; that by two immutable things, in which it is impossible for God to lie (ἐν οἷς ἀδύνατον ψεύσασθαι θεόν), we may have a strong encouragement, who have fled for refuge to lay hold of the hope set before us: which we have as an anchor of the soul, a hope both sure and stedfast and entering into that which is within the veil". The saying ends as it has begun on the note of Christ's person and work on behalf of the believer. The first stanza stressed Christ's death for us and our death with him from which the attendant promise of life with him flows. The saying closes with the underlying faithfulness of Christ in which relationship he ever remains to us in spite of our

the faithfulness and truth of God still stands in the promise that "the righteousness of God" comes "through faith in Jesus Christ unto all them that believe; for there is no distinction" (Rom. 3:22).

[56] Other N.T. passages use πιστός in connection with God but are not as pointed in their application as the above, but do nevertheless have the same positive note, with the possible exception of Revelation (see Heb. 11:11; 1 John 1:9, faithful to forgive our sins; Rev. 1:5; 3:14; 19:11).

[57] Cf. Arndt-Gingrich, s.v., p. 107, H. Riesenfeld, op. cit., pp. 208 and 216, and H. Schlier, TDNT, I, pp. 469 and 471.

own faithlessness. Even though Peter denied (ἀρνέομαι) him, Christ's faithfulness restored that denier. Our faithlessness does not remove his faithfulness to forgive and restore; indeed, to us who "confess our sins, he is faithful (πιστός) and righteous to forgive us our sins, and to cleanse us from all unrighteousness" (1 John 1:9). The faithful saying (2 Tim. 2:11 ff.) very faithfully and forcefully presents the critical points of the believer's life and the concomitant blessings and warnings. Affirming our death with Christ (συναπεθάνομεν), it reminds us of our need to persevere for him (ὑπομένομεν) but it also warns us of a future possibility of denial (ἀρνησόσεθα) and last it comforts us who are not yet perfect and thus who at times are faithless (ἀπιστοῦμεν) with the faithfulness of Christ.

But what now of the origin and extent of the saying? In this aspect of our discussion we need to bear in mind two factors. The first is that the saying is quoted because of its reference to enduring (ὑπομένομεν, 2 Tim. 2:12; cf. ὑπομένω, 2:10). This is the linguistic and ideological connection. The second factor is that the saying itself must be understood primarily on the background of its first words (συναπεθάναμεν) which probably most particularly give indication of its original setting. The concept of dying with Christ is more fully developed in Romans 6 than anywhere else in the N.T. We have already noted above the great similarity between 2 Tim. 2:11 and Rom. 6:1 ff., especially verse 8. And it is abundantly evident in Romans 6 that Paul relates our having died with Christ to baptism (cf., e.g., Rom. 6:3 and 4). It would be therefore most appropriate to conjecture that our saying was utilized in connection with a baptismal setting. In that setting by means of this saying are unfolded before the eyes of those to be baptized the various ramifications of the Christian life. And that with which the saying begins is that which is signified by baptism, viz., our union with Christ, the fact that we have died with Christ and the fact that we live with Christ.

The great similarity between 2 Tim. 2:11 and Romans 6:8 also points in the direction of the origin of the saying. If, as the letter would seem to demand, 2 Timothy was written from Rome, then the church in Rome would appear to have developed the saying (at least 2 Tim. 2:11) by reflexion on and utilization by contraction of Romans 6:8[58]. The terms

---

[58]   Romans 6:8: εἰ δὲ ἀπεθάνομεν σὺν Χριστῷ, πιστεύομεν ὅτι καὶ συζήσομεν αὐτῷ· 2 Timothy 2:11: εἰ γὰρ συναπεθάνομεν, καὶ συζήσομεν·
2 Timothy 2:11 would seem to be a contracted form of Romans 6:8, omitting those elements which are obvious from the context of the saying, i.e. σὺν Χριστῷ referred to by means of the συν- verb, πιστεύομεν ὅτι stated already in the designation of the saying πιστὸς ὁ λόγος, and finally αὐτῷ not stated explicitly as being superfluous in a terse saying.

of the second statement of the saying provide very little basis for any fruitful conjecture, except for the fact that the second statement so exactly parallels the first in form that almost all commentators acknowledge that they go together and belong to the original saying.

The similarity of the third statement to the words of Jesus is so striking that the relationship comes immediately to mind (Mt. 10:33; Lk. 12:9). The tradition is that common to Matthew and Luke but not in Mark. And although the saying is not in the form of either Matthew or Luke, because it is expressed on the lips of Christians not on the lips of Jesus, nevertheless it is nearer in form to that of Matthew than that of Luke[59]. There would seem to be little doubt that this part of the saying reflects the words of Jesus. But who has combined this statement influenced by Jesus' own words with that of 2 Tim. 11, 12a, verse 11 at least seemingly influenced by Paul's own words in Romans 6:8?

Easton argues with some vigor that "the faithful saying extends only through v. 12a". As the reason for this decision he says that "not only is the tone of vv. 12b-13 out of place in a triumphant hymn but — as can easily be verified by reading the Greek aloud — the two couplets have a rhythm and an assonance (almost a rhyme) quite absent from what follows"[60]. The latter contention of Easton may be granted in part, but with the reservation that such a consistency of rhythm and assonance may not have been a necessity for the saying as a whole. It must not be forgotten that the εἰ plus the verb pattern is consistent throughout the saying in its present form. Further, there may be reasons why the last two couplets have a different rhythm. And of equal importance to that of Easton's observation is the fact that the form of the last two lines is still in a similar style (leaving aside for the moment 13b) to the first two—as can easily be verified by looking at the printed Greek text.

The heart of Easton's objection rests in his statement that "the tone of vv. 12b-13 (is) out of place" in the hymn. Is the tone indeed out of place? Do the last two statements not fit with the first two? Or to put the problem another way, who is most likely to have written these statements? Were they added by Paul or were they part of the saying Paul quoted?

It must be noted, in relation to Easton's observation, that the last two statements do differ from the first two in relation to the apodosis.

---

[59] Matthew 10:33 Luke 12:9 2 Timothy 2:12
ὅστις δ' ἂν ἀρνήσηται ὁ ἀρνησάμενος εἰ ἀρνησόμεθα
... ἀρνήσομαι κἀγώ ... ἀπαρνηθήσεται ... κἀκεῖνος ἀρνήσεται
Cf. Swete, op. cit., p. 4.
[60] Easton, ad loc.

The first two use a verb form with συν- and a verb in the first person plural ("we"). The last two statements use a verb in the third person singular ("he") and emphatic pronoun ἐκεῖνος. But this is not just a difference of style or rhythm or assonance, but a difference necessitated by the inherent responses of the apodosis to the protasis. In the first two statements the protasis is followed by verbs in the apodosis that express some resultant activity with Christ, hence συν- and a verb with the first person plural. But the last two statements emphasizing in the protasis negative actions on our part toward Christ are responded to in the apodosis by Christ's (ἐκεῖνος) response to that action of ours, hence a verb in the third person singular. Granting the protases of the last two statements, it would be virtually impossible to express the apodoses in the same form as that of the first two statements, *i.e.*, by a compound verb in the first person plural with συν. And this explains at once a difference in rhythm, tone and assonance. And in this connection, it should not be forgotten that the content of the thought communicated as well as the available vocabulary has even caused the second protasis of the first two statements to break with the pattern of the συν verbs. The form of the last two statements are not arbitrarily different, but are different because of what they express. At the same time the protasis of the last two statements are in the same form as the first two, εἰ with a verb. A consideration of form or tone, without regard to the substance in view, is an erroneous guide, for it fails to deal adequately with the fact that content has its effect upon form, and structure, and thus even upon rhythm and tone.

If the author of the Pastorals has added verses 12b and 13 himself, we must ask the reason why. In effect, we must ascertain whether it is more plausible that they were part of the saying or that they were added by the author of the Pastorals? Now it cannot be denied that the latter is a possibility. The vocabulary does not exclude that possibility. The vocabulary is not completely lacking in the Pastorals or in Paul elsewhere. But the problem arises to explain the reason for such an addition, and for such an addition that seems to add to the saying and use its form. The relationship to the immediate context is not fully apparent. The questions of denial and faithlessness are not evident in the immediate context. It may be argued that Paul adds these statements to warn Timothy and to strengthen his appeal in verses 1 ff. But that this is the relationship is doubtful. And it would have the further complication of making these words in verses 11 ff. have a double reference, *i.e.*, to verse 10 and to verses 1 ff. The other alternative is that he added the words as a warning to strengthen his own words in verse 10. But this also is dubious. We may question why Paul would add to the saying, imitate its form, and have his own words seem to fall, at least for the reader, under the formula "faithful is the saying". For as the verses now stand they would seem to be intended as part of the "hymn" and thus part of the faithful saying.

On the other hand, does not the saying in its present entirety, verses 11-13, present a coherent whole (contra Easton)? Would it not have been appropriate in a baptismal setting to bring in the word of warning as well as the final word of encouragement that Christ remains faithful? Does not the fact that Paul quotes the first line "if we died with him..." which is not directly germane to that which he wishes to underscore also show the plausibility of continuing the hymn to the end or at least to this terminus point?

The fact that stanza 12b is a reflection of the saying of Jesus bears upon the question under consideration. Paul never reflects on this saying anywhere else in his writings. It would seem therefore more plausible to think that it has been incorporated in the saying by others and not here and now all at once by Paul.

The cumulative effect of the probabilities would seem to point to the fact that the last two stanzas were originally a part of the saying. The form bespeaks this conclusion and so do the other considerations. The least that can be said is that the last two stanzas are part of the saying as we now have it.

The question still remains concerning 13b, "for he cannot deny himself" (ἀρνήσασθαι γὰρ ἑαυτὸν οὐ δύναται), which has been set aside momentarily during the previous discussion of the last two statements (verses 12b and 13). There are scholars who think that the entire "hymn" is quoted by the author except for verse 13b which is then added by the author himself[61]. The main argument against its inclusion is one from style and form. It elongates that last statement and makes it out of balance with the others, it is contended. Hence some advocate that it is an explanatory appendix.

It may well be asked if this is an adequate criterion to exclude verse 13b from the "hymn" and affirm that the author of the letter added it himself. Since the original source of the saying is not now extant, it is an impossibility to assert that its rhythmical scheme was uniform throughout, or that it was consistently modeled on the rhythm and structure of verses 11-12a[62]. Even these preceding phrases are of different lengths[63], depending in fact upon the ideas expressed in them.

[61] Gealy with hesitancy, Hanson, Hendriksen, Lock, von Soden, and Spicq. Even some of these speak of this only as a possibility. Compare especially Gealy's discussion of the arguments for and against.

[62] Cf. Gealy, ad loc.

[63] Using the present day syllabification of the words the following lengths for the phrases emerge: Verse 11: protasis 8, apodosis 5, total 13.

Verse 12:	„	6,	„	7,	„ 13.
Verse 12b:	„	6,	„	9,	„ 15.
Verse 13:	„	5,	„	7,	„ 12.
Verse 13b:					total 12.

It is noteworthy that the lengths of protases, apodoses and particularly the

And yet for all that, verse 13b on the basis of length determined by syllabification corresponds to those that precede[64]. Certainly if a reference to Christ preceded this portion of the "hymn", as the συν- form of the verbs and the occurrence ἐκεῖνος would lead one to think, then it would seem likely that that statement itself would not conform to the shape (εἰ etc.) or the length of the statements presented here. It may well be that the preceding statement concerning Christ is balanced off by this concluding statement in verse 13b both in its content and more specifically in its form and length. The "hymn" would then begin and end with a striking statement concerning Christ.

Again the question must be asked as to which is the most plausible explanation, an addition by Paul or a part of the original saying? And again it must be acknowledged that an addition by Paul is not absolutely impossible. Neither the vocabulary, style nor the idealogical content rule out the possibility of verse 13b coming from Paul's mind and hand. But then the question must be asked as to why he added this statement. Did he feel that the "hymn" as it stood, particularly verse 13, lacked this statement? Or did he have in mind something in the preceding verses that this thought would support? The latter would seem to lack any basis in the context itself. Verse 13b gives the reason (γάρ) why Christ remains faithful (verse 13). It is rather self-evident that verse 13b finds its rationale as the explanation of the latter part of verse 13a. Did verse 13 originally stand as it is without 13b as the terminus point of the "hymn" (or this section of it)? In a sense the latter part of verse 13a ("he abides faithful") may well stand by itself as the counterpart of the protasis of verse 13. But the content of the previous statements of the saying would seem to indicate that verse 13b was necessarily and inherently part of the saying. In the preceding three statements the apodosis follows almost automatically or axiomatically from the protasis. Why shall we live with Christ?, because we have died with him. Why shall we rule with Christ?, because we have remained faithful. Why will Christ deny us?, because we have denied him. But why Christ remains faithful is not to be found in the reason that we are unfaithful. Therefore the reason inherent in each case in the other statements must for the fourth statement be given by adding this additional statement: "for (γάρ) he cannot deny himself". The reason that "he remains faithful" (ἐκεῖνος πιστὸς μένει) is "because he cannot deny himself" (ἀρνήσασθαι γὰρ ἑαυτὸν οὐ δύναται). The saying itself as a whole and especially the fourth statement thus demand this concluding phrase of verse 13b. The explanation of verse 13b is more plausible as an original part of the saying than as an addition by Paul.

overall lengths of each statement are approximately the same. In its overall length verse 13b corresponds to the preceding statements.

[64] See the preceding note.

And again it must be noticed that verse 13b as it now stands is presented as part of the saying. The saying would therefore seem to consist of four stanzas (verse 11-13) including verse 13b.

What of the origin of the saying as a whole? 2 Timothy 2:11 ("if we died with him, we shall also live with him") would seem to point to a baptismal setting for the entire saying. And this verse would also seem to be shaped by the reflection of the church at Rome on Paul's statement in Rom. 6:8 and its relation to baptism (Rom. 6:2 & 3). This hypothesis is strengthened by the fact that 2 Timothy is most probably written from Rome. These factors all merge together; the parallel is found in the letter to the church at Rome (6:8), and there it is in connection with baptism, and 2 Timothy is written from Rome. The second statement ("if we endure, we shall also reign with him") would seem to be added to forcefully remind the ones being baptized of their need not only to have been spiritually united with Christ in his death but also to live for and be faithful to Christ in their life. The third statement then brings in the terrible possibility which is before them of denying rather than remaining stedfast for Christ. And this statement reflects the influence of the words of Jesus himself (Mt. 10:33; also Lk. 12:9). The fourth statement is then added as a final word of comfort to deal faithfully with the real problem in life of our faithlessness. What if we do not always remain stedfast? Does our every "denial" cause Christ to deny us forever? No, if we are faithless, he abides faithful, for he cannot deny himself. And with these words the saying comes to a well-rounded presentation of the truth and with these words of comfort it concludes. The Christ with whom we have died remains faithful to us, not in the final analysis because of our faithfulness, but because he cannot deny himself.

It remains to consider the suggestion of Spicq and others that Paul has utilized a hymn in both what precedes and in what follows. In that which precedes Paul has largely adapted the hymn and worked in his own thought and expressions, suggests Spicq. Then when he gets to verse 11 he proceeds to quote that portion of the hymn forthwith. This hypothesis has some merit in that there are a few phrases in that which precedes that might be from a hymn, e.g., verse 10, "Remember Jesus Christ, risen from the dead, of the seed of David". And further it has the plausibility of providing the antecedent for the συν- verbs and the connection for the γάρ in verse 11 by the fact that Jesus Christ is mentioned in both verse 8 and verse 10 preceding. However, its plausibility stops with these considerations. That which precedes verse 11 is admitted by all, even Spicq, to be so intertwined with specific references of Paul ("I" and "my") that any untangling and disengaging of any reference to a hymn is virtually impossible. And not only are there these personal references

136

("I" and "my") but also the other references are in different persons, *e.g.*, "you" (second singular, verses 7 & 8), and "they" (verse 10) than the "we" characteristic of verses 11 ff. And even if verse 8, for example, is a reference to some known statement we cannot with definiteness say that it originally belonged together with verses 11 ff. It would appear moreover that the writer did not intend to refer to the distant verse 8 but only to verses 11 ff. by the position of his formula in verse 11. And this would be in accord with his practice elsewhere, where the formula would seem to refer to that immediately adjacent to it and then only to that on one side of the formula. The known factors surrounding the formula in verse 11 give every reason for the reader to think that the writer was referring exclusively to verses 11-13.

CHAPTER VII

CONCLUDING PERSPECTIVES

Those portions of the Pastoral Letters designated by the formula πιστὸς ὁ λόγος are as follows:

"Christ Jesus came into the world to save sinners" (1 Tim. 1:15).

"If a man seeks the office of a bishop,
he desires a good work" (1 Tim. 3:1).

"bodily exercise is profitable for (a) little;
but godliness is profitable for all things,
having promise of the life which now is,
and of that which is to come" (1 Tim. 4:8).

"When the kindness of God our Savior, and his love toward man, appeared,
not by works done in righteousness which we did ourselves,
but according to his mercy he saved us,
through the washing of regeneration and renewing of the Holy Spirit,
which he poured out upon us richly, through Jesus Christ our Savior;
that being justified by his grace,
we might be made heirs according to the hope of eternal life"
(Titus 3:4-7).

"If we died with him, we shall also live with him:
if we endure, we shall also reign with him:
if we shall deny him, he also will deny us:
if we are faithless, he abides faithful;
  for he cannot deny himself" (2 Tim. 2:11-13)[1]

---

[1] The sayings are quoted in the form in which they are rendered in the *American Standard Version* with a few minor exceptions such as the omission of any initial connective. The Greek texts for the sayings are as follows:

1 Tim. 1:15: Χριστὸς Ἰησοῦς ἦλθεν εἰς τὸν κόσμον ἁμαρτωλοὺς σῶσαι.

1 Tim. 3:1: εἴ τις ἐπισκοπῆς ὀρέγεται, καλοῦ ἔργου ἐπιθυμεῖ.

One realizes at once that the contents of the faithful sayings are somewhat diverse. But this in and of itself is instructive. 1 Tim. 1:15 focuses exactly on what Christ came to do, *i.e.*, to save sinners. 1 Tim. 3:1 exalts the office of a bishop and designates it as a good work. 1 Tim. 4:8 encourages godliness by showing that it has promise for this life and the next. Titus 3:4-7 expresses the saving act of God as it changes us here and now and also makes us heirs of eternal life. 2 Tim. 2:11-13 proceeds from our death with Christ to encourage and warn us about ethical responsibilities to and for Christ in this life.

1 Tim. 1:15 depicts pointedly Christ Jesus as Savior. He is the one who has come to save sinners. This and no other reason is given as the purpose for Christ's coming. 1 Tim. 1:15 specifies explicitly the incarnation ("came into the world") and in doing so embraces all that the Johannine phrase implies concerning the person and work of the one who has come. The second part of the saying in synoptic terminology describes the condition of men and the action Christ Jesus has wrought to make them whole and deliver them from their condition. This saying pinpoints the act of God in history in Christ Jesus for man's salvation. In a few words it defines who the Savior is and what we men are. With one telling verb ("to save") it describes the whole work of Christ Jesus and its effect upon us lost men.

In Titus 3 the Trinitarian form makes its appearance with the references to God our Savior, the Holy Spirit and Jesus Christ our Savior. The movement within the saying proceeds from the action on God's part in history (his kindness and love toward man appearing), to the action within us by His Spirit (he saved us). The latter receives the primary emphasis and the former is set forth as the basis for this action. The eschatological motif is seen in the movement from the appearance through the application to the culmination (heirs of eternal life). Within the saying itself, emphasis is laid on the mercy of God as the ground of our

1 Tim. 4:8 : ἡ σωματικὴ γυμνασία πρὸς ὀλίγον ἐστὶν ὠφέλιμος,
ἡ δὲ εὐσέβεια πρὸς πάντα ὠφέλιμός ἐστιν,
ἐπαγγελίαν ἔχουσα ζωῆς τῆς νῦν καὶ τῆς μελλούσης.

Titus 3:4-7 : ὅτε ἡ χρηστότης καὶ ἡ φιλανθρωπία ἐπεφάνη τοῦ σωτῆρος ἡμῶν Θεοῦ,
οὐκ ἐξ ἔργων τῶν ἐν δικαιοσύνῃ ἃ ἐποιήσαμεν ἡμεῖς
ἀλλὰ κατὰ τὸ αὐτοῦ ἔλεος ἔσωσεν ἡμᾶς
διὰ λουτροῦ παλιγγενεσίας καὶ ἀνακαινώσεως πνεύματος ἁγίου,
οὗ ἐξέχεεν ἐφ' ἡμᾶς πλουσίως διὰ 'Ιησοῦ Χριστοῦ τοῦ σωτῆρος ἡμῶν,
ἵνα δικαιωθέντες τῇ ἐκείνου χάριτι
κληρονόμοι γενηθῶμεν κατ' ἐλπίδα ζωῆς αἰωνίου.

2 Tim. 2:11-13 : εἰ συναπεθάνομεν, καὶ συζήσομεν·
εἰ ὑπομένομεν, καὶ συμβασιλεύσομεν·
εἰ ἀρνησόμεθα, κἀκεῖνος ἀρνήσεται ἡμᾶς·
εἰ ἀπιστοῦμεν, ἐκεῖνος πιστὸς μένει,
ἀρνήσασθαι γὰρ ἑαυτὸν οὐ δύναται.

salvation, and this is pointedly highlighted by repudiating our works as a basis. Having laid this ground work, the saying then directs our attention to how we are saved, *i.e.*, by the work of the Holy Spirit. At the same time it connects the Holy Spirit's work with the work of Jesus Christ as Savior and shows that the Holy Spirit is poured forth by him because he is the Savior. And finally, not only does it speak of our inner transformation but also of our present (justified) and future (heirs) standing before God. From beginning to end the saying makes it abundantly plain that our salvation is totally of God.

Let us turn to a comparison of 1 Tim. 1:15 and Titus 3:4-7. The central thrust of each is exactly the same as is evidenced by the central verb in each (σῴζω). Thus we may say that they are both definitely soteriological. But the differences are also instructive within this recognized framework. 1 Tim. is terse and objective ("sinners"); Titus 3:4-7 is lengthy and personal ("us"). The formula at 1 Tim. 1:15 specifically calls for a response, "worthy of all acceptation". Titus 3:4-7 recognizes that those who use the saying have responded ("our Savior"), and the words added to the formula (verse 8) urge the careful maintenance of good works based on the fact that they have already believed God. Although both sayings focus on man and his salvation, they do that also in terms of emphasis. 1 Tim. 1:15 places almost all the emphasis on the incarnational action of Christ Jesus in accomplishing the salvation of sinners. Titus 3:4-7, although it begins with this emphasis (verse 4) and builds upon it (also verse 6b), focuses much more in depth on the application of the salvation. 1 Tim. 1:15 spoke of Christ Jesus saving sinners. Titus 3:4-7 specifies and delineates how that salvation accomplished is applied in terms of the experience and standing of those sinners who are thus saved. Hence it speaks of the washing of regeneration and renewing of the Holy Spirit which was poured out upon us richly (verses 5 & 6). And thus it speaks of being justified and of being heirs (verse 7).

The sayings might be criticized in terms of their lack of a specific mention, in so many words, of the death, burial and resurrection of Jesus Christ[2]. On the one hand this would be a failure to recognize that which is implicit in the phrases such as "Christ Jesus came into the world to save sinners". On the other hand it would be a failure to remember that these are not evangelistic sermons (*kerygma*) but "faithful sayings", known and in large measure used by and within the believing community. Faith[3] also has been noted as missing from the sayings. But that element

---

[2] One must be slow to draw hard and fast conclusions about omissions from the faithful sayings in view of the fact that we have only parts of some of them. If one would include the "saying" or "hymn" of 1 Tim. 3:16, one would then bring into consideration Christ's resurrection or ascension ("received up in glory") and faith ("believed on in the world").

[3] *E.g.*, Easton, *ad* Titus 3:7.

is either implied in the sayings ("our Savior"), or mentioned in an enlargement on the citation-emphasis formula (Titus 3:8), or urged by the words, "worthy of all acceptation".

1 Tim. 1:15 and Titus 3:4-7 place all the stress on what God has done. He saved us. 2 Tim. 2:11-13 also stresses the work of Christ in the συν-verbs, and especially in the 11th verse which speaks of the fact that we have died with Christ and shall live with him.

But there is a difference between 1 Tim. 1:15, Titus 3:4-7 on the one hand and 2 Tim. 2:11-13 (and 1 Tim. 4:8) on the other. In the former sayings man is seen as passive. In 1 Tim. 1:15 "sinners" is the object of the verb. In Titus 3:4-7 any action of man in saving himself by works is negated. The pronoun is the object of the verb ("saved us"), or is used with the preposition and the verb ("poured out upon us"), or is the subject of a passive verb ("we might be made heirs", *cf.* the passive participle, "being justified"). In Titus 3:4-7 man is seen as wholly passive and as a recipient of God's salvation. This is not the case in 2 Tim. 2:11-13 (nor 1 Tim. 4:8). Here man is seen as active and responsible. Here the verbs are active, and in the protases "we" is the subject. Each protasis presents a conditional situation (εἰ, "if we"). Although the redemptive work of Christ for and in man is presented as basic, primary and pervasive, the accent is on man's response both in the initial act of union with Christ and in the continuing acts of living for Christ ("if we endure"). The saying moves with the soteriological as foundational ("if we have died with him, we shall also live with him") to the problematics of the ethical of experiential ("if we endure", "if we shall deny him", "if we are faithless"). The apodoses based as they are on the conditions of the protases show the crucial importance of man's actions and responses, and especially in relation to Christ. This saying with its heavy note on man's responsibility shows the redemptive and Christological setting of N.T. ethics, and it views one's activity in life in relation to Christ. It begins with the basic question of one's union with Christ and life with Christ. Only then does it speak of our need to endure for him. And finally it ends with Christ's faithfulness to us even when we are faithless.

I Tim. 4:8 also focuses on man's needed activity. Godliness is seen as involving the response of man. In its contrast to bodily exercise the saying thinks of the needed spiritual exercise on the part of man. The introductory words in the context (verse 7b) even use the phrase, "exercise yourself unto godliness". This saying, like that of 2 Tim. 2:11-13, relates godliness to this life ("we shall also live with him", 2 Tim. 2:11) and life to come ("we shall also rule with him", 2 Tim. 2:12). The promise is set forth in 2 Tim. 2:11 ff. by means of apodoses in the future tense related to the respective protasis with the correlation emphasized by the use of "also" (καί). The first two statements of 2 Tim. 2:11 ff. bear the form of "if we" answered by the words "we shall also". That note of promise and resultant profitableness is set forth in 1 Tim. 4:8 explicitly by using the words "profitable" and "promise".

On the surface 1 Tim. 4:8 seems much less Christ oriented. But it only seems so. Godliness bespeaks a relationship to Christ because in these letters it is rooted in Christ (*cf.* 1 Tim. 3:16). Thus it has a power that comes from Christ and only degenerates into a form when one denies the power thereof (2 Tim. 3:5). Godliness is the characterization of those who love God (2 Tim. 3:4) and thus who live with and for Christ. 2 Tim. 2:11 says that such a living with Christ comes from our response of dying with Christ. The saying of 1 Tim. 4:8 also recognizes the need for response not only in the basic understanding inherent in the word godliness as used by Christians but also in the words added to the formula, "worthy of all acceptation". When godliness is real, not just a form, it manifests the power of God at work within and through the believer.

Both 2 Tim. 2:11-13 and 1 Tim. 4:8 stress what we must do and be. One more directly and one more indirectly on the background of Christ's saving work and his power within us.

The delineation of the work of Christ in the three sayings is diverse and noteworthy (1 Tim. 1:15; Titus 3:4-7; 2 Tim. 2:11-13). All relate that work to the salvation of sinful mankind. 1 Tim. 1:15 speaks in a compressed way of the great deed of Christ coming to save sinners. The emphasis would appear to be on the historical act of Christ Jesus coming into the world. Through this great act in history, with all that it involves, Christ Jesus saves sinners. Titus 3:4-7 encompasses this element of 1 Tim. 1:15 but then builds on it. It refers not only to the appearing in history of God's kindness and love toward man but also of that which has taken place within those who are saved. And the saying views the entire sweep of the history of salvation, from Christ's coming until our inheritance of eternal life as his heirs. Thus Titus 3:4-7 relates in particular concerning Jesus Christ our Savior that he has poured out the Holy Spirit upon us richly and that he is the one who has provided God's grace by which we were justified. And further, Titus 3, in distinction from either of the other two (1 Tim. 1:15; 2 Tim. 2:11-13), presents all three persons of the Trinity in their relationship to the process of man's salvation. The work of the Father and especially that of the Holy Spirit are emphasized, although each are related to Christ as pivotal. In 2 Tim. 2:11-13 the stress is returned simply to Christ as in 1 Tim. 1:15 but also with a difference. The 2 Tim. 2:11-13 saying relates the believer unto Christ in terms of the συν-verbs. What Christ has done (died, lived), the believer has experienced with him, or will experience with him (reign). 2 Tim. 2:11-13 and Titus 3:4-7 thus present two ways of viewing Christ's redemption in relation to his people. 2 Tim. 2:11-13 presents it under the figure of the believer experiencing his salvation in and with Christ in terms of Christ's death and resurrection. Christ is seen there as the representative of his people and they in turn are caught up in and benefit from his saving activities. When Christ died, we died also with him. When Christ lived (arose), we lived also with him. Titus 3:4-7 on the other hand sees the believer experiencing the work of Christ more in terms of the believer's life and history. Jesus Christ our Savior pours the Holy Spirit upon us here and now. The washing and renewing is that which we experience at a particular time in our life. We are saved here and now by the application to our lives by the Holy Spirit of what Christ has done for us as our Savior. This comparison and contrast is illustrative and helpful in showing the two ways in which the N.T. sees the gap bridged between Christ's coming to save once years ago and his saving us here and now many years later. They are not contradictory or mutually exclusive. One is not preferable to the other. They are both needed. Each perspective highlights a particular aspect of the truth.

At this point we must pause and reflect on certain other differences that have been manifested by these four sayings. In each category there is a rather lengthy saying with a corporate "we" structure (Titus 3:4-7; 2 Tim. 2:11-13). The "liturgical" aspect would seem to lie on the face of these sayings as indicated by this aspect. The other two sayings (1 Tim. 1:15; 1 Tim. 4:8) are much more brief and terse statements which are less personal in the sense that they do not have within them the "we" aspect. Take the statement: "Christ Jesus came into the world to save sinners" (1 Tim. 1:15). The reference to sinners is more general than the possible but more personal "us". Likewise 1 Tim. 4:8: "for bodily exercise is profitable for little; but godliness is profitable for all things, having promise of the life which now is, and of that which is to come". Here again there is no reference to "us" or "we". Noteworthy in connection with this is the fact that only with these two less personal or more general sayings are the words "and worthy of all acceptation" used. Or to put it the other way, the addition to the formula is missing from the sayings that lay stress on the personal "we" aspect. What significance does this have?

The briefer and more objective sayings (1 Tim. 1:15; 1 Tim. 4:8) would seem to have a "non-liturgical" outward look, whereas the longer and "we-type" sayings (Titus 3:4-7; 2 Tim. 2:11-13) would seem to have a more inward and "liturgical" perspective. The latter have within them the human response (the "we"). The former have no direct reference to the needed response but this is specifically requested in the addition to the formula "and worthy of acceptation". Thus 1 Tim. 1:15 and 1 Tim. 4:8 may have been used in a more evangelistic or catechetical setting in which the response was urged by the words "and worthy of acceptation". Titus 3:4-7 and 2 Tim. 2:11-13 do not have the addition to the formula urging acceptance because they already express that acceptance within themselves (and probably also in the setting in which they were used). The words "and worthy of all acceptation" are therefore words that urge the human response of faith and obedience. They are used when that response is not evident within the saying and they are not added when that response is evident within the saying.

What of the saying in 1 Tim. 3:1 in connection with the addition or omission of the words "and worthy of all acceptation"? Here the words are not found. Why not? The answer lies in the nature of the saying and its limited or specific application to a particular group of people. This is not a general truth which must be fully embraced by all everywhere in faith and/or obedience. Rather it is a saying which seeks to commend the office of the bishop as a good work. It is indeed commended in a sense to the community as a whole but it is not a truth which one must personally embrace and apply directly and specifically to oneself. The particular response which is in view is the encouragement of those who should seek the good work of serving as a bishop. And thus the absolute qualification "worthy of all acceptation" would be out of place in connection with 1 Tim. 3:1.

I Tim. 3:1 by itself constitutes a unique category, *i.e.*, ecclesiastical or church governmental. "If a man seeks the office of a bishop, he desires a good work". The purpose of this saying is stated so concisely and clearly in its own words that any summary would be redundant. What may seem striking is that this saying is concerned with church order in general and the office of a bishop in particular. This is only if one does not take into account the interest and concern for church government and officers already in the N.T.[4] It would be more striking if no saying had arisen about the bishop in the early church in view of the pervasive role of the bishop-presbyter (pastor-teacher) as the key permanent officer in the N.T.[5] One would almost expect a saying on church government in the midst of a letter that is so taken up with ordering the church of God (chapters 2 and 3, and 4:17 ff.; especially chapter 3 and particularly 3:14-16) and this is all the more so when one finds them on other matters. And yet the balance within the Pastoral Letters (one out of five), which

[4] For an affirmation of the interest and concern for church government and officers in the N.T. on the background of an intensive and extensive study, including a discussion and evaluation of the opposite position, see H. N. Ridderbos, *Paulus*, pp. 479-543, and also "Kerkelijke order en kerkelijk recht in de brieven van Paulus" in *Ex Auditu Verbi* (a festbundel for G. C. Berkouwer, Kampen: Kok, 1965), pp. 194-215.

[5] See, *e.g.*, Acts 11:30; 14:12; 15:2,4,6,22,23; 16:4; 20:17 ff. esp. verse 28; 21:18; 1 Cor. 12:28; Eph. 4:11 ff.; Philip. 1:1; 1 Thess. 5:12 f.; 1 Tim. 3:2 ff.; 5:1, 2,17,19; Titus 1:5 ff.; Heb. 13:7,17; James 5:14; 1 Peter 5:1 ff.

may well reflect the balance within the sayings at large, is that which one might expect in view of the proportionate amount of space devoted to this subject in the N.T. as a whole.

Perhaps the main question which may be raised is not that 1 Tim. 3:1 is regarded as a saying but that it is regarded as a *faithful* saying. This is in part due to the fact that a truth about church government is regarded by some as having nothing in it which makes it worthy of being designated as faithful. This in turn is founded on a view that thinks of a faithful saying as one that is strictly soteriological, or at least theological or ethical. But the hard fact remains that I Tim. 3:1 is designated by the words πιστὸς ὁ λόγος.

This in itself should caution us against separating church government from the "spiritual" concerns and the faith of the church. The first reference to elders in the book of Acts (at the end of Paul's first missionary journey) is in a context which expresses the very concerns of all these sayings:

> 21 And when they had preached the gospel to that city, and had made many disciples, they returned to Lystra, and to Iconium, and to Antioch, 22 confirming the souls of the disciples, exhorting them to continue in the faith, and through many tribulations we must enter into the kingdom of God. 23 And when they had appointed elders in every church, and had prayed with fasting, they commended them to the Lord, on whom they had believed.
>
> (Acts 14:21-23)

In this passage we find the basic soteriological proclamation (verse 21). And there is the response of faith (verses 21 and 23). Next there is the confirmation and exhortation "to continue in the faith, and that through many tribulations we must enter into the kingdom of God" (verse 22). Paul returns to these churches which he had established and to those areas where his very life was in danger to appoint "for them elders in every church" (verse 23). This appointment of elders is for no other reason than that the elders might aid the church and its members in the obedient response of verse 22[6]. Thus this key passage in Acts ties together the very elements which are in the Faithful Sayings including 1 Tim. 3:1.

The officers in the N.T. are virtually always seen in connection with the faith and life of the people of God. Eph. 4:11 ff. says they are given

---

6   "In these cities they strengthened the young churches which they had so recently planted, putting their administration on a firm basis by appointing suitable members as elders, who would be true spiritual guides to their brethren, and giving them further instruction and encouragement in face of the hardship and persecution which they would inevitably have to face as they maintained their Christian witness", F. F. Bruce, *Commentary on the Book of the Acts* (*N.I.C.N.T.*, Grand Rapids: Eerdmans, 1954), in commenting on Acts 14:22-23, page 296.

by Christ to the church "for the perfecting of the saints ... till we all attain unto the unity of the faith ...". According to 1 Thess. 5:12 their work is to admonish. In Hebrew 13:7 they are men "that spake unto you the word of God". And in Heb. 13:17 they are also those who shall give an account for the souls of those under them. In the Pastoral Letters the officers are those who hold "to the faithful word (πιστοῦ λόγου) which is according to the teaching, that he may be able both to exhort in the sound doctrine, and to convict the gainsayers" (Titus 1:9). 2 Tim. 2:2 expresses the thought thusly: "And the things which you have heard from me among many witnesses, the same commit to faithful men, who shall be able to teach others also". Faithful (πιστοῖς) men, officers (elders-bishops/pastors-teachers) were those who were most responsible for teaching the truths of the faithful sayings. Is there any wonder that the saying "if a man seeks the office of a bishop, he desires a good work", is characterized as a faithful one?

The breadth and emphasis of the faithful sayings must be related to other statements or summaries of the Christian faith, and in particular to the so-called *kerygma*. C. H. Dodd in his influential book, *The Apostolic Preaching and Its Development*[7], attempted a crystallization of the primitive Christian preaching[8] and designated it by the Greek word κήρυγμα[9]. As a summary of the *kerygma* in common between Paul[10] and the preaching of Acts[11] he gives the following[12]:

The new Age of fulfilment has dawned by the coming of Christ[13]

---

[7] C. H. Dodd, *The Apostolic Preaching and Its Developments* (London: Hodder & Stoughton, 1936).

[8] Hailed by A. M. Hunter in his *The Unity of the New Testament* (London: SCM, 1944), p. 22, as "one of the most important and positive contributions to New Testament science in our generation".

[9] Κήρυγμα. A word meaning *proclamation, announcement* or *preaching* by a herald. The word itself only occurs eight times in the N.T. and never in Acts. It has come to be used however as the technical term to designate the essential core of the early Christian preaching and message, particularly that of the Book of Acts but also that of Paul.

[10] In Paul's letters, Dodd, *op. cit.*, p. 28.

[11] Especially the early speeches of Peter, Dodd, *op. cit.*, p. 36.

[12] *Op. cit.*, p. 50. Discussion continues about the exact form and content of the *kerygma*. For a modern discussion of the *kerygma* with a critique of Dodd and others see R. H. Mounce, *The Essential Nature of New Testament Preaching* (Grand Rapids: Eerdmans, 1960), especially but not exclusively chapter five, pp. 60 ff.

[13] In Dodd's summary of the Pauline *kerygma*, *op. cit.*, p. 28, and that of Acts, p. 38 and 45 there is also reference to prophecies fulfilled and a New Age that is inaugurated by the coming of Christ. Hence this has been added to his summary.

the Davidic descent of Jesus, guaranteeing His qualification for Messiahship;

His death according to the Scriptures;

His resurrection according to the Scriptures;

His consequent exaltation to the right hand

of God as Lord and Christ;

His deliverance of men from sin into new life;

and His return to consummate the new Age.

How do the "faithful sayings" compare with the *kerygma?* The faithful saying of 1 Tim. 1:15 refers to the work of Christ in a much briefer way than does the *kerygma*. This is not strange when one reflects that this is a one phrase statement being compared with the outline of a speech. 1 Tim. 1:15 does draw together at once Christ's coming and the salvation of sinners. In this it is similar to the *kerygma*. One senses in the sayings the background of the *kerygma*. For example, 2 Tim. 2:11 ff. may speak of one's death *with* Christ because one already knows of the death *of* Christ. It may speak of one's life *with* Christ because one already knows of the resurrection *of* Christ. And it may speak of one's reigning with Christ because one already knows of the ascension and exaltation of Christ. And 1 Tim. 1:15 may also speak of Christ's coming to save sinners without saying how this is accomplished because his death and resurrection are well-known.

But the sayings do not completely build upon the previous *kerygma* without any transition. No, quite the contrary. The sayings are not purely ethical and hortatory. They do on the other hand apply Christ's work to the believer and encourage and exhort him on that basis. Although the emphasis is far more on the believer and his life, it is still couched in the eschatological emphasis seen in the *kerygma*. The new age is inaugurated (Titus 3:4), Christ has come into the world (1 Tim. 1:15), and thus we shall not only live now (Titus 3:5; 1 Tim. 4:8; 2 Tim. 2:11), but also in the age to come we as heirs shall receive the inheritance of eternal life (Titus 3:7; 1 Tim. 4:8) and rule with Christ (2 Tim. 2:12). The soteriology of the faithful sayings certainly explicitly makes the salvation of man their main thrust as does the *kerygma*. The faithful sayings differ from the *kerygma* in laying less explicit stress on the objective work of Christ (*e.g.*, death and resurrection) and also in less explicit stress on faith and repentance. The first difference however would be virtually eliminated if the saying of 1 Tim. 3:16 were included among the faithful sayings. And the latter difference is in part minimized when one realizes that "and worthy of all acceptation" is indeed a request for response. The differences are not so much of kind as of degree. And even those differences must be described on the background of the differences within the sayings, *i.e.*, those that urge acceptance ("worthy of all acceptation") and those that are the "we-type".

The most significant difference between the *kerygma* and the faithful sayings lies in the fact that the former is a rather well-defined summary for evangelism whereas the latter cover various aspects of the life and work of the church and are concerned with the Christian life as well. Faithful sayings range through the gamut of a brief expression of the basic purpose of Christ's coming (1 Tim. 1:15), a well-rounded expression of God's salvation of the believer (Titus 3:4-7), an exhortation to godliness (1 Tim. 4:8), an encouragement to live for Christ because one has died with Christ (2 Tim. 2:11-13), to a statement about the office of the bishop (1 Tim. 3:1). Although there is diversity in the various expressions of the *kerygma* in the N.T., the range of diversity found in the faithful sayings is in the nature of the case completely lacking. It is this diversity that reminds us that the early church was interested in edification as well as evangelism, in sanctification as well as conversion, in church government as well as preaching. And these sayings, with some of their non-Pauline elements, show us that this concern was that of the primitive church in general and not just that of Paul. They caution us not to oversimplify the early church and also not to relegate justification, regeneration or the new birth, renewal, etc., to just one element of the church.

The place of the teaching of the faithful sayings is wrapped up with the date of the Pastoral Letters. And this in turn is related to the question of authorship. But do not these sayings themselves present another problem to the question of authorship? Of the problems which these sayings may present, the one to which we now turn our attention consists of that of the great and original theologian Paul using the crystallized expressions of others as an aid to communicate the message which he would write. Are not the sayings incongruous to a Pauline authorship when seen in this light? As a matter of fact, however, Paul has demonstrated in his earlier writings his recognition of and dependence upon the "tradition" which he has received from others[14]. Therefore, in a formal sense the utilization of that which he has received from others and which he passes on need not be a problem.

But the problem does remain in a material sense. In his earlier letters

[14] See for example 1 Cor. 11:2,23 ff.; 15:1 ff.; 2 Thess. 2:15; 3:6. For a discussion of "tradition" in this sense see the following and the literature cited therein: H. Ridderbos, *The Authority of the New Testament Scriptures* (Grand Rapids: Baker, 1963), pp. 17 ff.; B. Gerhardsson, *Memory and Manuscript* (Uppsala, 1961), pp. 288 ff.; and O. Cullmann, *The Early Church* (London: SCM, 1956), pp. 54 ff. The last is an English translation of *Die Tradition* (Zurich, 1954). See for a discussion of *paradosis* in Paul, in the Thessalonian Letters and in the area indicated in the title the recent article of R. Schippers, "The Pre-Synoptic Tradition in 1 Thessalonians II 13-16", in *Novum Testamentum* VII (1966), pp. 223-234, an issue written in honor of Prof. Dr. G. Sevenster.

he has not used the formula "faithful is the saying". Nor do his earlier letters seem to utilize sayings as such. Those letters relate "tradition" about the life and ministry of Jesus, rather than "sayings" formulated by the church iteself. What explains the difference? We have made some progress with the problem when we have recognized the difference in that which is transmitted. The tradition referred to in the earlier letters is essentially that handed down and received from eyewitnesses. It is a witness. It is not a "saying" or aphorism, but the relating of that which has occurred. These traditions are not sayings and they are not referred to as such, but rather as that which is received and handed down. Further, whatever creedal/liturgical material[15], comparable to a saying, is found in Paul is used in an inconspicuous way. It is not cited and emphasized by a formula. It must be ferreted out, because whatever has been used has been unobtrusively worked into his letters. But now the sayings are clearly marked by a formula and are much more evidently cited and emphasized as sayings in their own right[16]. These are fixed sayings used and designated as such.

Another factor which enters into the picture is that of time. It takes time for a saying to arise in the Christian community, and furthermore it takes time for a saying to become generally recognized and accepted. The same is true in regard to the development of a formula of reference. Indeed a formula of reference would hardly develop until several sayings had been well-known. Hence this time factor accounts in part for their absence from the earlier letters and their occurrence in the Pastorals. A further consideration is Paul's growing concern[17] with the need of passing on the truth to others as he comes to the end of his life[18]. This growing concern makes him more inclined to communicate able summaries of Christian truth and commend them to the church and especially to the elders. He says the latter should be those who hold "to the faithful word which is according to the teaching, that he may be able both to exhort in the sound doctrine, and to convict the gainsayers" (ἀντεχόμενον τοῦ κατὰ διδαχὴν πιστοῦ λόγου, ἵνα δυνατὸς ᾖ καὶ παρακαλεῖν ἐν τῇ διδασκαλίᾳ τῇ ὑγιαινούσῃ καὶ τοὺς ἀντιλέγοντας ἐλέγχειν, Titus 1:9). And in the midst of this concern he commends these faithful words and exemplifies them in these letters.

[15] See among others the work of O. Cullmann, *The Earliest Christian Confessions* (London: Lutterworth Press, 1949) which appeared in 1943 under the French title *Les Premieres Confessions de Foi Chretiennes* and also that same year in the German edition *Die ersten christlicher Glaubensbekenntnisse*, 2nd ed. 1949.

[16] The noteworthy emergence of 1 Tim. 3:16, although not designated by the formula, "faithful is the saying", is an example in these letters of this trend.

[17] A concern evidenced already in the N.T. *Cf.* H. N. Ridderbos, *Paulus*, 1966, p. 487 f.

[18] See for example, Titus 1:9; 2 Tim. 1:13; 2:2,14; 3:14 ff.; and 4:1 ff.

Finally, it is not without significance that these faithful sayings occur only in letters written to Paul's co-laborers and assistants, Timothy and Titus, and not in letters written directly to churches. It may well be that Paul is using the weight of well-known faithful sayings to aid Timothy and Titus in carrying out their instructions. This conjecture is strengthened by noting the two factors of either the position of most of the sayings and/or more particularly the words of admonition that follow them. In the case of three of the sayings (1 Tim. 4:8,9; 2 Tim. 2:11-13; and Titus 3:4-8) the sayings are followed by a specific charge on the part of Paul to them to teach these things. 1 Tim. 4 : 11, "these things command and teach". 2 Tim. 2:14, "Of these things put them in remembrance...". Titus 3:8, "...and concerning these things I desire that you affirm confidently...". In the case of 1 Tim. 3:1 the saying leads off an important chapter on church officials, especially bishops. And Titus 3:4-7 gives the theological basis for the ethical admonition of Titus 3:1 and 2. Only 1 Tim. 1:15 seems to lack either of the afore-mentioned contextual characteristics.

But perhaps the solution to the difference between faithful sayings in the Pastorals and not in the other Pauline letters is also to be found in part in the larger problem of noticeable differences in style, vocabulary, etc. This difference has led C. F. D. Moule to propose recently that Luke was the amanuensis of the Pastoral Letters[19]. Several basic factors undergird this proposal. First of all amanuenses were used in letter writing in the day, and this usage seems to be exemplified in the N.T. and in Paul. Second, there are many striking similarities between the Pastorals and Luke in the general area of vocabulary. Perhaps this proposal may also help explain in part the presence of faithful sayings in the Pastorals, and perhaps also at the same time the solution to the sayings' question may throw light on this proposal.

How could Luke's role as an amanuensis help explain the presence of the faithful sayings? Just because he was the type of man who would collect and utilize such items. Luke's interest in and concern for what others have said and done is displayed most evidently in his prologue to his gospel (Luke 1:1-4)[20]. This interest and concern, and research therein, is not only set forth in his own self-testimony but it is also plentifully

---

[19] C. F. D. Moule, *The Birth of the New Testament* (New York: Harper & Row, 1962), p. 175, 220, 221; much more fully from the same author, "The Problem of the Pastoral Epistles: A Reappraisal", *Bulletin of the John Rylands Library*, 47 (1965), pp. 430-452. The latter is the Manson Memorial Lecture delivered in the University of Manchester on 30 October 1964.

[20] "Forasmuch as many have taken in hand to draw up a narrative concerning those matters which have been fulfilled among us, even as they delivered them unto us, who from the beginning were eyewitnesses and ministers

evidenced on the pages of Luke and Acts. In no other Gospel is there the reproduction of what others have said such as we find in Luke's Gospel in the "Magnificat" of Mary (Lk. 1:46-55)[21], the "Benedictus" of Zacharias (Lk. 1:67-79)[22], and the "Nunc dimittis" of Simeon (Lk. 2:29-32)[23]. Throughout the Book of Acts Luke relates the speeches that were given. And within the speech of Paul to the Ephesian elders at Miletus (Acts 20:17 ff.) Luke specifically includes the quotation of a word (λόγος) of Jesus on the part of Paul[24]. This phenomenon is more striking than it may at first seem because it preserves one of the two[25] words or sayings of Jesus not found in the Gospels within the N.T. And this saying is preserved by Luke in the situation of Paul giving instruction to elders. The *Sitz im Leben* is somewhat like that of the Pastoral Letters. In them Paul gives instructions to Timothy and Titus with a particular concern for the elders and uses faithful sayings. In Acts 20 when he instructs the elders of Ephesus he uses a saying of Jesus. Furthermore, it must be remembered that Luke's summary of the action and message in Acts 14:21-23 (see above) coupled with his summary of the message originally preached by Paul virtually coincides with or encompasses the content, message and stress of the faithful sayings. Luke, perhaps more than any other candidate for the amanuensis of the Pastoral Letters, would have had an eye and an ear for faithful sayings. Luke as an amanuensis may thus also help explain the presence of faithful sayings in the Pastorals[26].

of the word, it seemed good to me also, having traced the course of all things accurately from the first, to write unto you in order, most excellent Theophilus; that you might know the certainty concerning the things wherein you were instructed" (Luke 1:1-4). For a discussion of Luke's prologue see especially N. B. Stonehouse, *The Witness of Luke to Christ* (Grand Rapids: Eerdmans, 1953), pp. 24-45.

[21] "And Mary said" (Καὶ εἶπεν Μαριάμ), Lk. 1:46.

[22] "And his father Zacharias was filled with the Holy Spirit, and prophesied, saying" (Καὶ Ζαχαρίας ... ἐπροφήτευσεν λέγων), Lk. 1:67.

[23] Simeon "blessed God, and said" (εὐλόγησεν τὸν Θεον καὶ εἶπεν), Lk. 2:28.

[24] "remember the words of the Lord Jesus, that he himself said, It is more blessed to give than to receive" (μνημονεύειν τε τῶν λόγων τοῦ κυρίου Ἰησοῦ ὅτι αὐτὸς εἶπεν, Μακάριόν ἐστιν μᾶλλον διδόναι ἢ λαυβάνειν), Acts 20:35.

[25] See J. Jeremias, *Unknown Sayings of Jesus* (London: S.P.C.K., 1957), p. 4 f.

[26] The presence of faithful sayings in the Pastorals also helps in part to explain the unique vocabulary of the Pastorals. And the unique words in the sayings may be the origin or at least the impetus to the use of those same unique words elsewhere in the Pastorals. On this basis 11 words occurring 31 times in the Pastorals which are not found in the other ten Paulines are accounted for. Likewise 3 "Hapax Legomena" occurring 7 times in the Pastorals are accounted for. This factor too would need to be taken into consideration in evaluating the criticism of P. N. Harrison in his work, *The Problem of the Pastoral Epistles* (London: Oxford University Press, 1921), pp. 18 ff., and Appendix IV, pp. 185 ff.

The faithful sayings reflect the faith and commitment of the early church and at the same time the various realms of emphasis. Those that most closely approach the *kerygma* display the tendency of drawing together the so-called *kerygma* and *didache*, i.e., especially Titus 3:4-7; 2 Tim. 2 : 11-13. The sayings are definitely rooted in the person and work of Jesus Christ. This is seen first of all in the explicit mention of Christ in three or them (1 Tim. 1:15; Titus 3:4-7; 2 Tim. 2:11-13). But it is also evident in the fact that most of the sayings reflect a saying or teaching of Jesus. (1 Tim. 1:15; 4:8; 2 Tim. 2:11-13, esp. verse 12). Even 1 Tim. 3:1 in its insistence on the office of the bishop as a good work or a commendable service may reflect Jesus' teaching that service, not exercising authority or lording it over others, was to characterize his disciples (Mk. 10:42-45; Mt. 20:25-28; Lk. 22:24 ff.; *cf.* also Jn. 13:12 ff.). If this latter is true, then all the sayings are christological in one of the two senses expressed above. But even if not, then at least all but this one saying on the office of bishop are christological. Not only are the sayings christological in the double sense mentioned, but in their fullest form, Titus 3:4-7, the trinitarian motif is evident.

The faithful sayings continue to highlight to the church the three important areas of emphasis: soteriology (esp. 1 Tim. 1:15 & Titus 3:4-7), godly living (esp. 1 Tim. 4:8 & 2 Tim. 2:11-13) and church order (1 Tim. 3:1). Well may the church again today say in reference to each of these sayings, "faithful is the saying".

BIBLIOGRAPHY

Abbott-Smith, G., *A Manual Greek Lexicon of the New Testament*, Edinburgh: T. & T. Clark, 3rd ed., 1937.
Aland, K., *Synopsis Quattuor Evangeliorum*, Stuttgart: Württembergische Bibelanstalt, 2nd ed., 1965.
Aland, K., Black, M., Metzger, B.M., Wikgren, A., editors, *The Greek New Testament*, New York: American Bible Society, 1966.
Alford, Henry, *The Greek Testament*, Volume III, Cambridge: Rivingtons, 5th ed., 1871.
Arndt, W. F., and Gingrich, F.W., *A Greek-English Lexicon of the New Testament and Other Early Christian Literature*. A translation and adaptation of Walter Bauer's *Griechisch-Deutsches Wörterbuch* ... 4th revised and augmented ed., 1952, Chicago: University of Chicago Press, 1957.

Barclay, W., *More New Testament Words*, New York: Harper, 1958.
Barr, J., *The Semantics of Biblical Language*, London: Oxford University Press, 1961.
Barrett, C. K.,*The Pastoral Epistles (The New Clarendon Bible)*, Oxford: Clarendon, 1963.
Beckwith, I. T., *The Apocalypse of John*, New York: Macmillan, 1922.
Behm, J., ἐκχέω, ἐκχύν(ν)ω, *TDNT*, II, pp. 467-469.
——, καινός ... ἀνακαίνωσις, ἐγκαινίζω, *TDNT*, III, pp. 447-454.
——, *Die Offenbarung des Johannes (Das Neue Testament Deutsch*, 11), Göttingen: Vandenhoeck & Ruprecht, 6th ed., 1953.
Bengel, J. A., *Gnomon of the New Testament*, A New Translation by C. T. Lewis & M. R. Vincent, New York: Sheldon & Co., 2 Volumes, 1864.
Bernard, J. H., *The Pastoral Epistles (Cambridge Greek Testament)*, Cambridge: University Press, 1906.
Bertram, G., ἔργον κτλ. *TDNT*, II, pp. 635-655.
Beyer, H. W., ... ἐπισκοπή, ἐπίσκοπος, κτλ. *TDNT*, II, pp. 599-622.
Boismard, M.-E., "Une liturgie baptismale dans la Prima Petri", *Revue Biblique* 63 (1956), pp. 182-208, 64 (1957), pp. 161 ff.
Bornemann, W., "Der I Pet. — eine Taufrede des Silvanus?", *Zeitschrift für die neutestamentliche Wissenschaft* 19 (1919-20), pp. 143 ff.
Bouma, C., *De Brieven van den Apostel Paulus aan Timotheus en Titus (Kommentaar op het Nieuwe Testament*, XI), Amsterdam: Bottenburg, 1946.
Bover, J. M., "Fidelis Sermo", *Biblica* 19 (1938), pp. 74-79.
——, "Uso del adjectivo singular πᾶς en San Pablo", *Biblica* 19 (1938), pp. 411-434.

Bruce, F. F., *The Acts of the Apostles*, London: Tyndale, 2nd ed., 1952.

———, *Commentary on the Book of the Acts (The New International Commentary on the New Testament)*, Grand Rapids: Eerdmans, 1954.

———, *Commentary on the Epistles to the Ephesians and the Colossians (The New International Commentary on the New Testament)*, Grand Rapids: Eerdmans, 1957.

———, *The Speeches in the Acts*, London: Tyndale, 1944.

Büchsel, F., γίνομαι ... παλιγγενεσία, *TDNT*, I, pp. 681-689.

———, θυμός, ἐπιθυμία, ἐπιθυμέω κτλ., *TDNT*, III, pp. 167-172.

Bultmann, R., "Bekenntnis- und Liedfragmente im I Pet.", *Coniectanea Neotestamentica XI in honorem A. Fridrichsen*, 1947, pp. 1 ff.

———, *Theology of the New Testament*, New York: Scribners, 2 volumes, 1955.

———, von Rad, G., and Bertram, G., ζάω, ζωή, κτλ., *TDNT*, *II*, pp. 832-875.

———, and Rengstorf, K. H., ἐλπίς κτλ., *TDNT*, II, pp. 517-535.

———, and Weiser, A., πιστεύω, πίστις, πιστός κτλ., *TWNT*, VI, pp. 193-230. English translation in *Faith (Bible Key Words)*, London: A. & C. Black, 1961.

Burton, E. DeWitt, *Syntax of the Moods and Tenses in New Testament Greek*, Edinburgh: T. & T. Clark, 3rd ed. 1898, reprinted 1955.

Bijbel, Nieuwe Vertaling op last van het Nederlandsch Bijbelgenootschap bewerkt door de daartoe benoemde Commissies, Amsterdam: Het Nederlandsch Bijbelgenootschap, 1953.

Calvin, J., *Commentaries on the Epistles to Timothy, Titus, and Philemon* translated from the original Latin by the Rev. William Pringle, reprinted Grand Rapids: Eerdmans, 1948.

Carrington, P., *The Primitive Christian Catechism*, Cambridge: University Press, 1940.

Chrysostom, J., *The Homilies of St. John Chrysostom on Timothy, Titus, and Philemon*. The Oxford Translation edited, with Additional Notes, by Rev. Philip Schaff (*Nicene and Post-Nicene Fathers*, Vol. XIII), Grand Rapids: Eerdmans, 1956.

Cremer, H., *Biblico-Theological Lexicon of New Testament Greek*, translated from the latest German edition by William Urwick, Edinburgh: T. & T. Clark, 1895.

Cullmann, O., *Baptism in the New Testament (Studies in Biblical Theology*, 1), Chicago: Allenson, 1950. The English version of *Die Tauflehre des Neuen Testaments*, 1948.

———, *The Christology of the New Testament*, Philadelphia: Westminster, 1959.

———, *The Earliest Christian Confessions*, London: Luttersworth Press, 1949. This book was first published in French, *Les Premieres Confessions de Foi Chretiennes*, 1943, and in the same year in German, *Die ersten christlicher Glaubensbekenntnisse*, 2nd ed., 1949.

———, *The Early Church*, London: SCM, 1956, pp. 54 ff. (This portion of the book is an English translation of *Die Tradition*, als exegetisches, historisches und theologisches Problem, Zürich: Zwingli, 1954).

Debrunner, R., Kleinknecht, H., and others, λέγω, λόγος, κτλ., *TDNT*, IV, pp. 69 ff.

Dey, J., ΠΑΛΙΓΓΕΝΕΣΙΑ, *Ein Beitrag zur Klärung der religions-geschichtlichen Bedeutung von Tit. III, 5*, Münster, 1937.

Dibelius, M., and Conzelmann, H., *Die Pastoralbriefe (Handbuch zum Neuen Testament, 13)*, Tübingen: J. C. B. Mohr, 3rd ed., 1955.

Dio Chrysostom edited by H. L. Crosby (*The Loeb Classical Library*), IV, Cambridge: Harvard University Press, 1946.

Dittenberger, W., *Sylloge Inscriptionum Graecarum*, Volumes I-IV, Leipzig, 1915-1924, reprinted 1960.

Dodd, C. H., *The Apostolic Preaching and Its Developments*, London: Hodder & Stoughton, 1936.

Duncan, J. G., "Πιστὸς ὁ λόγος", *Expository Times*, xxxv (1923), p. 141.

Düsterdieck, F., *Handbook to the Revelation of John*. Translated from the 3rd ed. of the German by Henry E. Jacobs. New York: Funk & Wagnalls, 1887.

Easton, B. S., *The Pastoral Epistles*, London: SCM, 1948.

Eadie, J., *A Commentary on the Greek Text of the Epistle of Paul to the Ephesians*, Edinburgh: T. & T. Clark, 3rd ed., 1883.

——, *A Commentary on the Greek Text of the Epistles of Paul to the Thessalonians*, London: Macmillan, 1877.

Ellicott, C. J., *The Pastoral Epistles of St Paul*, London: Longman, 3rd. ed., 1864.

Fairbairn, P., *The Pastoral Epistles*, Edinburgh: T. & T. Clark, 1874.

Falconer, R., *The Pastoral Epistles*, Oxford: Clarendon Press, 1937.

Fausset, A. R., *A Commentary on the Old and New Testaments* by Jamieson, Fausset, and Brown, Vol. VI, Grand Rapids: Eerdmans, 1948.

Feine, P., *Jesus Christus und Paulus*, Leipzig: Hinrichs, 1902.

Fiebig, P., *Berachoth. Der Mischnatractat "Segenssprüche" ins Deutsche übersetzt ..., Ausgewählte Mischnatractate in deutscher Ueber-setzung*, 3, Tübingen: J. C. B. Mohr, 1906.

Field, F., *Notes on the Translation of the New Testament*, Cambridge: The University Press, 1899.

Foerster, W., ἄξιος κτλ., *TDNT*, I, pp. 379-380.

——, "Εὐσέβεια in den Pastoralbriefen", *New Testament Studies* 5 (1958), pp. 213-218.

——, Ἰησοῦς, *TDNT*, III, pp. 284-293.

——, σέβομαι, ..., εὐσέβεια κτλ., *TWNT*, VII, pp. 168-195.

Foerster, W., and Fohrer, G., σῴζω κτλ., *TWNT*, VII, pp. 966-1024.

Frame, J. E., *The Epistles of St. Paul to the Thessalonians (The International Critical Commentary)*, New York: Scribners, 1912.

Funk, R. W., *A Greek Grammar of the New Testament and Other Early Christian Literature* (A Translation and Revision of the ninth-tenth German edition of F. Blass and A. Debrunner incorporating supplementary notes of A. Debrunner), Chicago: The University of Chicago Press, 1961.

Gealy, F. D., *1 and 2 Timothy, Titus (The Interpreter's Bible, 11)*, Nashville: Abingdon, 1955.

Gerhardsson, B., *Memory and Manuscript, Oral Tradition and Written Transmission in Rabbinic Judaism and Early Christianity (Acta Seminarii Neotestamentici Upsaliensis XXII)*, Uppsala, 1961.

Greijdanus, S., *De Brief van den Apostel Paulus aan de Gemeente te Rome* (*Kommentaar op het Nieuwe Testament*, VI), 2 volumes, Amsterdam: Bottenburg, 1933.

——, *Het Heilig Evangelie naar Beschrijving van Lucas* (*Kommentaar op het Nieuwe Testament*, III), 2 volumes, Amsterdam: Bottenburg, 1940, 1941.

——, *De Openbaring des Heeren aan Johannes* (*Kommentaar op het Nieuwe Testament*, XIV), Amsterdam: Bottenburg, 1925.

Grosheide, F. W., *De Brief aan de Hebreeën* ... (*Commentaar op het Nieuwe Testament*), Kampen: Kok, 2nd ed., 1955.

——, *Commentary on the First Epistle to the Corinthians* (*The New International Commentary on the New Testament*), Grand Rapids: Eerdmans, 1953.

——, *Het Heilig Evangelie volgens Johannes* (*Kommentaar op het Nieuwe Testament*, IV), 2 volumes, Amsterdam: Bottenburg, 1950.

——, *De Tweede Brief aan de Kerk te Korinthe* (*Commentaar op het Nieuwe Testament*), Kampen: Kok, 2nd ed., 1959.

Grundmann, W., δέχομαι ... ἀποδοχή κτλ., *TDNT*, II, pp. 50-59.

Grundmann, W., and Bertram, G., καλός, *TDNT*, III, pp. 536-556.

Guthrie, D., *The Pastoral Epistles* (*The Tyndale New Testament Commentaries*), London: Tyndale Press, 1957.

——, *The Pauline Epistles*, New Testament Introduction, Chicago: Inter-Varsity Press, 1961.

Hahn, F., *Christologische Hoheitstitel*. Ihre Geschichte im frühen Christentum (*Forschungen zur Religion und Litteratur des Alten und Neuen Testaments*, 83), Gottingen: Vandenhoeck & Ruprecht, 1963.

Hanse, H., ἔχω κτλ., *TDNT*, II, pp. 816-832.

Hanson, A. T., *The Pastoral Letters* (*Cambridge Bible Commentary*), Cambridge: University Press, 1966.

Harrison, P. N., *The Problem of the Pastoral Epistles*, London: Oxford University Press, 1921.

Hatch, E., and Redpath, H. A., *A Concordance to the Septuagint and the other Greek Versions of the Old Testament*, Oxford: Clarendon Press, 3 volumes in 2, 1897, reprinted 1954.

Hauck, F., μένω ... ὑπομένω, ὑπομονή, *TDNT*, IV, pp. 574-588.

Hendriksen, W., *Exposition of I and II Thessalonians* (*New Testament Commentary*), Grand Rapids: Baker, 1955.

——, *Exposition of the Gospel according to John* (*New Testament Commentary*), 2 volumes in 1, Grand Rapids: Baker, 1961.

——, *Exposition of the Pastoral Epistles* (*New Testament Commentary*), Grand Rapids: Baker, 1957.

——, *More Than Conquerors*, An Interpretation of the Book of Revelation, Grand Rapids: Baker, 7th ed., 1954.

Hermetica, Volume I, edited by Walter Scott, Oxford: Clarendon Press, 1924.

Hicks, B., "On Some Political Terms Employed in the New Testament", *The Classical Review* 1 (1887), p. 4.

Hodge, C., *A Commentary on the Epistle to the Ephesians*, Grand Rapids: Eerdmans, reprint, n.d.

——, *An Exposition of the First Epistle to the Corinthians*, Grand Rapids: Eerdmans, reprint 1956.

Holtz, G., *Die Pastoralbriefe* (*Theologischer Handkommentar zum Neuen Testament*, XIII), Berlin: Evangelische Verlagsanstalt, 1965.

Holtzmann, H. J., *Die Pastoralbriefe*, Leipzig: Engelmann, 1880.

The Holy Bible, newly edited by the American Revision Committee A. D. 1901, *American Standard Version,* Grand Rapids: Christian Reformed Publishing House.

The Holy Bible, Revised Version, Oxford University Press and Cambridge University Press, 1885.

Hughes, P. E., *Paul's Second Epistle to the Corinthians (The New International Commentary on the New Testament)* Grand Rapids: Eerdmans, 1962.

Hunter, A. M., *Paul and His Predecessors,* London: SCM Press, 2nd rev. ed., 1961.

———, *The Unity of the New Testament,* London: SCM, 1944.

Huther, J. E., *Pastoral Epistles (Meyer's Commentary on the New Testament),* English translation of the 4th German edition, Edinburgh: T. & T. Clark, 1893.

Jeremias, J., *Die Briefe an Timotheus und Titus (Das Neue Testament Deutsch,* 9), Göttingen: Vandenhoeck & Ruprecht, 6th ed., 1953.

———, *Unknown Sayings of Jesus,* London: S.P.C.K., 1957.

Johnson, P. C., *The Epistles to Titus and Philemon (Shield Bible Study Series),* Grand Rapids: Baker, 1966.

Jones, R. B., *The Epistles to Timothy (Shield Bible Study Series),* Grand Rapids: Baker, 1959.

Käsemann, E., "Sätze heiligen Rechts im Neuen Testament", in *Exegetische Versuche und Besinnungen,* II, Tübingen: J. C. B. Mohr, 1960. The article was first given at the 9th general meeting of the *Studiorum Novi Testamenti Societas* in Marburg on 8 September 1954 and then was published in *New Testament Studies* I (1954-55), pp. 248-260.

Kelly, J. N. D., *A Commentary on the Pastoral Epistles (Harper's* or *Black's New Testament Commentaries),* New York: Harper & Row, 1963.

———, *Early Christian Creeds,* London: Longmans, Green & Co., 1950.

Kent, H. A., *The Pastoral Epistles,* Chicago: Moody Press, 1958.

Kilpatrick, G. D., H ΚΑΙΝΗ ΔΙΑΘΗΚΗ, London: The British and Foreign Bible Society, 2nd ed. with revised critical apparatus, 1958.

Kittel, G., and Friedrich, G., editors, *Theologisches Wörterbuch zum Neuen Testament,* Volumes I-VII and other volumes in preparation, Stuttgart: Kohlhammer, 1933—. English translation *Theological Dictionary of the New Testament* by G. W. Bromiley, Volumes I-IV and others in process, Grand Rapids: Eerdmans, 1964—.

Kramer, W., *Christ, Lord, Son of God (Studies in Biblical Theology,* 50), Naperville, Illinois: Allenson, 1966.

de Kruijf, T. C., *De Pastorale Brieven:* Vertaald en toegelicht *(Het Nieuwe Testament vertaald en toegelicht* onder redactie van W. Grossouw e.a.), Roermond/Maaseik: Romen en Zonen, 1966.

Lategan, B. C., *Die Aardse Jesus In Die Prediking van Paulus* volgens sy briewe, Rotterdam, 1967.

Lenski, R. C. H., *The Interpretation of St. Paul's Epistles to the Colossians, to the Thessalonians, to Timothy, to Titus and to Philemon,* Minneapolis: Augsburg Publishing House, 1937.

Liddell, H. G., and Scott, R., *A Greek-English Lexicon,* A New Edition Revised and Augmented throughout by H. S. Jones with the assistance of R. McKenzie *et al.,* Oxford: Clarendon, 9th ed., 1940.

Liddon, H. P., *Explanatory Analysis of St. Paul's First Epistle to Timothy*, London: Longmans, Green, & Co., 1897.

Lightfoot, J. B., *Saint Paul's Epistle to the Philippians*, 1913, reprinted Grand Rapids: Zondervan, 1953.

Lock, W., *The Pastoral Epistles (The International Critical Commentary)*, Edinburgh: T. & T. Clark, 1924.

Lohmeyer, E., *Die Offenbarung des Johannes (Handbuch zum Neuen Testament)*, Tübingen: J. C. B. Mohr, 1926.

Lohse, E., *Die Offenbarung des Johannes (Das Neue Testament Deutsch, 11)*, 8th ed., 1st new ed., Göttingen: Vandenhoeck & Ruprecht, 1960.

Martin, R. P., "Aspects of Worship in the New Testament Church", *Vox Evangelica* II, London: Epworth, 1963, pp. 6-32.

——, "The Composition of I Peter in Recent Study", *Vox Evangelica*, London: Epworth, 1962, pp. 29-42.

——, "A Footnote to Pliny's Account of Christian Worship", *Vox Evangelica* III, London: Epworth, 1964, pp. 51-57.

——, *Worship in the Early Church*, Westwood, N.J.: Revell, 1964.

McCasland, S. V., "Christ Jesus", *Journal of Biblical Literature* 65 (1946), pp. 377-383.

Meyer, H. A. W., *Handbook to the Gospels of Mark and Luke*, translated from the 5th ed., of the German, 2 volumes, Edinburgh: T. & T. Clark, 1880.

Milligan, G., *St Paul's Epistles to the Thessalonians*, Grand Rapids: Eerdmans, reprinted 1953.

Morgenthaler, R., *Statistik des neutestamentlichen Wortschatzes*, Zürich: Gotthelf, 1958.

Morris, L., *The First and Second Epistles to the Thessalonians (The New International Commentary on the New Testament)*, Grand Rapids: Eerdmans, 1959.

Moule, C. F. D., *The Birth of the New Testament*, New York: Harper & Row, 1962.

——, "The Nature and Purpose of I Peter", *New Testament Studies* 3 (1956-57), pp. 1 ff.

——, "The Problem of the Pastoral Epistles: A Reappraisal", *Bulletin of the John Rylands Library* 47 (1965), pp. 430-452.

——, *Worship in the New Testament (Ecumenical Studies in Worship, 9)*, London: Luttersworth Press, 1961.

Moulton, J. H., and Milligan, G., *The Vocabulary of the Greek New Testament illustrated from the Papyri and other Non-Literary sources*, London: Hodder & Stoughton, 1930.

Moulton, W. F., and Geden, A. S., *A Concordance to the Greek Testament*, Edinburgh: T. & T. Clark, 3rd ed., 1926.

Mounce, R. H., *The Essential Nature of New Testament Preaching*, Grand Rapids: Eerdmans, 1960.

Murray, J., *The Epistle to the Romans (The New International Commentary on the New Testament)* 2 volumes, Grand Rapids: Eerdmans, 1959, 1965.

Nauck, W., *Die Herkunft des Verfassers der Pastoralbriefe*. Inaugural-Dissertation zur Erlangung des Doktorgrades. Unpublished, Göttingen, 1950.

Nestle, E., et Aland, K., *Novum Testamentum Graece*, Stuttgart: Württembergische Bibelanstalt, 25th ed., 1963.

New American Standard Bible New Testament, Nashville: Broadman, 1963.
The New English Bible New Testament, Oxford & Cambridge University Presses, 1961.
The New Testament, A New Translation by James Moffatt, New York: Doran, 1913.
Oepke, A., γυμνός ... γυμνασία, *TDNT*, I, pp. 773-776.
——, εἰς, *TDNT*, II, pp. 420-434.
——, λούω, ἀπολούω, λουτρόν, *TDNT*, IV, pp. 295-307.
Oldfather, W. A., and Daly, L. W., "A Quotation From Menander in the Pastoral Epistles?", *Classical Philology* 38 (1943), pp. 202-204.
van Oosterzee, J. J., *The Pastoral Epistles (Commentary on the Holy Scriptures* by J. P. Lange, 11) translated from the German, Grand Rapids: Zondervan, reprinted 1960.

Parry, R. St John, *The Pastoral Epistles*, Cambridge: The University Press, 1920.
Pfitzner, V. C., *Paul and the Agon Motif*. Traditional Athletic Imagery in the Pauline Literature. (Supplements to *Novum Testamentum*, Volume XVI), Leiden: E. J. Brill, 1967.
Plummer, A., *The Second Epistle of St. Paul to the Corinthians (The International Critical Commentary)*, New York: Scribner, 1915.

Reicke, B., "The Constitution of the Church in the Light of Jewish Documents", in *The Scrolls and the New Testament* edited by K. Stendahl, London: SCM Press, 1958, pp. 143-156.
Reicke, B., and Bertram, G., πᾶς, ἅπας, *TWNT*, V, pp. 885-895.
Rengstorf, K. H., ἁμαρτωλός, ἀναμάρτητος, *TDNT*, I, pp. 317-335.
The Revised Standard Version of the Holy Bible, New York: Nelson, 1952.
Ridderbos, H. N., *The Authority of the New Testament Scriptures*, Grand Rapids: Baker, 1963. (English translation of *Heilsgeschiedenis en Heilige Schrift*, 1955).
——, *The Coming of the Kingdom*, Philadelphia: Presbyterian & Reformed, 1962.
——, "Kerkelijke orde en kerkelijk recht in de brieven van Paulus" in *Ex Auditu Verbi* (feestbundel G. C. Berkouwer), Kampen: Kok, 1965, pp. 194-215.
——, *De Pastorale Brieven (Commentaar op het Nieuwe Testament)*, Kampen: Kok, 1967.
——, *Paul and Jesus*, Philadelphia: Presbyterian & Reformed, 1958.
——, *Paulus. Ontwerp van zijn Theologie*, Kampen: Kok, 1966.
——, "The Structure and Scope of the Prologue to the Gospel of John", *Novum Testamentum*, VIII (1966), pp. 180-201.
Riesenfeld, H., "The Meaning of the Verb ἀρνεῖσθαι", *Coniectanea Neo-testamentica*, XI, Lund: Gleerup, 1947, pp. 207-219.
Robertson, A., and Plummer, A., *The First Epistle of St Paul to the Corinthians (The International Critical Commentary)*, Edinburgh: T. & T. Clark, 2nd ed., 1914.
Robertson, A. T., *The Epistles of Paul (Word Pictures in the New Testament*, Volume IV), Nashville: Broadman, 1931.
——, *A Grammar of the Greek New Testament in the Light of Historical Research*, London: Hodder & Stoughton, 3rd ed., 1919.
Robinson, J. A., *St. Paul's Epistle to the Ephesians*, London: Macmillan, 2nd ed., 1928.

The Roman Antiquities of Dionysius of Halicarnassus edited by E. Cary (The Loeb Classical Library), II, Cambridge: Harvard University Press, 1939.

Sasse, H., κοσμέω, κόσμος κτλ., TDNT, III, pp. 867-898.

Schippers, R., Getuigen van Jezus Christus in het Nieuwe Testament, Franeker: Wever, 1938.

——, "The Pre-Synoptic Tradition in 1 Thessalonians II 13-16", Novum Testamentum VIII (1966), pp. 223-234 in the volume written in honor of Professor G. Sevenster.

Schlatter, A., Die Kirche der Griechen im Urteil des Paulus. Eine Auslegung seiner Briefe an Timotheus und Titus, Stuttgart: Calwer, 1936.

Schlier, H., ἀμήν, TDNT, I, pp. 335-338.

——, ἀρνέομαι, TDNT, I, pp. 469-471.

Schmidt, K. L., et al, βασιλεύς, βασιλεία κτλ., TDNT, I, pp. 564-593.

Schneider, J., ἔρχομαι κτλ., TDNT, II, pp. 666-684.

Schniewind, J./Friedrich, G., ἐπαγγέλλω, ἐπαγγελία κτλ., TDNT, II, pp. 576-586.

Schweizer, E., Church Order in the New Testament (Studies in Biblical Theology, 32), London: SCM Press, 1961.

Scott, E. F., The Pastoral Epistles (The Moffatt New Testament Commentary), London: Hodder & Stoughton, 1936.

Selwyn, E. G., The First Epistle of St. Peter, London: Macmillan & Co., 1955.

Septuaginta edited by Alfred Rahlfs, Stuttgart: Württembergische Bibelanstalt, 2 volumes, editio septima, 1935.

Sevenster, G., De Christologie van het Nieuwe Testament, Amsterdam, 2nd ed., 1948.

Sickenberger, J., "Das in die Welt Kommende Licht", Theologie und Glaube 33 (1941), pp. 129-134.

Simpson, E. K., The Pastoral Epistles, Grand Rapids: Eerdmans, 1954.

Smelik, E. L., De Brieven van Paulus aan Timotheüs, Titus en Filemon (De Prediking van het Nieuwe Testament), 3rd ed., Nijkerk: Callenbach, 1961.

Smyth, H. W., Greek Grammar revised by G. M. Messing, Cambridge: Harvard University Press, 1959.

Soden, H. von, Die Briefe an die Kolosser, Epheser, Philemon; die Pastoralbriefe (Hand-Commentar zum Neuen Testament, Dritter Band, Erste Abtheilung), Freiburg i. B. und Leipzig: J. C. B. Mohr, Zweite Auflage, 1893.

——, Die Schriften des Neuen Testaments in ihrer ältesten erreichbaren Textgestalt. 4 volumes. Teil 1, Abteilung 1-3, Berlin: Verlag von Alexander Duncker, 1902-1910; Teil 2, Text mit Apparat, Göttingen: Vandenhoeck und Ruprecht, 1913.

Souter, A., Novum Testamentum Graece, Oxford: Clarendon, 2nd ed., 1947.

Spicq, C., Les Épitres Pastorales (Études Bibliques), Paris: Gabalda, 1947.

——, "Gymnastique et morale d'après 1 Tim., IV, 7-8", Revue Biblique 54 (1947), pp. 229-242.

——, "La Philanthropie hellénistique, vertu divine et royale (à propos de Tit. III, 4)", Studia Theologica 12 (1958), pp. 169-191.

Staab, K., Pauluskommentare aus der griechischen Kirche, Münster, 1933.

Stählin, G., νῦν, TDNT, IV, pp. 1106-1123.

Stonehouse, N. B., *The Witness of Luke to Christ*, Grand Rapids: Eerdmans, 1953.

Sukenik, E. L., *Megillot Genuzot*, metok genizeh gedumah senimtseah bemidbar yehudah seqirah seniyah, Yerusalayim, hotset Musad Bialik [c 1950] (Hidden Scrolls from the midst of the ancient genizah which was found in the wilderness of Judah, Jerusalem, Bialik Institute [c 1950]).

Swete, H. B., *The Apocalypse of St John*, Grand Rapids: Eerdmans, 3rd ed. 1909, reprinted 1954.

———, "The Faithful Sayings", *Journal of Theological Studies* xviii (1917), pp. 1-7.

Tasker, R. V. G., *The Greek New Testament*; being the text translated in *The New English Bible*, 1961. Edited with introduction, textual notes, and appendix. Oxford & Cambridge University Presses, 1964.

Taylor, V., *The Names of Jesus*, London: Macmillan, 1954.

Thayer, J. H., *A Greek-English Lexicon of the New Testament*, Edinburgh: T. & T. Clark, 4th ed., 1901.

Theodore of Mopsuestia, *In Epistolas S. Pauli Commentarii*, The Latin version with the Greek fragments, with an introduction, notes and indices, by H. B. Swete, Cambridge: University Press, 2 volumes, 1880.

Tischendorf, L. F. C. von, *Novum Testamentum Graece ... editio octava critica maior ...* Lipsiae: Giesecke & Devrient, 2 volumes, 1869-1872.

Torrey, C. C., "Χριστός", *Quantulacumque* edited by Casey, Lake & Lake, London: Christophers, 1937, pp. 317-324.

Trench, R. C., *Synonyms of the New Testament*, London: Kegan & Co., 12th ed., 1894.

Turner, N., *A Grammar of New Testament Greek* by J. H. Moulton, Volume III, Syntax, Edinburgh: T. & T. Clark, 1963.

van Unnik, W. C., "L'usage de σῴζειν 'sauver' et de ses dérivés dans les Évangiles synoptiques", *La Formation des Évangiles* (*Recherches Bibliques*, II), Desclée de Brouwer, 1957, pp. 178-194.

Vine, W. E., *The Epistles to Timothy and Titus*, London: Oliphants, 1965.

Vos, G., *The Self-Disclosure of Jesus*, Grand Rapids: Eerdmans, 1954.

Wagner, W., "Über ΣΩΖEIN und seine Derivata im Neuen Testament", *Zeitschrift für die neutestamentliche Wissenschaft* VI (1905), pp. 205-235.

Walder, E., "The Logos of the Pastoral Epistles", *The Journal of Theological Studies* xxiv (1923), pp. 310-315.

Warfield, B. B., *The Lord of Glory*, New York: American Tract Society, 1907.

———, "The Saving Christ", *The Person and Work of Christ*, Philadelphia: Presbyterian & Reformed, 1950, pp. 549-560.

———, "Some Exegetical Notes on I Timothy", *The Presbyterian Review* viii (1887), pp. 500-508, 702-710.

Weiss, B., *Die Briefe Pauli an Timotheus und Titus* (*Kritisch-exegetischer Kommentar über das Neue Testament*, XI. Abteilung), Göttingen: Vandenhoeck & Ruprecht, 7. Auflage, 1902.

Westcott, B. F., and Hort, F. J. A., *The New Testament in the Original Greek*, 2 volumes, Cambridge: Macmillan, 1890.

Wetstein, J. J., *Novum Testamentum Graecum*, Amsterdam: Dommerian, 1752, and reprinted since then.

White, N. J. D., *The First and Second Epistles to Timothy, The Epistle to Titus* (*The Expositor's Greek Testament*, Vol. 4), Grand Rapids: Eerdmans, 1961.

Windisch, H., "Zur Christologie der Pastoralbriefe", *Zeitschrift für die neutestamentliche Wissenschaft* 34 (1935), pp. 213-238.

Wohlenberg, G., *Die Pastoralbriefe* (Zahn's *Kommentar zum Neuen Testament*, XIII), Leipzig: Deichert, 2nd ed., 1911.

Wuest, K. S., *The Pastoral Epistles in the Greek New Testament*, Grand Rapids: Eerdmans, 1952.

Ysebaert, J., *Greek Baptismal Terminology: Its Origins and Early Development* (*Graecitas Christianorum Primaeva* I, edited by C. Mohrmann and J. G. A. Ros), Nijmegen: Dekker & Van de Vegt N.V., 1962.

Zahn, Th., *Introduction to the New Testament* translated from the 3rd German edition, 1909, 3 volumes, reprinted Grand Rapids: Kregel, 1953.

SCRIPTURE INDEX

164